Ideology
and Foreign Policy

To Ingela
for her ultimate affirmation

Ideology
and Foreign Policy
Problems of Comparative
Conceptualization

Walter Carlsnaes

Basil Blackwell

British Library Cataloguing in Publication Data

Carlsnaes, Walter
    Ideology and foreign policy: problems of
    comparative conceptualization.
    1. International relations — Philosophy
    I. Title
    327.1 '01   JX1305
    ISBN 0–631–15229–6

Library of Congress Cataloging in Publication Data

Carlsnaes, Walter.
    Ideology and foreign policy.
    Bibliography: p.
    Includes index.
    1. International relations–Research. I. Title.
    JX1291.C29   1987   327'.072   86-13651
    ISBN 0-631-15229-6

Typeset in 11 on 13 pt Ehrhardt
by Joshua Associates Limited, Oxford
Printed in Great Britain by
T. J. Press Ltd, Padstow

Contents

Of course, I should not dream of
quarrelling about a term. But . . .

Sir Karl Popper

Preface

This book represents the second stage in a projected three-pronged exploration of various aspects of the concept of ideology in political analysis. In the work preceding this study, the emphasis was placed on the roots and the historical development of the concept, and especially on a philosophical and methodological critique of its major meanings and usages in the history of political ideas. In line with this historical and critical thrust, it did not propound a conceptualization of its own. This omission is rectified in the present study. It does not, however, attempt to go beyond this point of conceptual reconstruction, except by way of implication or occasional asides. In other words, this analysis will probably not satisfy the impatient reader who wants to be done as quickly as possible with 'mere' conceptual problems in favour of the 'real' issues of an empirical theory of ideology. He or she will have to await the final instalment in my long liaison with this concept.

This is also a study in the craft of foreign policy analysis and of some of its underlying methodological problems. As such it is probably more philosophical in both tone and substance than is customary within this subdiscipline of political science. My defence for resorting to this somewhat alien discourse rests on the view that the crisis that has undermined the comparative study of foreign policy during the past decade and a half has its roots not so much in problems of research design or technique as in shortcomings of a fundamentally metatheoretical nature. Hence, whether we like it or not, the cure for this condition will necessarily entail swallowing a healthy dose of the philosophy of social science. However, I have tried to make this potion as small and palatable as possible.

Although at first glance the table of contents may suggest a disjointed structure of analysis, this is an impression that I hope will be quickly dispelled. To ensure this, the underlying logic of this book is explained towards the end of the first chapter. It is nevertheless possible to approach the three middle chapters as separate discussions of three different types of methodological issues in political science. Indeed, none of them needs to be viewed as necessarily dealing only with problems within the subdiscipline of foreign policy analysis. Although this is most evident in the chapter on ideology, the same holds for the discussion of the implications of the concept of action for political analysis, as well as for the explanatory model presented in chapter 3. These chapters in fact address general philosophical and methodological issues in political science, even though in the first instance they do so with specific reference to the analysis of foreign policy.

This study owes its genesis to my halcyon years as a doctoral student at Princeton University, where I was first introduced to the problems of comparative foreign policy analysis. Since I subsequently happened to complete my doctoral studies at Oxford with a dissertation in which the term 'foreign policy' did not occur even a single time, I would like to regard this book as a suitable, if belated, recompense for that double defection. It is to Oxford, however, that I am indebted for my sustained interest in the concept of ideology, and especially for my belief in the necessity of grounding all systematic empirical studies on a sound philosophical basis. In a special sense I thus owe the particular form, method and subject matter of this study to a symbiosis of the two intellectual traditions – the 'scientific' and the 'philosophical' – which I continue to associate with these two extraordinary institutions of higher learning.

Skytteanum, the ancient building housing the equally ancient Department of Government at Uppsala University, is an excellent place to write serious books in. The animated discussions that I have pursued with its occupants over the years have not always been enlightening or profound; but when fruitful, I have usually been on the receiving end. If this is not always reflected in the contents of the present study, the fault is undoubtedly my own. I have also received much help and stimulation from a host of other people and institutions, both in Sweden and elsewhere. Although I shall not mention any names here, I hope that all of them will remain aware of both my gratitude and my penchant for returning for more.

Finally, there have always seemed to exist a number of obvious reasons for being enamoured of Ingela. As for myself, one predominates at present: that after all our years together she has at last made an honourably married man of me. This is, surely, an entirely fitting reason for dedicating this book to her lovely person.

1

Introduction

The present-day popularity of the concept of ideology in the comparative analysis of foreign policy is noteworthy for at least two reasons. The first pertains to the relatively recent origins of this prominence, despite a recognized – if not always eminent – pedigree stretching back for almost two centuries. Not many decades ago the characterization of a person, a policy or a state in 'ideological' terms almost invariably signified disapprobation in one form or another, and was hence reserved mainly for purposes of attack or invective rather than for dispassionate analysis. Today there is little left of this legacy: few and far between are the foreign policy scholars who have not, at one point or another (and often at many), used the term when discussing their subject matter; and most of the time they have done so without any disrespectful implications.[1]

There are undoubtedly various factors that can be adduced to account for this rise in the term's popularity. A major one is the nature of twentieth-century politics itself, which since the first decades of this century, and particularly after the First World War, has taken on a character distinctly different from the political perturbation of the previous century. Domestically, political life has become increasingly far-reaching and 'democratic' in the sense of both active participation and ostensible availability; and this is a development which has been accompanied – and often precipitated – by an open battle between various doctrinal or ideational groups, all clamouring for at least a public hearing, and many for much more as well. Many observers of these historical developments have equated them with the rise and consolidation of what is termed 'ideology' or 'ideological' politics. 'Our age has been the age of ideology,' two leading scholars thus claim, echoing many others. 'Ideological commitments have tended to dominate political behaviour.'² With regard to the international system, a similar break between the past and the present has become accepted as a commonplace historical fact. Michael Brecher, for example, writing about some of the salient characteristics of what he calls the 'multiple revolution' in the international system during this century, notes that

> in the Europe-centered nineteenth-century system, interstate conflict was for limited power, prestige, and profits, with exceptions – notably, Napoleonic France. The coming of Fascism, Nazism and Communism, however, sundered the value consensus of the international system ... Ideology and power become intertwined, each strengthening the intensity of the other; the result was to aggravate the tendency of actors to seek unlimited power, now possible because of the technological revolution.³

Apart from these changes during the present century – changes primarily within and between Western societies – it is also significant to note that the popularity of 'ideology' as a purportedly neutral concept of analysis has on the whole been coeval with the political awakening and international emergence of the non-Western peoples. Indeed, this awakening itself is often conceived of as being deeply 'ideological' in nature, at least in the sense that it is viewed as a political movement – or a series of movements – primarily inspired and guided by ideas and ideals, particularly those associated with liberty and equality as expressed in the principle of self-determination.⁴ Here the pertinent historical watershed is not so much the First World War as the Second, despite President Wilson's reverberating formulation of the principles of national self-determination already during the second decade of this century. And it was the end of the Second World War that sounded the beginning of what became known as the Cold War, at the heart of which an 'ideological' confrontation of the first order was said to lie, not only penetrating into all aspects of Big Power relationships, but also deeply affecting their interactions with other states, particularly with the newly emerging indigenous regimes of Africa and Asia. 'Ideological' warfare became the order of the day, and it was fought on all available fronts.

The second and more disturbing reason which makes this belated regard for the concept of ideology noteworthy is that it has achieved prominence despite a remarkable elusiveness in meaning. Indeed, the more esteem the term has acquired, the fuzzier its contours seem to have become. Already in the 1950s, in one of the first major studies of 'ideology', Arne Naess felt compelled to raise this issue in his conjecture that

> the movement of the term 'ideology' into social science, social psychology and political science will, within a generation, be followed by a movement in the other direction. It will continue to be used in headlines, in summaries and popularizations, but scarcely in statements intended to express . . . theories, hypotheses or classifications.[5]

More recently this scepticism has become even more pointed and explicit. One scholar thus notes 'a lack of agreement regarding even the basic properties of ideology', while another has claimed that since 'ideology' today 'points to a black box', one is 'entitled to wonder whether there is any point in using it for scholarly purposes'.[6] Daniel Bell, in a dour mood of biblical castigation, is even more emphatic in his curt dismissal of it as an 'irretrievably fallen word'.[7] But despite such occasional murmurings the visibility of the concept has continued to increase each year, which undoubtedly reinforces the assumption – among scholars and the public alike – that it constitutes a significant tool in political analysis; and hence that any doubts on this score are merely the consequence of semantic squabbles devoid of any real substance. But is this really the case? This query leads us straight to the core of this analysis and to the reason for pursuing it in the first place.

A THE PROBLEM

Let it be stated immediately that this study proceeds from the basic assumption that definitional or conceptual contentions cannot, a priori, be brushed aside as meaningless exercises in semantic nitpicking. To do so is indeed to beg a very fundamental question, inasmuch as 'semantical differences are usually symptoms which reach into the core of the matter.'[8] Or as Richard Rudner has put it:

> There is . . . a view as widespread as it is curious (celebrated in the indiscriminate use of the phrase 'merely verbal') that to be concerned with linguistic analyses or with logical analysis of any discourse, or with linguistic problems at all, is to overspecialize or even trivialize, one's concerns. No doubt this disparaging view of linguistic concerns has its genesis in the conviction that very few real and pressing problems can be construed as 'merely matters of language.' But, whatever the genesis of such a view may be, it is surely mistaken.[9]

The ensuing analysis is based on the proposition that the concept of ideology is thoroughly problematic in the sense just intimated, and that it is hence in need of rigorous analysis *qua* concept if there is to remain any point in retaining it as a full-fledged scholarly tool in the study – comparative or otherwise – of foreign policy. Even a quick perusal of a representative (if haphazardly chosen) sample of the relevant literature ought to leave little doubt as to the imperativeness of such an examination. The fact is that in this literature 'ideology' functions happily as a convenient and much used word for speaking not only about the *nature* or *essence* of foreign policy, or a major *approach* in its analysis, but also about a significant *factor* determining its substance. And even when its usage is confined to any one of these functions, the term most of the time appears to mean different things to different scholars.

1 The first type of usage is also the oldest, while at the same time bearing the imprint of the major international confrontations of this century. It is based on the view that the foreign policy of a state is essentially an expression of its peculiar ideology – that such policies in some sense or other constitute an 'ideological' extension of sovereign societies and their basic values into the international arena. This is the position expressed, for example, by Felix Gross in the 1950s, and although his definition of foreign policy as a set of ideas which 'reflects the culture' and hence the 'ideology' of a society is no longer as common as it once used to be, Kenneth W. Thompson and Roy C. Macridis could still maintain twenty years later (in one of the most widely used texts on foreign policy) that 'to

the present day it is perhaps the prevalent approach.' This definition of foreign policy 'maintains that a democratic regime pursues one type of foreign policy, an autocratic government another, a communist government a third, and a democratic socialist administration still another.'[10] Ole R. Holsti, in a more recent analysis of approaches to the study of foreign policy, has described this view in somewhat greater detail:

> Foreign policy is the external manifestation of domestic institutions, ideologies, and other attributes of the polity. The notion that political, economic, and other internal institutions determine the nature of foreign policy is an old one, extending back to Kant and earlier. Contemporary advocates of this position include, among others, 'hard-line' analysts who attribute all Soviet or Chinese foreign policy behaviour to the imperatives of Marxism–Leninism and communist totalitarianism. Many revisionist American historians adhere to a comparable position – that the institutional requirements of capitalism are not only a necessary but also a sufficient explanation for the nature of American foreign policy.[11]

But this view is not only applied to whole societies or states, but it is also to be found in the analysis of individual statesmen and their foreign policies. Thus, for example, Woodrow Wilson's general policy not to recognize any new Latin American regimes that had not been established by strictly constitutional means is often explained in terms of the liberal values that he saw embedded in the American governmental system, and which – in his view – it was incumbent upon him as president to promote elsewhere. This 'totalitarian hold of a Lockean world view' (to cite Louis Hartz's apt characterization) led him to eschew 'acting for the sake of interests. He castigated American corporations. He helped bring down Huerta, the Mexican leader most favourably disposed toward American investors during the first decade of the revolution. For Wilson, democracy was more important than oil, silver, or copper, especially if it triumphed through his efforts.'[12] A similar case has been put forward for the Truman Doctrine and its application during the bitterest years of the Cold War.[13] Or as Stephen D. Krasner has described this notion with reference to twentieth-century American foreign policy as a whole: 'After the Second World War, and between 1912 and 1920, broader foreign policy aims primarily involved ideological objectives. During these periods American leaders were moved by a vision of what the global order should be like that was derived from American values and the American experiences – Lockean liberalism and a nonrevolutionary, democratic, prosperous historical evolution.'[14]

Furthermore, this view of the ideological nature of foreign policy is often contrasted with the notion of interest, as has already been suggested above. Franz Schurmann's massive *The Logic of World Power* perhaps represents the most ambitous effort to juxtapose these two concepts and to draw out their implications for – to use the words of the subtitle to his book – 'the origins, currents, and contradictions of world politics'.[15] In this analysis of twentieth-century American history he posits and expounds on two basic types of foreign policy. Imperialism, the first of these, is by nature an ideological outgrowth, since it 'is an emanation not of the realm of interests but of the realm of ideology'.[16] Against this type of policy he places expansionism, which entails 'the natural tendency of productive interest to go beyond national boundaries in search of new accretions to their property'.[17] The politics (or 'realms') of interest and ideology thus constitute two different and competing types of policy; but in contrast to Krasner's view, these are not mutually exclusive but have, on the contrary, coexisted over the years, albeit with a tendency for the agencies of interest to contain the agencies of ideology.

This usage of 'ideology' can also be found in another guise in the literature on international politics, differing only in terms of its function as a universally legitimizing factor in the international system, in contrast to a factor expressive of the individuality of particular nation–states (or societies). Herbert C. Kelman thus speaks of the 'nationalist ideology' which provides 'the basic set of assumptions that govern the relationship of a nation–state to other states in the international system', while embodying 'the principle that a political system must in some fashion be representative of the population under its control.'[18] Evan Luard, while using the term in a similar manner, has expressed a somewhat different view when he notes that between '1815 and 1914 the ideology of nationalism promoted a bitter competition among states', albeit that 'there existed at the same time a highly developed system of consultation among the very powers which were most strongly competing, to find the means of accommodation between them.'[19] In a sense, of course, this 'nationalistic' interpretation of ideology underpins the previous viewpoint: it legitimizes different sovereign states to 'express' different 'ideologies', as long as their governments 'legitimately' represent their citizens. De Gaulle was perhaps the last great exponent of this doctrine in Europe, while the foreign policies of the newly emerged states often continue to be described in terms of it, both by their own governments and by Western scholars.[20]

2 The second major use of the concept of ideology in the international studies literature bears on *how* foreign policies are analysed, not on their nature or substance. Thus, for example, Thompson and Macridis (in their collection mentioned earlier) make a fundamental distinction between the 'ideological' and the 'analytical' approach in the comparative study of foreign policy. The former refers to the notion that foreign policy should be considered 'a function of a political system in action or of the preferences or convictions of political leaders', while at the heart of the latter lies the viewpoint that 'policy rests on multiple determinants, including the state's historic tradition, geographical location, national interest, and purposes and security needs', all of which have to be taken into account by the political scientist.[21]

Bernard C. Cohen, in an important encyclopaedic contribution to foreign policy studies, also uses 'ideology' to designate one of the major approaches to be found in the literature on this subject. But the meaning he gives to the term is quite different from the one just cited. He contrasts it with 'rationality', describing ideology as 'a concern for democratic control of foreign policy making which generally . . . reflects a belief that foreign policy decisions should be made by politically responsive or responsible individuals or groups', while the rational approach signifies 'a concern for the organization and structure of policy making which generally . . . reflects a belief that certain policy making relationships or arrangements can be found that are . . . more "rational" than others.'[22] Here the distinction or emphasis is clearly normative rather than descriptive; but in so far as it purports to describe the way scholars look at foreign policy, it is at the same time an analytical classification pertaining not to how political life should be, but to how it is viewed.

A more explicitly prescriptive usage, and one not confined merely to scholars, is to be found in some philosophical discussions concerning the kind of international order that confronts states in their dealings with one another. As a study on the 'ideology and practice of international order' has put it, a conception of this order 'is almost inevitably going to be a prescriptive one embodying certain value preferences, for the simple reason that order itself is not normatively neutral . . . What is order for the Great Powers may not be order for the small ones. What is order for the satisfied states may well not be order for the dissatisfied ones.'[23] More specifically, this author refers to two normative traditions in this question, namely, the Kantian and the Rousseauian, and describes their respective positions in terms of utopianism and realism, adding that 'we shall refer to utopianism as the ideological impetus to reform the international order and to realism as the main source of resistance.'[24] Furthermore, while 'utopian thought, like ideology generally, was deemed to be at an end' during the 1950s and 1960s, 'thought about international-order reform has experienced a resurgence during the 1970s, to such an extent that we might be tempted to equate the intellectual mood of the present time with the utopian impulse of the post-1918 decade.'[25] In this usage we thus have a direct coupling with a more general discussion about the purported role of ideology in politics as such, a debate which has been pursued almost unabatedly ever since Raymond Aron, Daniel Bell, Seymour Martin Lipset, Edward Shils and others initiated it almost three decades ago.

3 The third distinctive way in which 'ideology' is used is also the most prevalent; and it is on this analytical level – the causal-explanatory – that the term really comes into its own as a Pandora's Box which, once opened, lets out an extraordinary melange of different notions of varying size and colour. If we differentiate broadly between the substance, sources, processes and outcomes of foreign policy, and give the literature little more than a cursory examination, we find that 'ideology' is used extensively by scholars to describe and/or explain not just one or other of these aspects of

foreign policy, but in some instances all of them. Let us briefly look at some examples of each of these usages.

In the analysis of the *substance* of foreign policies, i.e., their goals, objectives, purposes, and so on, we will immediately discover an old and hallowed tradition linking these to 'ideology' in one way or another. This is of course not surprising, given the notion referred to above that foreign policy basically constitutes an ideological phenomenon. But it is also present even when such 'theoretical determinism' (to use K. J. Holsti's phrase) is neither specified nor implied.[26] 'The term ideology,' Thompson and Macridis thus write, 'applies not only to the manner in which objectives are shaped, but also to how given objectives will be pursued.'[27] Most often this usage of the concept is phrased in terms such as the 'external ideological goals in Soviet foreign policy' or 'an aggressive ideological orientation in foreign policy'; and sometimes these goals are contrasted with domestic ones, as when Vernon V. Aspaturian writes that 'a new variable in Soviet policy is the contradiction between enhancing economic prosperity at home and fulfilling international ideological commitments', while in other instances no such conflict is perceived.[28]

Some authors ascribe ideological foreign policy goals only to certain types of regimes, while others tend to universalize the concept by extending it to the analysis of the foreign policies of most if not all systems of government. 'Ideologies,' Stanley Hoffmann thus writes on the one hand, 'in so far as they deal with international affairs, are, typically, revolutionary – whether the revolution consists of pushing the hands of the clock forward or backward.' Hence, he notes, the 'United States is not an ideological nation, and its policies are not ideological.'[29] This is also the view expressed by Henry Kissinger in his immensely influential *Nuclear Weapons and Foreign Policy*, in which he makes a similar distinction between status quo and revolutionary powers, of which only the latter – i.e., the Soviet Union and China – are driven by ideology to pursue single-minded and ineluctable imperialist goals.[30] In a somewhat similar vein Richard W. Cottam distinguishes between 'cultural' and 'ideological' messianism in his discussion of foreign policy motivation. The former is pre-eminently represented by British imperialism, and primarily involves a 'civilizing' role (the 'white man's burden', in

Rudyard Kipling's famous phrase), while the latter is narrower in scope and more 'politicizing' by nature. In Cottam's view this type of foreign policy is typified by the actions of post-Second World War Soviet Russia.[31] Gabriel A. Almond, on the other hand, referring to American foreign policy and its aims, claims that:

> there is ... a general ideological consensus in the United States in which the mass of the population and its leadership generally share ... The advocates of the American foreign policy consensus are, in general, agreed that the primary aims of American policy, both domestic and foreign, should turn on a reconciliation of individual freedom and mass welfare of a primary material kind.[32]

This subsumption of all foreign policies – including those of the US and other Western states – under the ideological umbrella has become increasingly prevalent during the last two decades, perhaps as a consequence of the periodic pursuit of policies of *détente* and accommodation rather than Cold War confrontation.

But while to some scholars, like the ones cited above, the ideological aims or purposes contained in foreign policies are seen as genuine and potent, others view them with distrust or scepticism. Hans Morgenthau has thus claimed that the ideological element in the substance of foreign policies is little more than a façade – a more or less intentional disguise 'for the true nature of policy'. 'While politics,' he adds, true to the 'realism' with which his name is so closely associated, 'is necessarily pursuit of power, ideologies render involvement in that contest psychologically and morally acceptable to the actors and their audience.'[33] This process is also sometimes referred to in terms of 'nationalistic universalism', which occurs when 'strong powers ... wrap ... national-interest objectives in ideological garb such as fascism, Marxism, or even liberalism.'[34] Along somewhat similar lines, but writing of a more specific form of foreign policy, another scholar notes that an 'ideological commitment is often added to an alliance already firmly grounded on specific common or complementary interests. In this case it will probably strengthen the alliance ... If, however, a community of interests is absent, an alliance based on ideology alone will be stillborn.'[35] Or as Werner Levi has put it, 'Statesmen act in order to satisfy interests, not to make ideology function.'[36]While many more examples can be found to illustrate this goal-oriented function of ideology, these will suffice for the present purposes.

The *sources* of foreign policy, or the *inputs* into a foreign policy system, are usually regarded as those factors which directly or indirectly impinge upon, determine, affect or influence the substance, processes or outcomes of the external behaviour of states. Among these the concept of ideology often plays a prominent role. This is the case, for instance, with all those scholars who view foreign policy in terms of 'theoretical determinism', or as a process of democratic determination. Thus, to cite Almond again, 'foreign policy consensus is founded upon a consensus of fundamental attitudes and ideology', shared by both the public and the decision-makers.[37] 'At the level of mass opinion,' he clarifies this claim elsewhere, 'these "psycho-cultural" characteristics condition patterns of thought and mood on foreign policy problems. At the elite level they affect patterns of policy-making.'[38] Similarly, R. Barry Farrell asserts that among 'the factors which most affect the way in which those who shape foreign policy are influenced in defining what is important and how they should look at the world are (1) ideology . . .', and adds that ideology 'in all probability plays a more important role in influencing the foreign policies of closed societies than it does open societies'.[39] John Galtung, writing about 'Foreign Policy Opinion as a Function of Social Position', notes that 'people have, more or less explicitly, social cosmologies, and their foreign policy attitudes have somehow to be compatible with them.'[40] He distinguishes broadly between two such cosmologies in terms of 'absolutistic' and 'gradualist' orientations, and – thus giving the term a much narrower definition than most scholars – classifies 'ideology' under the former as a deductive system which affects attitudes towards the formulation of policy in certain special ways. However, by tying 'ideology' to specific social positions (particularly those on the periphery), whose occupants tend to have only a marginal influence on foreign policy elites, he at the same time plays down the direct influence of this factor.[41]

'Ideology' has also been used to denote an exogenous factor with respect to the societies whose policies it affects. One scholar, denouncing 'the type of diplomacy which tends to characterize a world in which international relations are highly ideological', thus notes that 'Responses to behaviour are determined by the ideology of the source of the behaviour, not by an objective evaluation of the nature or intent of the behaviour itself.'[42] In summary, what these examples illustrate is that 'ideology' in its input version has not only been couched in terms referring to both domestic and external factors, but has also been posited as both an important and marginal factor in the explanation of policy making. In addition, some view it with approbation, while others tend to find it a hindrance to 'good', 'sound' or 'rational' policy.

When we come to the analysis of foreign policy *processes*, dealing with all the diverse ways in which decisions are arrived at, we find what are perhaps the most recent attempts to link the concept of ideology to the study of foreign policy. In this context Kissinger, in a widely quoted essay, speaks of three important 'styles' of foreign policy making, namely, the 'charismatic–revolutionary', the 'ideo-logical' and the 'bureaucratic–pragmatic'.[43] These categories also refer to leadership 'types', i.e., to the different predispositions of elites. 'In the ideological mode of policy making,' K. J. Holsti writes, in agreement with Kissinger, '. . . policy reflects a constant tension between the bureaucratic elements, with their traditional ways of dealing with problems, and the older revolutionary traditions which emphasize long-range goals and actions abroad involving high risks.'[44] Brecher, in a sophisticated framework which he has used empirically in his prize-winning work on the foreign policies of Israel, has in a similar vein introduced the notion of an 'attitudinal prism', which is part of the 'psychological environment' within which policy processes take place. One of the important components of this 'prism' is 'ideology', which in turn affects the 'images' which elites form of reality and upon which they act, thereby constituting the prime pivot around which foreign policy decisions revolve.[45] They do so for the simple reason (and here he appreciatively quotes Kenneth Boulding) that it 'is what we think the world is like, not what it is really like that determines our behaviour'.[46] 'Indeed,' Brecher adds, 'elite images are not less real than the reality of their environment and are much more relevant to an analysis of the foreign policy flow.'[47] That foreign policy decision-makers are no less prone than others to the effects of this type of 'cognitive behaviourism' is, of course, not entirely unexpected. Indeed, some would maintain that they are rather more than less impressionable in this respect.[48]

Finally, with reference to the *outcomes* or *outputs* of foreign policy, 'ideology' has been variously used not only to describe certain forms of input into the international system, but also to explain why certain types of the international system have been superseded by others. Rudolph J. Rummel, exemplifying the first usage, speaks of 'ideology patterns' in characterizing and explaining votes at the UN; thus the 'positive loading for votes with the U.S. and negative loading for votes with the U.S.S.R. suggests that this is bipolar factor, indexing behaviour associated with opposing ideological positions.'[49] This 'ideological dimension' relates foreign policies to the international system in the sense that it becomes an independent variable in the explanation of certain patterns of behaviour within that system. In this connection Hedley Bull has not only spoken of 'successive ideological conflicts' as 'a cause of . . . major wars', but has also averred:

> If we assume that in the future as in the past there will be constant change and variety in the ideologies that are espoused in different parts of the world, then the attempt to remould a state's system on principles of ideological fixity and uniformity is likely to be a source of disorder, and we are driven back to the principle that order is best founded upon agreement to tolerate ideological differences, namely the principle upon which the present states system is founded.[50]

Mortan A. Kaplan, however, has claimed that the 'rise of . . . new international ideologies . . . sounded the death knell for the "balance of power" international system.'[51] This second type of output usage is also closely tied to the 'theoretical determinism' referred to earlier; in a sense it is simply an expression of this doctrine in terms of an input–output model.

What we have above are more or less randomly picked examples of how the concept of ideology has been used in international relations literature with reference to one or other of the selected dimensions of foreign policy. Thus we have seen that some scholars have tied 'ideology' only to the substance of foreign policies, while others have used it primarily as an input variable; to a third group it has served to explain certain aspects of the processes involved in foreign policy decision making, and a fourth group has viewed it mainly in terms of the outcomes of such behaviour. However, we also find instances in which the term plays a more encompassing and overarching role, linking the concept not just to this or that dimension of foreign policy but to all of them. Three such examples will suffice for purposes of illustration.

K. J. Holsti, first of all, writes that 'Ideologies not only establish foreign policy goals, evaluative criteria, and justifications for actions, but have important effects on perceptual processes as well', and he goes on to give five ways in which 'Marxism–Leninism as an ideology has great consequences in Soviet foreign policy', touching upon all the dimensions mentioned above.[52] 'In American foreign policy,' he adds, 'liberal values and doctrines play a similar role, though they are much less evident as guides to social and political analysis.'[53] Similarly, Zbigniew Brzezinski and Samuel Huntington, writing about the 'value and viability of ideology', claim that 'Ideology and political beliefs play significant roles in the Soviet and American political systems. Ideology gives the Soviet leaders a framework for organizing their vision of political development; it sets limits on the options open to them as policy makers; it defines immediate priorities and long-range goals; and it shapes the methods through which problems are handled.'[54] And expanding on this description of the role of ideological beliefs, they add that their 'impact . . . is most visible and most important in the field of foreign affairs. Here, consequently, the ways in which political ideas shape their approaches to these problems are relatively clear.'[55] Our third example comes from the European side of the Atlantic. F. S. Northedge, speaking generally about ideology, defines it as 'the prevailing political orthodoxy of a state', and then applies this notion specifically to foreign policy:

> We may distinguish between various functions of ideology in foreign policy: to bind the country together psychologically, to provide a scale of values by which its people may know what to strive for and what to repudiate; a frame of reference enabling men to make sense of the otherwise bewildering world they inhabit and justify their government's efforts to grapple with it; a prism through which states perceive the international realities on which their foreign policy must work.

Without ideology a nation does not exactly perish, but it can hardly know what to approve and disapprove.[56]

These three examples from the literature not only illustrate a usage of 'ideology' which is as wide in scope as it is in content, but they also bring us back to our starting-point: the omnibus – and hence 'black box' – character of the term, and the query, which ineluctably impinges on the mind as a consequence of this condition, whether it means anything significant and substantive at all.

For if 'ideology' can signify all of these things, can it mean anything at all in and by itself? And if it means some of these things to some scholars, and other things to others, can it possess a distinctive meaning of its own which at least a cross-section of scholars can agree upon? And if so, how is one to establish a defini-tion which is persuasive enough to warrant such acceptance? This is the thrust of the questions which this study will tackle and attempt to answer.

B   THE LOGIC AND METHODOLOGY OF THE ANALYSIS

These queries, involving both semantic and conceptual ramifica-tions of the first order, cannot, or at least ought not to, be considered in isolation. For the problem with 'ideology' is not only semantic but also in a crucial sense *philosophical* and *methodological*, i.e., it is an issue which can only be resolved in terms of the type of inquiry which falls within the ambit of the philosophy of social science rather than within an empirical subdiscipline. More specifically, it raises the question of the role – broadly speaking – of psychological, cognitive, ideational, normative and related factors in theories of foreign policy; and in so doing it implicates some of the most fundamental and controversial issues, not only in the comparative analysis of foreign policy as a subdiscipline, but in the field of political science as a whole. Clearly, it makes a significant difference, with respect to such a term as 'ideology', if we propose to pursue the analysis of foreign policy in terms of, say, a structural–functional, or a behavioural, or a Marxist, or a game-theoretic, or a systemic, or a bureaucratic, or a decision-making or any other equally contending 'theoretical' approach. For these obviously 'offer different accounts of those features crucial for explanation and the causal relations which hold', as Charles Taylor has written.[57] Consequently, before attempting to explicate a particular concept belonging to this larger – and much debated – subdiscipline, it behoves us first to discuss and clarify the latter in terms of the type of philosophical or metatheoretical approach which we intend to apply.

This is not, however, always recognized within the literature. For despite the fact that the discussion and explanation of international politics is hampered – sometimes crucially, as we have seen above – because participants are talking about different things while using similar terms, they are, as Kenneth N. Waltz has noted, at the same time disinclined 'to treat the question of meaning as a problem that can be solved only through the articulation and refinement of theories. The tendency instead is to turn the problem of meaning into the technical one of making terms operational. That won't help.'[58] With this I can only fully agree. Thus, before addressing the problems surrounding the concept of ideology, we must first ask ourselves what we mean, methodologically, when speaking about 'foreign policy' as our dependent variable, and what we intend to accomplish by positing a 'comparative' framework for its analysis and explanation. As we shall have occasion to note below, the answers to these queries – which of necessity must be couched in philosophical terms – are by no means self-evident or unproblematic.

My argument here is, in other words, that the semantic problem connected with 'ideology' is symptomatic of a more fundamental problem in the field of foreign policy analysis; and that the latter must first be resolved before the former can be successfully tackled. 'Ideology' has shown itself to be one of the most attractive and pliable terms in the social sciences; and it will remain a promiscuous bedfellow – with an exceptionally variegated offspring – until clear and commonly acceptable conceptual and theoretical structures exist in terms of which this semantic profligacy can be contained. Therefore, if our aim is to achieve more than a temporary ameliora- tion of the present condition of our concept, we must of necessity deal with these larger methodological issues first.

Hence, in the following two chapters I will address myself exclusively to these before returning, in chapter 4, to the concept of ideology itself and, in the last chapter, to a consideration of what role it can play as an analytical instrument in the explanation of foreign policy. More specifically, the next chapter will limit itself to a consideration of our dependent variable, i.e., the nature of *foreign policy actions*, while the third will be reserved for a methodological discussion of the *method of comparison* and, more importantly, an *explanatory model* to which it can be linked. And while chapter 4 will deal exclusively with the *conceptualization of ideology* as an explanatory variable, these various – and seemingly independent – issues will be briefly brought together in chapter 5.

I should immediately add, however, that although my aim is to argue for a specific explanatory role for 'ideology', the present book will not deliver all the requisite – and perhaps anticipated – goods in this respect. By limiting itself to the *conceptual* problems of such an endeavour, as the book's subtitle underlines, it will on the whole leave aside the *empirical* issues surrounding the function of ideology in practice. This aspect will be only briefly discussed in the final chapter, even though it is obviously central to the role of ideology as an explanatory concept. For inasmuch as the link between this function of ideology in politics – including foreign policy – and its use as concept in explanatory analysis depends on the elaboration of a *theory of ideology*, it will have to await further elaboration in a different context.

Before proceeding with the tasks outlined above, a few additional introductory remarks will be offered, dealing with some of the general methodological presuppositions and assumptions underlying this study. My intention here is not, however, in the first instance to lay bare the various normative premises which undoubtedly suffuse this analysis, but rather to indicate some of my particular methodological preferences with respect to the comparative study of foreign policy. The philosophical issues and controversies connected with the term 'value' – 'that unfortunate child of misery', as Abraham Kaplan quotes Max Weber – are in any case too complex to be given anything but the most cursory attention here.[59] Instead, I shall address myself to some selected problems associated with what A. James Gregor has called 'metapolitics', that is, the conceptual language of political science.[60]

The first of these concerns the 'theoretical' ambition undergirding this study. The word 'theory' is, needless to say, as ubiquitous a term in political science as it is ambiguous, vague, and above all, inconstant and fickle. Given this, and in order to forestall any misunderstandings, I will briefly indicate in what sense it will be used in the following chapters.

In a somewhat vague manner we can differentiate between two poles in the use of this term in political science. Anatol Rapoport thus speaks of a 'stronger sense', on the one hand, according to which 'a theory must contain logically deduced propositions, which, if referring to portions of the real world, must be in principle verifiable'; and of 'weaker' one, in terms of which 'a theory can simply be a preparation of a conceptual scheme in which a theory in the stronger sense will one day be developed.'[61] In a similar vein, though writing a decade later, Harry Eckstein distinguishes between a 'hard' and 'soft' line on theory, adding that while 'positions range between them, they have recently been rather polarized, more often on, or very near, the extremes than between them.'[62] The hardliners' view on theory is that it consists 'solely of statements like those characteristic of contemporary theoretical physics (or, better, considered to be so by influential philosophers of science)', while the extremists at the other pole regard it as 'any mental construct that orders phenomena or inquiry into them'.[63] In view of this situation, I fully agree with Eckstein that although we could avoid confusion by simply employing the appropriate qualifying adjective each time we use the term 'theory', this would not solve the problem regarding another and more germane question, namely, what we perceive to be *good* theory in our discipline. In addition, he also gets my full support when he avers that neither of these poles represents a viable solution to the problem. The problematic nature of 'theory' is, in short, not simply semantic or terminological, but methodological; and therefore it needs to be argued in terms of the basic desiderata of the philosophy of social science rather than with reference to immediate research considerations.

Eckstein gives us such an argument for a 'middle' position, or rather, one that 'is neither hard nor soft but does come closer to the hard than the soft extreme'.[64] Thus he argues that it 'seems better to label as theory any constructs designed to realize the same ends and formulated with the same animus as those which characterize the fields in which hard theory has been developed ... On this basis, theory is characterized by a telos, or animus, of inquiry rather than by the particular form of statements.'[65] He lists these 'theoretical' ends or goals (on which I shall not elaborate here) under the following headings: regularity, reliability, validity, foreknowledge and parsimony.[66] This teleological conception of theory seems to me to be an obviously sensible and fruitful delineation and delimitation of its utility in political science; and it is in this sense that the term will be used in this study, with the added clarification that in more concrete and succinct terms, this view of 'theoretical' activity and its aims corresponds with what is usually referred to as the creation of empirical generalizations. In a previous essay Eckstein in fact defined theory in this more concise manner. Theories, he thus wrote there, 'are testable (that is, falsifiable) generalizations stating relations among concrete phenomena or, more broadly, abstract forms approximated in concrete experience'.[67] In the eyes of the hardliners this is obviously, 'theoretically' speaking, an unsatisfying definition; but it is certainly not inexact, and for our purposes it is clearly more practicable than theirs, while it avoids the mushiness which characterizes the term in so much of the literature. This does not imply, however, that the meaning that Rapoport gives to the weaker conception is unimportant for 'theory' in our sense; on the contrary, such mental constructs as classificatory or analytical schemas, frameworks, typologies, conceptualizations, etc., are certainly not to be slighted simply because of their 'pretheoretical' nature. Their fruitfulness, however, depends on the contributions they make to theoretical explanations as defined above. I should add that much of what will follow in the ensuing pages belongs to the pretheoretical rather than to the theoretical sphere of inquiry. I hope, however, that the theoretical animus motivating these investigations will be both apparent and justified.

The meaning given to the concept of theory above, and its specification in terms of both a scientific goal and a semantic stipulation defined with reference to it, also contains an additional methodological distinction which should be made clear from the outset, particularly since it applies specifically to the analysis in this book. Generally speaking, one of the most decisive differences between the natural and the social sciences lies in the fact that while

the former has a language of its own, the latter to a large extent
shares its terminology with those whose actions and behaviour
constitute the object of the analysis in question. 'The language of
political inquiry,' Felix Oppenheim thus writes in the introductory
sentence to his contribution to one of the more recent handbook
additions to our disciplinary library, 'has long been the language of
everyday life, as used by politicians and citizens.'[68]It is obviously this
fact, and not any perverse or other wayward inclination, that has
persuaded the editors of that handbook to distinguish between, and
thus alot separate extensive treatments on, the 'logic' and the
'language' of political inquiry.[69]However, this distinction – and in
particular its implications – has not always been fully appreciated
within our discipline. Often it has been ignored altogether, and in
other instances fudged; and when neither of these has been the case,
it has still received such scant attention from scholars that the result
has been more or less the same. Usually the 'language' of political
science has been taken for granted without second thought, while its
'logic' has been assumed to be a question determined mainly by the
techniques at hand, the pliability of the available data, and the
scholar's particular technical proficiences and/or predilections.

However, we shall not go into the details of this problem here, nor
indulge in the questionable pleasures of an extensive litany. Rather, I
simply want to offer one or two suggestions in order to clarify the
relevance of this distinction to our present concerns. The first is that
the logic of political inquiry is more fundamental to analysis than is
language. This is one of the reasons why I will treat the question of
what constitutes a 'comparative analysis' of 'foreign policy' before
trying to delve into the problematic nature of 'ideology'. But
although logic precedes language, it is obvious that without a 'good'
language no logic – however excellent – will get us very far. In this
sense they are interdependent and indeed feed on each other. Thus
although chapter 4 will primarily focus on linguistic problems, it will
become apparent that these also impinge on the previous chapters,
and that logic – I certainly hope – will not be absent in chapter 4. To
a large extent the nexus between the two is the requirement that
there exists a clear link between the logic of comparison and
comparative concepts, while the methodological import of the two
are clearly distinguished. And it is apparent that certain concepts of

political science fall within the first category, while others belong to the second. The difference, given the present context, can perhaps be put as follows: we do not ordinarily speak of one thing as being more 'foreign policy'-like than another, while in ordinary discourse it seems quite natural to say that something is more – or less – 'ideological' than something else. This difference can also be clarified by speaking, respectively, of categorical and comparative concepts; and it is primarily with reference to the desiderata of the former that I shall analyse 'foreign policy', and in terms of the latter that 'ideology' will be conceptualized.[70]

The observant reader will already have become cognizant of some aspects of the general tenor of my views on the logic of inquiry; and for a somewhat more detailed analysis of these he or she is referred to the next chapter, where I will try to defend a position in the philosophy of social science which is neither wildly novel nor, probably, enormously exciting. As to the language of political science, however, I must make some further preliminary remarks here, since I believe that despite what has been said above about the metatheoretical pre-eminence of the logic of enquiry, it is our linguistic deficiencies which at the present time are more prominent within the discipline.[71] It is for this reason (amongst others) that Oppenheim surely is correct when he claims that 'the elucidation of the language of political science is by no means an idle exercise in semantics, but is in many instances a most effective way to solve substantive problems of political research.'[72] For the same reason Karl Popper must be said to be skating on very thin ice indeed when he enjoins that 'Linguistic precision is a phantom, and problems connected with the meaning or definition of words are unimportant ... Words are significant only as instruments for the formulation of theories, and verbal problems should be avoided at all costs.'[73] A few pointers as to my own standpoint may be in order here.

First of all, if it is true (as Ludwig Wittgenstein has claimed) that 'the meaning of a word is its use in a language', it is equally true that 'language is a historic deposit', and that in a given historical period – such as our own – we find not only one but various languages layered on various levels in human discourse.[74] Hence to pass unawares (or nonchalantly) from one of these to another is bound to cause us considerable grief and consternation. An obvious referent here for my disapprobation is the semantic miscreant usually referred to as 'ordinary usage'. I will have more to say about the mischief that it has caused when analysing 'ideology', but a few caveats may already be appropriate at this point.

The first of these is that the use of ordinary language is unavoidable; and in view of this we all do well to heed J. L. Austin's advice: 'Ordinary language is *not* the last word, in principle it can everywhere be supplemented and improved upon or superseded. Only remember, it is the *first* word.'[75] The use of the language of daily intercourse is certainly to be preferred to that penchant for semantic obfuscation on the part of some social scientists which seems to be rampant in much of the 'technical' literature. This, however, does not mean, given a *ceteris paribus* clause, that ordinary language is necessarily superior to some other language. Rather, the pertinent question here is surely: 'Which are the concepts that are to be taken over from ordinary language into the language of political science?'[76] And equally surely, this is a question which ordinary language cannot answer by itself. It is here that the logic of inquiry comes in; for it is only in terms of the latter that the requisite distinctions between levels of language can be made, and with reference to which we can determine the function of language on each of these. This is thus not a brief against the immense richness and intellectual evocativeness of language as ordinarily spoken (or rather, when spoken well), or against the inherent soundness of the vocabulary of everyday speech. Nor is it an argument in favour of an artificial language replete with neologisms, or of what Giovanni Sartori disparagingly calls 'novitism'.[77]

It is, however, an argument against the regrettable practice, all too common among political scientists (but certainly not only amongst them), of attempting to settle a conceptual dispute simply by appealing either to the ordinary language of day-to-day discourse or to the terminological practices of fellow scholars. The former, while philosophically not an entirely suspect practice, is unacceptable in so far as it builds on the highly questionable assumption that the language of political science is – and ought to be – wholly coterminous with that of politics. As to the latter, its dubiousness has already been amply illustrated in the first part of this chapter.

Finally, if theories 'are the artifacts of deliberative language use', and if the clarification of 'the language of political inquiry consists . . . in constructing an adequate scientific language out of elements of ordinary discourse', then it is clear that a choice has to be made with regard to how 'deliberative' we want to make our concepts, and how 'open' they should be in order to remain 'adequate'.[78] My view is that this question cannot be settled a priori, but that we should always to some degree aim at open-textured definitions in order to avoid the dangers of 'premature closure'. As Gregor has noted, 'concepts whose meanings are arbitrarily and unalterably fixed can be stultifying'; hence our explications should be couched in terms approximating rather than exhausting a specific meaning.[79] At the same time, as Kaplan has advised us, we ought to see to it that the 'initial contexts of application . . . provide enough closure to contain usable empirical meaning', i.e., one which will provide a substantive yield in inquiry.[80] In other words, our definitions should *not* be 'indefinite' or 'open' to such an extent that the dimensions specifying the boundaries of a concept cannot be pinpointed in a relatively precise operational or empirical manner. 'Indefiniteness' in this sense is surely the straightest path to that most classic of fallacies, namely, the fallacy of equivocation.

Rather, the kind of premature closure which is at issue here and against which we should be on our guard is that type of conceptual specification which entices us to attempt to solve empirical problems simply by resorting to stipulative or definitional explication. At the same time, an awareness of this danger should not lead us to commit the opposite error, that of eschewing clearly specified demarcations of meaning. Hence, although Oppenheim's precept that we should 'steer a middle ground between vagueness and rigidity' in our conceptualizations is perhaps easier proffered than practised, it is nevertheless my ambition to do precisely this in the ensuing pages.[81] I will also try to avoid cluttering them with an abundance of definitional minutiae, since my aim is to present the skeleton of our subject matter, not all of its many muscles, nerves and tissues.

2

Foreign Policy Actions

If, as I intend to argue in the next chapter, the main purpose of the comparative study of foreign policy is to generate empirical generalizations, then the first order of business is to delimit our subject matter. That is to say, before we can proceed to analyse foreign policies in these terms, it is essential to specify the class or universe of cases (or phenomena) which we propose to consider in our research. As an analytical procedure this belongs to what F. S. C. Northrop has referred to as the 'natural history stage of inquiry'; and for our purposes it can perhaps best be pursued in terms of what Giovanni Sartori – following in Aristotle's footsteps – calls 'definition by analysis', i.e., 'the process of defining a term by finding the genus to which the object designated by the term belongs, and then specifying the attributes which distinguish such an object from all the other species of the same genus'.[1] This is the essence of the taxonomical method of classification (hallowed in Latin as analysis *per genus et differentiam*); and I fully agree with Sartori (and Harry Eckstein) that its frequent neglect in much of contemporary social science has contributed substantially to our methodological and disciplinary problems in the study of politics, including foreign policy.[2]

The main reason for the necessity of classification is that only on the basis of a taxonomical *Ausgangspunkt* can we speak about comparability at all. Obviously, before comparing anything we must know what we are comparing. Or, as Arthur Kalleberg has written about the logic of inquiry underlying the comparative method, science 'must know what is not, or what is not this but that – in short, science must first of all discriminate.'[3] In other words, a proper classification constitutes the most basic type of conceptualization in the comparative analysis and explanation of whatever concrete phenomena may capture our scholarly interest or fancy. Thus, although it may be a naïve belief, as John Gunnell has averred, that there is 'necessary and natural progression in any science from taxonomy or description and classification to explanatory theory', it is certainly not simple-minded to maintain that no explanations – comparative or otherwise – can be posited without their being grounded in the most basic form of concept formation entailed by the method of definitional classification.[4] And although, as Kalleberg also has noted, concept formation 'as a general problem in philosophy . . . is extremely complex inasmuch as it covers questions of definition, classification, comparison, measurement, and empirical interpretation', he is surely right when he adds that the basic objective of conceptualization is the analysis of 'questions of definition and especially of the criteria of classification to be used in developing the basic concepts of political science, concepts of the attributes of political phenomena'. For not 'only is it necessary to resolve this question prior to engaging in the questions of comparison and measurement, but it is precisely on this most basic level that it is possible to see most clearly the nature of the misunderstandings held by antagonists on both sides of the controversy about a behavioural science of politics.'[5] It is thus not merely due to reasons inherent in the logic of inquiry that the priority and importance of classificatory conceptualization have to be stressed, but also, as we shall see shortly, because of the philosophical implications involved in opting for certain definitions of meaning (or class attributes) while rejecting others. By defining a universe of phenomena we also posit, on the most fundamental level, our conceptual view of the nature of politics and social life – a view implicating a philosophical stance of the first order and one containing a host of methodological ramifications. Furthermore, as Murray Edelman has written, to 'place an object in one class of things rather than another establishes its central characteristics and creates assumptions about matters that are not seen.'[6] For these reasons we do well to pay careful heed to how, and on the basis of what philosophical and methodological considerations, we define our basic conceptual categories.

Delimitation is a form of classification – indeed the first step in the process – and in the comparative analysis of foreign policy the basic delimitation which must be made before any other classification (and eventual comparison and explanation) can proceed is that of the *unit of analysis*: the answer to the question, in our case, of what constitutes the class (or universe) of phenomena which we wish to call 'foreign policy'.[7]

> The choice of unit [Johan Galtung has written] is probably the first decisive choice made in most investigations. Once made, it is hard to reverse: the procedure will be built up around this choice. For that reason it is essential to have a clear picture of the spectrum of possible units, so that the choice based on the research problem may be a fruitful one, and not only a traditional one.[8]

In the contemporary literature on foreign policy it is embarrassingly easy to unearth a surfeit of choices that have been made in this matter; and I am afraid that most of them fall within Galtung's 'traditional' rather than 'fruitful' category (although I fail to perceive the logic of his epithets).

In particular I have in mind such 'actor' entities as the 'state' or 'nation–state', the 'decision-making unit' ('State department', 'Foreign Office', 'bureaucracy', 'elites', and so on), as well as such 'systemic' units as 'structures', 'processes', 'effects' or 'outcomes'. Prime examples of each are readily available in the literature, and thus need hardly be cited here. Nor shall I offer individual or particular arguments against these choices (which, furthermore, are often made subconsciously and are hence implicit rather than explicit), except to say that, although I by no means wish to claim that any of these concepts or constructs are a priori unfruitful or harmful to the field of foreign policy research as such, I reject the suggestion that any of them constitutes the unit of analysis in this field, i.e., the phenomenon which we wish to describe and to explain. When and if they enter into our analysis of foreign policy, I submit that they should do so only in some other – however honourable – capacity, and only after an explicit and formal definition of this unit has been provided.[9] Thus clearly an 'actor' (however defined) cannot be a 'foreign policy', nor can a 'process', a 'structure' or an 'outcome' be a 'foreign policy'. Rather, if we weld 'foreign policy' to any of these concepts, it is surely to qualify them in one way or another; but in so doing we have, of course, immediately changed our unit of analysis to something other than 'foreign policy' – that is, in each case we have then posited a universe of phenomena in which 'foreign policy' is used to classify either 'actors', 'processes', 'structures' or 'outcomes' into a respective subclass. In short, it has then become a classificatory criterion and not a unit of analysis.

Instead, I will argue in favour of the proposition that we should regard *foreign policy actions* as our unit of analysis. And I shall do so according to the taxonomical principle referred to above, that is, by a definitional analysis in terms of what Sartori calls ladder-climbing.[10] Or rather, I propose to *descend* a ladder of abstraction, starting from the most inclusive and universal category to the most specific. Such a descent involves the successive introduction of classificatory properties (or connotations) into the analysis, which as a result decreases the denotation (or extension) of the term in question; and its purpose here is to retain as universal a category or unit of analysis as possible – to allow for subsequent comparisons to be made – while at the same time unfolding a unit which is specific enough to make empirical generalizations and testability feasible.[11] The main aim is thus to propose a unit of analysis which ideally combines inclusiveness with specifity, the extensional requirements of the comparative method with differentiae which make comparisons meaningful. And in view of these requirements and the procedure indicated above, I shall start with a consideration of the concept of *action*, since – given the above proposition – this is prima facie the obvious genus of which 'foreign policy' is a species. It is also, I believe, the category most in need of elucidation, for reasons which, it is hoped, will become evident below.

But before doing so, a few additional comments on the nature of classificatory definitions may be in order. First of all, it is obvious that specifications of meaning cannot in themselves be either true or false. They are merely stipulated conventions – or attempts towards establishing such – serving particular and clearly specified pur- poses. Thus, as May Brodbeck has written, to 'criticize a concept on the ground that its definition is not "really" what the concept means makes sense only if the definition is proffered as an explication of how a term is already being used. In that case we are given not a definition – which is always stipulative – but a report, which may be true or false.'[12] My intention is obviously not to submit a report in this sense, even though such an exercise may in itself be illuminative in view of the conceptual disarray prevailing in our field. Rather, I will be arguing the case for a specific proposal in regard to 'foreign policy', i.e., a definition which one may take or leave at will. From this, and for obvious reasons, it also follows that I am proposing not an 'essentialist' but rather a 'nominalist' definition of our unit of analysis. Carl Hempel has distinguished between these two metatheoretical approaches to conceptualization as follows. Nominal definitions are 'characterized as a stipulation to the effect that a specified expression, the definiendum, is to be synonymous with a certain expression, the definiens, whose meaning is already determined', while an essential (or 'real') definition 'is not a stipulation determining the meaning of some expression, but a statement of the "essential nature" or the "essential attributes" of some entity'.[13] In other words, we will here be dealing not with the intrinsic nature or qualities of 'foreign policy', but merely with the establishment of a conceptual instrument by means of which relationships between given phenomena may be traced in terms of empirical generalizations.

Furthermore, when conceptualizing we should distinguish between theoretical and operational definitions, between what has also been called the 'unit of analysis' and the 'unit of observation'.[14] It is clear that the requirements for the two are different, in that theoretical (or formal) definitions of concepts state their meanings, while operational definitions contain statements regarding the 'operations' by means of which a 'meaningful' concept can be empirically specified and measured.[15] Or as Hempel has written, an operational definition of a concept 'is conceived as a rule to the effect that the term is to apply to a particular case if the performance of specified operations in the case yields a certain characteristic result.'[16] Given this distinction, I here take the position that the operationalization of a concept is typically a laboratory procedure in one form or another, and as such cannot provide us with the theoretical linkages which explanations call for and which only formal definitions can vouchsafe. That is to say, without formal or constitutive definitions of meaning we cannot hope to achieve the 'systematic import' – as distinguished from, but not unconnected with, 'empirical import' – which, in Hempel's view, is so basic to any fruitful conceptualization.[17] This does not mean, of course, that operational definitions are unimportant or unnecessary. It merely specifies that they implement formal definitions rather than replacing them – that, in Sartori's words, 'there must be a conceptualization before we engage in operationalization.'[18] In what follows I shall thus limit myself to the formal conceptualization of our unit of analysis, leaving the operational problem aside for the time being.

A FOREIGN POLICY AND THE CONCEPT OF ACTION

Nobody, I believe, would seriously care to dispute the supposition that 'foreign policy' constitutes a form of behaviour, and more particularly, a form of behaviour emanating from, or at least ascribable to, human beings. In other words, just as in any other sphere in which we work as social scientists, we are here concerned primarily with aspects of human instrumentality. Or as John Steinbruner has laconically put it: 'Presumably there is no one who would seriously contest that the human brain is the ultimate locus of decision making.'[19] However, if – following common philosophical practice – we define 'action' as purposive human behaviour, i.e., that class of behaviour which in one way or another involves a description of motives, purposes, reasons and intentions, and stipulate that 'foreign policy' should properly be classified solely in terms of this form of human instrumentality, some objections will perhaps be raised. And yet it seems evident to me that this is precisely what distinguishes the analysis of foreign policy from the different universe of cases designated as 'international politics', 'international relations', 'transnational politics', and so forth. In the latter we are dealing with a much more complex configuration of human and other factors, i.e., with relationships which are not necessarily or exclusively purposive and which as a result call for descriptions and explanations which essentially cover a different and much wider spectrum of phenomena on a higher level of analysis and abstraction. Thus the differences between, e.g., bipolar and multipolar international systems with regard to the presence or absence of stability are commonly – and properly – not explained in terms of action-oriented concepts; but the question, say, why state A's foreign policy is stable over time while state B's is fickle calls, I submit, for precisely such concepts.[20]

There are several reasons why we should consider 'foreign policy' in terms of the concept of action. The least important, perhaps, is that both intuitively and traditionally it has been treated in this way, although not always explicitly and in full cognizance of the philosophical and methodological implications of the concept.[21] A second and more weighty reason is that 'behaviour' *per se* has far too wide a denotation to serve any useful discriminatory purpose in this context: its scope ranges from the most purposeful to the most instinctive and somnambulic, from the running of the marathon to the jerking of a leg when the patellar tendon is tapped. A third and perhaps more controversial reason is that in positing 'action' as the genus of which 'foreign policy' is a species, we steer clear of such units of behaviour as are usually described in terms of the adjectives 'structural', 'functional', 'systemic', and so forth. These terms may serve a purpose in the subsequent theoretical exploration of foreign policy, but as descriptive designations for our central unit they are in my view quite inappropriate, simply because their meanings depend not on observables but on particular theories; for not only do they function as 'hypothetical constructs' in these theories, but they also derive their meaning from them. In all such cases of 'theoretical terms' their very systemic nature disqualifies them from acting as observable terms; for (as Abraham Kaplan writes) even 'to make the relevant observations already involves the theory . . . what begins as the effort to fix the content of a single concept ends as the task of assessing the truth of a whole theory'.[22] Or as Hempel has noted of theoretical terms, they usually 'purport to not directly observable entities and their characteristics . . . They function . . . in scientific theories intended to explain generalizations.'[23] And it is certainly not such a function that we seek from our basic units of analysis: to do so would be to confuse the difference between the empirical classification of phenomena and their explanation. Furthermore, while the distinction between theoretical and empirical terms is admittedly not clearcut at all times, methodologically it is generally acknowledged that the former cannot be reduced to, nor derived from, the latter.[24]

However, the most significant reason for treating our unit as a species of 'action' is that it forces us to face squarely some of the most fundamental philosophical problems surrounding the conduct of inquiry in this field. Indeed, by emphasizing the centrality of this concept we are at the same time forced to consider seriously the question of what constitutes explanation in an area of analysis suffused with purposive behaviour. And this is a query which, although often neglected by both foreign policy analysts and by political scientists generally (or, for that matter, by the social sciences as a whole), is obviously of prime methodological importance. Part of the reason for this neglect is a tradition (stretching back to Arthur Bentley and Charles E. Merriam) claiming sole legitimacy for 'behavioural' frameworks in the analysis of social and political phenomena; and in such positivistic or neo-positivistic approaches the concept of purpose as an explanatory (or 'causal') variable is notoriously lacking. Even when 'action-oriented' concepts have been present, as for example in the case of Talcott Parsons's and Neil Smelser's work on the 'general theory of action', 'action' itself very soon becomes submerged by the grander pursuit of 'general theory', which as a result (to use George Homan's pithy words, in an address pointedly entitled 'Bringing Men Back In') 'appear[s] to have no actors and mighty little action'.[25] Another reason is of course the fact that philosophers themselves have disagreed strongly about the methodological implications of 'action' and such 'action'-oriented terms as reasons, motives, intentions and purposes.[26] And this, in turn, is a function of the long debate about the basic premises of the philosophy of social science in general, and particularly about the nature and logic of explanation in this area of inquiry, which differs in some fundamental respects from the world of the natural sciences. The controversy has been about how the sciences of nature are related to the study of man and society; and ever since Wilhelm Windelband made his celebrated distinction between 'idiographic' and 'nomothetic' explanations in the late nineteenth century, this question has remained topical and controversial.[27] Hence it is perhaps not surprising that political scientists have in general tended to steer clear of these issues and the heat generated by them.

They have paid a price for so doing, however, and at times – indeed, all too often – it has been unnecessarily high.

This is not, however, the place to go into the intimate details of this exceedingly complex philosophical issue-area. Instead, I shall proceed as expeditiously as possible by merely outlining what I believe to be some of the more important methodological implications of regarding foreign policy as essentially 'action'-like in nature, while at the same time indicating how this bears upon the question of what constitutes explanation in this field of analysis.

1 First of all, I take the view that much of human behaviour – though obviously not all of it – is in principle amenable to 'causal' explication in terms of purposive concepts. In other words, I submit that explanations couched in terms of motives, intentions, beliefs and purposes are not, because of this, necessarily explanations of a non-causal kind. As against this position – sometimes referred to as the 'naturalist' claim – a number of philosophical arguments have been proffered. Here I shall briefly refer to five and give reasons why we should reject each one of them.

The first and perhaps most important is the assertion that intentions, etc., cannot be causes, since they are logically, not causally, linked to the action in question.[28] They cannot be causal, it is claimed, since it is a generally accepted Humean tenet that a cause must be a separate event from that which is its effect; that is to say, causes must be independent of, as well as antecedent to, their effects.[29] Two different versions of this thesis have been espoused. The first claims that since an intention and an intended behaviour – the action in question – are logically linked by way of identical or interdependent descriptions, it follows *ipso facto* that a relationship of contingency between the two is excluded, i.e., the former then cannot in a Humean sense cause the latter, since the two events are not susceptible to logically independent descriptions.[30] In effect, they can be said to refer to one and the same event. The other version is based on the assertion that an intention to 'perform' a given action cannot be specified except in terms of a disposition to perform the intended action, thereby indicating that the two are not logically independent.[31]

A second important argument against the naturalist position is that causes act *a tergo*, while this is not true of intentions, etc., which operate *a fronte*. In A. J. Ayer's apt imagery, 'causes push while motives pull', and because of this it is argued that the latter, due to their inherent teleological nature, cannot have a causal function.[32] Thirdly, it has been asserted that since behaviour based on purposive factors is rule-governed, it is not and cannot be expressed in terms of the causal explanatory model, which posits connections based on properties of generality rather than on purposive rule-following patterns.[33] The argument here is that we can predict human actions because we know the systems of rules which operate in given social settings; and hence, for this very reason, we cannot be offering a causal explanation. A fourth argument is that while reasons justify and make actions intelligible, causes do not; instead they necessitate the effects which we attempt to explain. In other words, causes posit connections between events in terms of relations of regularity, while reasons are related to actions in terms of justificatory relevance.[34] Causes are thus based on nomic connections, while reasons do not have such implications of generality: they are basically 'idiographic' as opposed to 'nomothetic' in character.

A final argument refers to the intentionality of purposive behaviour, which is said to distinguish it radically from behaviour causally explained. For while in the latter type of explanation any extensionally equivalent causal statement can be substituted for any other causal statement without any explanatory loss, this does not hold for the former, i.e., for behaviour based on a *specific* intention on the part of the agent. Thus, for example, we can say that somebody died because he ventured out onto a dangerous thoroughfare and was hit by a motor vehicle, but also that he died because his head was squashed by a skidding Harley–Davidson. Both of these alternative statements adequately characterize the causal antecedent, and are thus, as causal explanations, equally acceptable.[35] This does not hold, however, for particular actions explained in purposive terms. People often behave or act similarly – such as hurrying to a church or concert hall – for very different reasons, and hence only the pertinent motivating reason in each case adequately explains a particular person's behaviour. Thus going to a church or a concert hall can in one case constitute the act of yielding obeisance to God Almighty or to Gustav Mahler, while in another being an expression of particular architectural predilections; and sometimes people do the same thing for different reasons on different occasions. Or as a witty philosopher has expressed it, there 'are many ways to insult a bishop and many actions which a bishop would miscontrue if he took them for insults. A man can pray without kneeling and kneel without praying.'[36] In less sacerdotal but equally ecclesiastical terms, I. C. Jarvie has noted that people's 'reasons for going to church may have very little to do with what they are doing in going to church'.[37] Hence, it is claimed, explanations based on intentions cannot be causal in nature.

Let us now turn to a very brief and critical consideration of each of these five arguments. First of all, with regard to the logical connection argument, it seems evident to me that (a) we, at least in part, have to concede that intentions, purposes or reasons by their very nature are conceptually (or definitionally) related to their consequent actions, and that they in this sense obviously differ from causes defined in the strict Humean sense; but (b) that it does not follow from this that these concepts therefore cannot refer to causes. Instead, it can be claimed that they merely refer to causes of a somewhat different and special kind. Furthermore, this applies to both versions of the logical connection argument, as Donald Davidson has argued in his classic paper on this topic.[38] Also, the fact that there exists a partial definitional nexus between reasons and actions does not mean, as Felix Oppenheim has noted more recently, that they are equivalent in meaning.[39] Indeed, the distinction between causes and reasons is neither as transparent nor as cut and dried as many philosophers and other scholars have assumed. Thus, e.g., having a good 'reason' for doing something often gives us a good 'cause' for doing it.[40] Furthermore, when looking at purposive explanations we should always, as Don Locke has insisted, distinguish between an intention which an agent may have, and the fact that he has it. In his own words, 'it is the content of the agent's belief, what he believes, which constitutes his reason, the agent-reason ... But it is the existence of this belief, that he believes it, which provides the explanation, and will hence be the cause, if anything is.'[41] The causal fact is thus not the belief as such, but the different fact that one *has* that belief; and it is to this factual condition that we refer when we speak of an efficient cause. There is no logical condition between *this* event as the antecedent to an action, and the action itself: thus having a reason is one thing, and acting because of one's having this reason is obviously something else. Or as two other scholars have put it, 'while reasons cannot be causes (they *are* utterly different sorts of things), the *having* of reasons, the believing in reasons, the *giving* of reasons, etc., are all psychological events and, as such, nothing prevents them from figuring in causal explanations.'[42] This difference has also been referred to in terms of explanations having an 'in order to' and a 'because of' aspect, both of which figure prominently in purposive explanations. And it is clear that the logical connection argument, if pertinent, pertains only to the former.[43]

In so far as it contains the implication that an event can be explained only if a posited goal has actually been realized, the anti-naturalist argument in terms of an extreme 'push–pull' interpretation of teleology leads to patently absurd consequences. This is at least the case when and if this goal is viewed as the factor which quite literally determines the prior event that is to be explained. This view has also been referred to as teleology defined as temporally reversed efficient causation; and as such it is a standpoint against which Ayer's argument surely is sufficiently persuasive, namely, the supposition that even 'if men generally succeed in fulfilling their purposes, they do sometimes fail, and the explanation of their embarking on the action must be the same whether the purpose is fulfilled or not.'[44] Hence he rules out 'ends' *qua* '*future* ends' as a determinant of an action, since 'we cannot think it possible that an event may be pulled into existence by one that never exists at all.'[45] However, if it is not this extreme form of teleology that is at issue, then it seems to me – as in the case of Charles Taylor's arguments for the primacy of teleological explanations in human affairs – that we are simply dealing with explanations of the ordinary purposive kind. These, as I have already indicated, can be considered as genuine contingent antecedents of the particular action to be explained, and are hence causal in the sense adduced above.[46]

As to the rule-following argument, most consistently pursued by Richard Peters, it seems clear to me that while some aspects of social behaviour can be predicted and thus explained in terms of social norms and rules, there is an equally great – and certainly a more interesting – variety of actions which cannot be fitted into this felicitous pattern. And even if we could fit a piece of behaviour into such a pattern, we are still left with the question of *why* the person in question adheres to that pattern (or why somebody else doesn't); so that even if on this first level we are not speaking in terms of causal explanations, we can and must do so on the second level. In viewing a given person at a polling booth, we can with some confidence predict his or her overt behaviour *qua* voter; but knowledge of institutional or stipulated procedures and roles will be irrelevant, for example, in answering the far more interesting question of why this particular person voted for one party and not for another (or, for that matter, why he or she bothered to vote in the first place).[47]

The argument that the connection between reasons and actions is one of justification rather than causality has been most vigorously expounded by A. R. Louch in his book *Explanation and Human Action*.[48] Without elaborating on his arguments, I think that we can submit to his thesis that reasons justify and make actions intelligible, without at the same time having to conclude from this that such reasons cannot be causal antecedents. Here again the distinction between having a reason for pursuing an action, and actually performing the action in question because of one's having this reason, is pertinent; and it is probable that 'the more reason' we have for doing something, the more causally effective that reason will be (everything else being equal). Hence a reason can have both justificatory and causal power, and the connection between the two must surely be such that we can in principle assess the causal power in the light of the justificatory power.[49] Louch does not seem to have considered this possibility, perhaps because he does not submit or acknowledge the above distinction. This is certainly detrimental to his argument as a whole, namely, the notion that justificatory power is a necessary as well as a sufficient condition for a reason to have explanatory power. In my view the former attribution is justified, but not the latter.

As to the last argument above, i.e., that intentionality cannot be a causal factor due to the inherent specificity of all intentional behaviour, there is a simple answer. For in so far as it is true that only a particular and specific intention has the motivational property that brings about a certain behaviour, this seems to indicate *not* that such intentions cannot be causal antecedents, but rather that reasons are causes of a specific intentional kind with their own peculiar properties. However, I shall not attempt here to expound in any detail on the nature of these properties, since this is so tricky and complex a topic – and so keenly debated – that it is best left in the more capable hands of the professional philosopher. In this context it suffices merely to suggest that an appeal to a special form of causality when speaking about human actions is neither strange nor simply a convenient methodological *deus ex machina*. The fact is, rather, that the meaning of 'causality' itself is anything but transparent and unproblematic in the philosophic literature. As Paul Samuelson – somewhat curiously: but he is not a philosopher – has put it, causality 'apparently is one of those scaffoldings inside which you can build a sermon of any type'.[50] Furthermore, as R. F. Atkinson has noted (with specific reference to historiography):

> There has often been a tendency to dismiss non-regularity, non-Humean uses of 'cause' as merely confused, but I believe that the implication of the more careful recent discussions is that historians and other 'ordinary' speakers have no reason to allow themselves to be brow-beaten in this way. They should not be too ready to abide by restrictions, imposed in the name of Hume, philosophy, even science, on what they are otherwise inclined to say.[51]

In this matter we must, obviously, distinguish between different forms of causality; and although I shall not delve into this question here, the following threefold classification, made by Alisdaire MacIntyre, can serve both as a suggestion and to round off this discussion.

In an order ranging from the strictest to the least strict meaning of 'cause', MacIntyre distinguishes between: (1) the Humean view, according to which 'one event is the cause of another, if and only if events of the former type have uniformly been observed to precede events of the latter type, and events of the latter type have uniformly been observed to follow events of the former type ... The occurrence of the earlier event is both a necessary and a sufficient condition of the occurrence of the latter event'; (2) the meaning of 'cause' which 'is equivalent to "necessary, but not necessarily sufficient, condition" '; and (3) the sense in which 'cause is a lever, a means of producing some other event.' This sense 'brings out the importance for causality of the concept of what would have happened if the cause had not operated', and as such underlies the former two, since all 'causal explanation presupposes a background of generalizations about what occurs in the absence of the cause.'[52] To this I will simply add that usually, when speaking about causation in human affairs, we probably intend to refer to either or both of the latter two types, and not to strict Humean causality. And in the light of these two it is perhaps not so difficult to understand why reasons, while intentional to the core, can and do have causal powers; and why, although these are not causes of a strict Humean kind based on the principle of regularity, they are not so special as to be mystical. As William P. Alston has put it, 'We most naturally speak of causes where some agent does something which results in an interference with the natural operations or conditions of some *other* agent or substance.'[53] Or in Oppenheim's words, 'Causality is not a "positivistic" concept, but an indispensable building block of a conceptual scheme of political inquiry – whatever one's philosophy of action.'[54] In short, it seems eminently sensible to speak of intentions, purposes, etc., as behavioural levers; and to claim that although they may not necessarily be sufficient to bring about an action, they nevertheless constitute necessary antecedents to such actions.[55] Since we will have reason, in the following chapter, to return to this topic in more detail, I shall not elaborate further on it here.

2 The second major methodological implication of regarding foreign policy as a species of action-like behaviour does not flow logically from the naturalist position defended above; and yet it is closely connected with his tenet, since it rests on the assumption that actions are causally related to purposive antecedents. The implication I have in mind here is the view that explanations of actions must take their starting-point in the intentions, motives, purposes, etc., of the person or persons whose actions we are studying.[56] Or as MacIntyre has put it, attention to these purposive categories 'must precede attention to causes; description in terms of the agent's concepts and beliefs must precede description in terms of our concepts and beliefs.'[57] Brian Fay and J. Donald Moon have made

the same point when they note that 'because social phenomena are intentional, their very identity depends upon the concepts and self-understanding of social actors, and so in order to explain social behaviour social scientists are constrained to use the actors' framework.'[58] However, as they go on to argue, this is by no means the whole matter; and it is because Peter Winch takes this starting-point – the determination of the actors' own intentional framework – to constitute the whole task of the social sciences that his famous *The Idea of a Social Science*, while both necessary and enlightening (particularly when viewed in terms of the period when it was first published), must at the same time be considered to be so fundamentally misconceived.[59] We do not want *only* to describe 'actions' in this particularized sense, but also to account for the systematic regularities which certainly do abound in the social lives of human beings.

In my view this is best done along the lines of Kaplan's simple but seminal distinction – not unrelated to Alfred Schutz's phenomenological standpoint – between 'acts' and 'actions', and between 'act meaning' and 'action meaning'. An 'act' is the atom, so to speak, of behaviour, the discrete unit of behaviour encompassing all biophysical operations, movements and events which we observe, while an 'action' is a specification of the former in terms of the given perspective which gives 'acts' meaning and purpose from the viewpoint of the agent (or those interacting with him), thereby constituting an 'act meaning'. In Kaplan's words, 'An action is an act with a certain act meaning, as voting is the act of marking a ballot when this is performed in the framework of certain political institutions.'[60] 'Action meaning', on the other hand, refers not to the meaning of given 'acts' to the actor concerned, but to the significance of 'actions' for the scholar or social scientist studying them.

Two levels of analysis are thus involved here. To understand certain *acts* in terms of their meaning within a given purposive context of interaction is not the same as understanding the meaning of *actions* in terms of what we consider to be appropriate theories or generalizations regarding behaviour, purporting to explain not only particular acts but classes of behaviour in general. And the social scientist is necessarily involved in *both* of these forms of interpretation, as distinguished from the natural scientist, for whom the distinction made here is wholly inapplicable. Kalleberg thus writes:

> The world of nature as explored by the natural scientist does not 'mean' anything to the molecules, atoms, and electrons therein. The observation field of the social scientist, however, namely the social reality, has a specific meaning and relevance structure for the human being living, acting, and thinking therein. Thus the constructs of the social sciences are, so to speak, constructs of the second degree, namely constructs of the constructs made by the actors on the social scene, whose behaviour the social scientist has to observe and to explain in accordance with the procedural rules of his science.[61]

Or as Kaplan has put it, the social scientist must first 'strive at an act meaning, i.e., construe what conduct a particular piece of behaviour represents; and then he must search for the meaning of the interpreted action, its interconnections with other actions or circumstances.'[62] The former operation he calls a 'semantic explanation', i.e., an explanation (or interpretation) which construes an act as a certain action, which is then offered as an explanation of the action; while the latter is a 'scientific explanation', since it is based on references to theories or generalizations, or is fitted into some larger, comprehensive pattern of explanation. We can also refer to the former as a description of an action (in terms of Kalleberg's first-degree constructs); and my point here is that as long as we do not rigorously use such descriptions as the starting-point of analysis, any 'scientific' explanations that we may adduce will tend necessarily to be vacuous and probably silly.[63]

It is with regard to this aspect of the social scientific process that the concept or notion of *Verstehen* is pertinent, although not as understood by most logical empiricists, who have tended to identify it with a method whereby an observer (in Ernest Nagel's words) both introspects 'in light of his own "subjective" experiences the "internal meanings" of social action', and validates hypotheses relating to such actions.[64] This misunderstanding of the term builds on Wilhelm Dilthey's notions of empathetic understanding (as well as on the reception of R. G. Collingwood's subsequent writings), rather than on principle made famous by Weber. For while the former can quite properly be chastised for his appeal to introspection and intuitionism (and thus for committing what Richard Rudner calls the 'reproductive fallacy'), no such charge can be levelled against Weber.[65] Rather, in the latter's view this concept merely refers to the idea that actions must be understood and described in terms of their intentional antecedents, i.e., with reference to their subjective nature as purposive behaviour. 'Such understanding,' Gunnell writes in clarification of this notion, 'is subjective not because it is private or an imputation of one's beliefs and feelings to others but because it is directed toward an illumination of the ideational bases of actions', to which he adds that this 'does not involve an intuitive probe of either the individual or group psyche but rather an attempt to give a rational account of observed behaviour in situational–motivational terms'.[66] Or as Weber himself notes, *verstehende* understanding involves 'putting the act in an intelligible and more inclusive context of meaning'.[67] In short, it means that the most important initial step in an inquiry into the meaning of actions must start with an analysis of what meaning a given act has for the actor whose behaviour we wish to clarify.

And yet this dictum is often ignored in the analysis of foreign policy. An illuminating example is provided by James Rosenau and his extensive conceptualization of foreign policy in terms of the notion of 'adaptation'. This is a concept which commonly refers both to a state of mind and to a conscious goal-fulfilling process. Hence it embraces both man's ability to control his environment for his own purposes and the capacity of 'adapting' himself to its requirements; and in both senses it constitutes a norm of behaviour while at the same time being a function of an individual act or series of such acts. In other words, like all human behaviour, adaptive actions are not simply physical events but they also express certain attitudes and expectations, giving them the social and psychological significance which makes acts and interactions meaningful in a behavioural sense. In terms of Kaplan's distinction above, the word 'adaptation' can therefore refer both to adaptive acts and to adaptive actions on the part of the actor, the latter being a specification of the meaning which such acts have for an actor or those interacting with him. In other words, when we say that an act by actor A is an adaptive action, we are explaining this act in terms of its purposive meaningfulness within the perspective which guides A in his behaviour.

Now it is obvious that the notion that foreign policy actions can be explained in terms of adaptive behaviour in this sense – and any other sense would, it seems to me, involve stretching its meaning to the point of meaninglessness – is neither novel nor a priori unsound. It rests on the commonsense premise that statesmen, like all human agents, behave within a framework of action which is dictated both by the desire to control their environment and the need to adjust to its dictates. And like all human beings, they are either successful in this or they succumb to illusions, irrationality, sloth or circumstances beyond their control and thus fail to accomplish what they set out to achieve. The important thing to notice, however, is that in having explained given foreign policy undertakings in this sense, we have not really given a 'scientific explanation' (in Kaplan's sense) but rather a description of the foreign policy behaviour of individuals. The term does not function as an independent variable (or as a second-degree construct in Kalleberg's terminology), but merely describes an instance of 'adaptive' action *qua* purposive behaviour in a given case (i.e., as a first-degree construct with 'act meaning'). And as such there is nothing wrong with this kind of analysis, as long as we are aware of its limits.

However, when we turn to Rosenau's use of the concept, we are faced with a different situation. To illustrate this, I will cite from one of his most extensive articles on the topic, in which he also gives us one of his more elaborate expositions of the use to which he wants to put the concept. After having defined that 'For a national society, adaptation means that fluctuation in the basic interaction patterns that sustain its social, economic, and political life must be kept within limits minimally acceptable to its members', he classifies the politics of adaptation in terms of four mutually exclusive categories, and then explains as follows:

> In short, the type of adaptive balance a society seeks in any given era is conceived to be a basic premise – an organizing conception – that its foreign policy officials bring to every situation they face. They may not think in these terms and they may never have made an explicit choice among the four types of adaptation, but their thought processes are founded on and guided by one of the four orientations to how their essential structures and their environment do and ought to relate to each other, both in the immediate present and in the long run. Thus, while their explicit choices in, say, three specific situations may

lead simultaneously to a military attack, a diplomatic concession, and a neutral stance, such discrepant behaviour forms a consistent pattern viewed from the perspective of the adaptive balance being pursued.[68]

From this passage it is clear, first of all, that Rosenau is attempting to explain foreign policy decisions in terms of a framework which does not refer to *act meaning* but to *action meaning*, i.e., to second-degree constructs, since it is a construction of the latter type which provides the comprehensive pattern – the four mutually exclusive forms of 'adaptation' – into which actions can be fitted and thus be explained and understood. In short, here the concept of adaptation does not refer to the level of act meaning as posited in my discussion above, i.e., to the 'descriptive' level of analysis.

However – and this is where the problem enters in – Rosenau at the same time imputes this conception to individual actors, for whom it is said to function as a meaningful first-degree construct of the purposive kind. That is, the adaptive balance 'sought by a society' is a construction not only of the social scientist or the objective observer, since at the same time it is also said to operate within the mind of the actor whose actions constitute the subject matter of analysis. For although he admits that the particular form of behaviour that he imputes to an actor is not necessarily always a conscious one at any particular point of foreign policy decision making, Rosenau nevertheless speaks of it as 'a basic premise – an organizing conception – that ... foreign policy officials bring to every situation they face ... their thought processes are founded on and guided by one of the four orientations to how their essential structures and their environment do and ought to relate to each other.' Stated differently, the same 'organizing conception' is applied to the understanding of both acts and actions, which is the same as saying that people act foolishly because they are governed by foolishness. Such circles of interpretation are inevitable when the two levels of analysis described above are ignored, and when a construct is made operationally identical with both the dependent behaviour which it purports to explain and the independent variable that is said to explain the dependent behaviour. What we have here is the fallacy of reification, i.e., the mistake of treating second-degree constructs as first-degree constructs as well, or of imputing the scholar's concepts to concrete reality. In this case a second-degree teleological framework is imposed on a first-degree purposive world; and I cannot see how Rosenau can escape this logical sin as long as he speaks of 'adaptation' as a concept not primarily grounded in the concrete reality of purposive behaviour as exhibited and understood by the actors involved. It is *from* this world that we have to extrapolate 'theoretically', not *to* it that we can wilfully impute our own theoretical constructs.[69]

In this matter Charles Reynolds is surely right when he admonishes that

> the action theorist must be in a position to make generalizations about rational behaviour in a social situation which is not imposed upon the situation and on the actor, but which is derived from an understanding of the motives, objectives and the cognition of the nature of the situation itself, on the part of the actor. In short, there must be a conformity between the social mode and the social act, that is, between the theorist's explanation of typical action and the actor's understanding which prompted the action. Otherwise the theorist is imposing a rationalization upon the social action which he is seeking to explain, rather than advancing an empirical explanation.[70]

It is in the light of this dictum that it becomes clear that a fundamental confusion is contained in Rosenau's claim that foreign policy officials 'may not think in these terms ... but their thought processes are founded on and guided by one of the four orientations to how their [sic] essential structures and their environment do and ought to relate to each other ...' This statement is, first of all, an almost Freudian instance of Ruskin's so-called pathetic fallacy – i.e., the attribution of human characteristics to theoretical constructs – in the form of a grammatical slip in which possessive pronouns play havoc with both meaning and logic.[71] It also contains an attribution of extra-conscious and intellective causality to his analytical framework, which is both epistemologically and psychologically highly dubious; and Rosenau does nothing to substantiate it as a hypothesis about the psychic states of foreign policy officials. Apart from the difficulties involved in substantiating a proposition of this kind, such an operation would probably be irrelevant in the context of this type of analysis, since what he seems to be saying is that given his framework it follows logically, i.e., by definition, that the thought processes of foreign policy officials are indeed grounded in one of the four 'adaptive' orientations posited by him. But since this is the establishment of truth by definitional fiat, the proposition turns out to be nothing but a particularly illuminating instance of the question-begging which almost invariably follows when we commit this particular sin of reification. Hence the importance of the methodological stricture that we move from acts to actions, from act meaning to action meaning, rather than the other way round. Only in following such a procedure will we be able to avoid the deep-rooted problems generally involved in the imputational method – problems which, despite the corrective example of Karl Mannheim, are far too often overlooked in the social sciences.[72] And it is because Michael O'Leary, in his critique of Rosenau's concept of adaptation, seems to have missed this point that he can facilely claim that 'As so often happens, the difficulty stems from how the concept is operationalized.'[73] As I have tried to show, the problem here is much more fundamental and serious than this, since it is basically philosophical in nature rather than resolvable merely by appropriating the right research techniques.

3 Closely connected with both of the above methodological standpoints is a further issue, one which caused an extended debate some years ago (primarily amongst Anglo-Saxon philosophers), and which as a bone of contention is still with us today, if perhaps to a lesser degree than before. I shall only briefly touch upon it here, in order to indicate what I feel to be the pertinent relationship between it and the decision to treat foreign policy as a species of action. The issue I have in mind here is that of 'methodological individualism' – the claim, in the eighteenth century poet William Blake's sweeping affirmation, that 'Art and Science cannot exist but in minutely organized Particulars.'[74] As a fundamental tenet of modern social science it was first seriously introduced by Weber, while its major champions since then have included Karl Popper and F. A. von Hayek.

As a principle, methodological individualism has been closely associated with what we can loosely call the 'empirical' tradition in the philosophy of social science; and as a methodological requirement it is commonly juxtaposed against Émile Durkheim's 'positivist' view that in sociology (and in the social sciences in general) 'states of consciousness can and ought to be considered from without, and not from the point of view of the consciousness experiencing them', as well as against his claim – flowing from the above – that 'social facts' refer exclusively to collective concepts not defined in terms of, or with reference to, individual properties. In short, it is 'the collective aspects of the beliefs, tendencies, and practices of groups that characterize truly social phenomena'.[75] This position is usually referred to as 'methodological holism' or, in its extreme forms, as 'ontological holism'; and by Weber's standards it is a position which, as W. G. Runciman writes, 'is fatally vitiated by its illegitimate reification of collective concepts'.[76] Unfortunately the arguments for and against methodological individualism have, on the whole, been quite muddled; and yet it seems clear to me that, given a commitment to the primacy of 'action' in the causal analysis of behaviour, as well as to the tenet that the social scientist ought to begin with a description of the 'act meaning' type before embarking on explanations of 'actions', it follows that we should also commit ourselves to methodological individualism. However, in view of the puddly waters attending this issue-area, I should perhaps explain what I mean here by this principle.

First of all, there has been a confusion between explanatory and descriptive aspects of this debate, and particularly about what is meant by the 'reduction' of social phenomena to individual properties or characteristics. Here I take the view that the reduction involved is on the descriptive and not on the explanatory level, since if it were on the latter level, methodological individualism would be a doctrine supporting – or even identical with – psychologism. Now it is obvious not only that such an identification has been denied by both Weber and Popper, but that psychologism itself can be accepted only if empirical proof for its tenability can be adduced, something which as yet has not been the case.[77] It is due to this distinction that, for example, Joachim Israel, although explicitly a Marxist-oriented sociologist, is nevertheless able to endorse this principle.[78] It is also this, I believe, that is meant by Runciman's description of Weber's methodological individualism, i.e., the view that 'the task of the sociologist is to establish causal explanations of the social actions of individuals, in terms of the meanings of these actions to the individuals themselves.'[79] Furthermore, this does not in any way imply – as some critics seem to think – that collective concepts cannot be used in the social sciences (even concepts which are not precisely defined or definable in terms of individuals). Rather, it simply stipulates that when and if propositions employing collective concepts are used, they must be amenable to testing with reference to individual behaviour. It is in this sense that Ernest Gellner (to some extent a critic of methodological individualism) is right when he enjoins that 'History is *about* chaps. It does not follow that its explanations are always in terms of chaps.'[80] However, if by this he means to imply that this statement is an argument against methodological individualism, he is surely mistaken (as he is when he claims that this principle transforms social scientists into 'biographers *en grande série*').[81] Similarly Oppenheim, perhaps inadvertently, is less than fully clear when he avers, on the one hand, that the 'language of political science may include statements about political "wholes" provided that they can be verified by statements about individual political actors and actions', while, on the other, defining methodological individualists as those holding the view 'that collective terms can be explicated with the help of individual terms exclusively.'[82] The impression that this statement may create is that the former is a 'holistic' position as against the latter; and this is certainly not the case with regard to the methodological individualism defended here.

A confusion has also existed between this principle and what is properly called 'ontological' or 'metaphysical' individualism, i.e., the assertion that 'the only real entities in the social world are individual persons.'[83] The fact is, of course, that the doctrine here endorsed does not in any way deny the reality of social factors and circumstances; nor, as J. O. Wisdom emphasizes, does it dispense with the 'institutional' or 'situational' settings of social phenomena.[84] It merely asserts that only individuals – or individuals in consort – can act purposively, and thus be described in terms of 'action'.[85] In any case, ontological individualism hinges on psychologism (with which it can perhaps even be equated, as Joseph Agassi has pointed out); and it is because Steven Lukes appears to have conflated these two forms of 'individualism' that his criticism of what he wrongly calls the 'methodological' kind seems in my view to strike at a straw man.[86]

A few additional comments on this doctrine may be called for here. First of all, it has at times been asserted that it states nothing but a truism, or that (to quote Runciman) it has been generally accepted as 'almost trivially true'.[87] As to the first claim, I believe it to be false; while the second, in my view, is certainly not applicable today (if it ever was). The falsehood creeps in if we assume that the concept of 'action' necessarily implicates a commitment to methodological individualism. The fact is that one can hold to the descriptive primacy of 'action' and still be either a 'methodological' or an 'ontological' holist: thus Marx, for example, whom I regard as an adherent of at least the former position, can at times be described as asserting the pre-eminence of 'action' *qua* praxis in sociology. And the same applies to some believers in psychologism. The latter claim has to be confronted by the fact that there are once again some strong movements of holism on the ascendancy, particularly in the form of various structural approaches.[88] In other words, methodological individualism is a principle that we are free to accept or to reject; it is not one which we willy-nilly acquire by becoming social scientists.

My second comment concerns the relevance of stressing this principle when writing about the analysis of foreign policy. To some it might seem a somewhat peripheral issue, not really pertinent to our field of study. Such a sentiment is, however, most certainly misplaced. Indeed, I know of few subfields within the social sciences in which an explicit need to stress constantly the reificatory dangers of holism is as evident as in that of foreign policy analysis.[89] How often have we not read that state A 'has done' this or society B that, or of the 'national interest' of 'nation' C and the 'ideology' of 'nation–state' D?[90] Admittedly, these are frequently merely instances of nothing worse than sloppy linguistic habits; but equally often, 'bad' language takes over our thinking, easily enticing us astray (and often unawares) into the fuzzy wastelands of reified holisms and other related methodological iniquities.[91]

Rosenau is here once again a case in point. He thus writes in the same essay quoted previously:

Considerable insight follows from an initial formulation that conceives national societies – like the single cell, the individual, group, or the organization – as entities that must adapt to their environment to survive and prosper. That is, if an entity is to maintain the boundaries that separate it from other entities, it must act toward the other entities in such a way as to keep its essential structures intact.[92]

This statement can be said, on the one hand, to represent a reformulation of the 'billiard-ball' view of international actors as separate, discrete and self-contained entities, a model or imagery which has deep roots in the traditional analysis of international politics, building on the old – and by now rather hackneyed – Westphalian conception of states as enclosed entities within an anarchical environment populated by a host of other, similar states. On the other hand, however, it also represents something else: a holistic conception *par excellence.* And the root of this methodological problem is the analogy or parallel which Rosenau explicitly draws between social psychology, on the one hand, and the 'new' field of national adaptation, on the other. For this analogy leads him to the highly dubious notion that the interaction patterns between a 'political actor' and its environment can be analysed in the same way that the social psychologist studies the interaction between the functioning of the individual and the social influences to which he is exposed.[93]

The difference between these two types of interaction and analysis is fundamental, of course, since the one deals with the individual as an organismic, concrete object of analysis, while a 'national society' (or any of the analytically defined 'political actors' of which he speaks) is obviously something quite different, that is, a construction of the mind. There is in fact no reason to assume that any of the entities to which he refers in the above extract 'act' similarly in a meaningful or comparable way, or that *homo politicus qua* individual can be equated or compared with 'groups', 'institutions' or 'national societies' *qua* actors. These latter are collective terms, and to treat them as if they 'designated individuals of a larger and more elusive kind than those ordinarily encountered in experience' is not only to commit the organismic fallacy, but to reify analytical constructs (also called the practice of misplaced concreteness, to use Alfred North

Whitehead's terminology).[94] And when we say that 'they' 'do' this or that, we are committing the pathetic fallacy as well.

It is precisely because of these dangers that the principle of methodological individualism needs constant stressing, and why we have to be so careful about using holistic language when trafficking with collective concepts. This is not to say that collective terms have no function in social science – on the contrary. But they should be treated with great care and (as Weber, above all, has warned us) only as conceptualizations of the dispositional properties of whole sets of individuals rather than – as the example quoted above – as some kind of socio-political organism or *Übermensch*. Or as Herbert C. Kelman has put it, 'while agreeing that the nation–state remains the basic unit of analysis in international relations, I would stress that individuals constitute the ultimate locus of action.'[95] In short, only the latter constitute the dramatis personae of international politics, and not any of the other second-order 'actor' constructs so ubiquitous in the theoretical literature. In this connection it is perhaps both interesting and edifying to note that Weber was so conscious of the dangers of holistic thinking that (according to Reinhard Bendix) he avoided, wherever possible, the use of nouns for collectivities or other social aggregates.[96]

It is also in the context of the principle of methodological individualism that we should view the importance – for foreign policy and general political analysis alike – of the so-called man–milieu hypothesis, most persistently and convincingly explored by Harold and Margaret Sprout.

> So far as we can determine [they write in explaining it], environmental factors (both nonhuman and social) can affect human activities in only two ways. Such factors can be perceived, reacted to, and taken into account by the human individual or individuals under consideration. In this way, *and in this way alone* . . . environmental factors can be said to 'influence,' or 'condition,' or otherwise 'affect' human values and preferences, moods and attitudes, choices and decisions. On the other hand, the relation of environmental factors to performance and accomplishment (that is, to the operational outcomes of results of decisions and undertakings) may present an additional dimension. In the latter context environmental factors may be conceived as a sort of matrix or encompassing channel, metaphorically speaking, which

limits the execution of undertakings. Such limitations on performance, accomplishment, outcome, or operational results may not –
often do not – derive from or depend upon the environed individual's
perception or other psychological behaviours.[97]

In short, what the Sprouts argue against is the belief or assumption –
contained in many works in the literature – that non-human,
environmental factors can directly determine or cause policies. Or
more specifically, they posit the proposition that the milieu (as they
also call the environment) can affect foreign policies in two ways
only: (1) in so far as it is perceived (or misperceived) by the
individual agent or agents concerned; or (2) as a limiting and
controlling factor on the outcome of the decisions made by these
agents.[98] Not only do I think that these two strictures are valid, but
also that they are very germane to the study of foreign policy.

In this connection the second, in particular, needs to be stressed,
since it should dispel any notion that methodological individualism
claims that everything that happens in a social system is directly the
intended result of human intention, and therefore can be explained
wholly in such terms. This is of course not the case at all. Indeed, as
both von Hayek and Popper have emphasized time and again,
intentional acts often have unintended (and, what is worse,
unwanted) consequences, many of which are as potent in human
affairs as intended consequences, and most of which are more problematic for the social sciences precisely because of their unpurposed
character.[99] Or as Anthony Giddens has put it: 'The escape of
human history from human intentions, and the return of the consequences of that escape as causal influences on human action, is a
chronic feature of human life.'[100] However, this fact does not negate
the principle defended here. Rather, it is only on the basis of it that
we can apperceive this distinction in the first place (and, parenthe-
tically, become immune to unwarranted conspiracy theories, as
Popper also points out in passing).[101]

4 A fourth point which needs to be stressed in this connection is
that although it is necessary, as I have argued, to specify actions in
terms of the purposive nature of the behaviour of individual actors,
this is by no means a sufficient determination if we aspire to
complete the explanatory picture of such actions. That is to say, the

argument that social phenomena are constitutively purposive, and thus that their explanation must necessarily constrain the social scientist to use the actor's framework of intentional reference, should not be taken to justify the conclusion that 'the beliefs, practices and actions which the social scientist encounters are congruent with one another in so far as they are explicable.'[102] Nor should the above tenets lead us to assume the extreme interpretative (or *Verstehen*) position, represented by some phenomenologists, of advocating that the explanations that we proffer must employ essentially the same concepts that would be utilized by an ideal, fully informed and self-consciously articulate participant in the behaviour that we wish to explicate.[103] These two propositions are based on a view of social life which, as Fay and Moon write, 'takes it to be, by definition, rational at some level and understandable in its own terms'; and as such it is not, and cannot sensibly be, a view that is true to life as experienced either by the participant or the observer.[104] For as the same two scholars note:

> people may systematically misunderstand their own motives, wants, needs and actions, as well as the nature of their social order, and – given what we have said about the constitutive role of self-understandings in social life – these misunderstandings may underlie and sustain particular forms of social interaction. In these situations, the actors' ideas may mask social reality as much as reveal it, and so the social scientist cannot confine himself to explicating the way in which the actors' concepts and self-understandings form a coherent whole.[105]

In order to understand these instances, the social scientist must be able to recognize not only the nature of the incoherencies of the actor's self-understandings, but also their social consequences.

Furthermore, the concept of action that is posited in this study should not be confused with the entirely different notion of rational action; nor, indeed, does it implicate or contain any specific reference to rationality itself as a constitutive element. Nevertheless, it would be silly to deny that my position does not adhere to a general presumption of rationality in regard to action. Hence, although actions as here understood can be both rational and irrational, it is obvious (as Jon Elster has written) that in order 'to gather the very evidence on which rationality could be denied in the case of a given individual, we must assume him to be rational if the outwardly observable behaviour is to be translatable into evidence.'[106] Obviously, purposive behaviour is often incongruent with objective reality (the notion of false consciousness is perhaps not wholly suspect here), and in the analysis of foreign policy – as in that of any intentional human activity – this factor is important both in the evaluation and in the explanation of it. Furthermore, we are interested not only in determining whether an action is irrational or not, but also in explaining what causes it to be irrational (or rational, for that matter). In other words, this normative determination immediately poses a causal query, namely, the question why, for example, a given foreign policy course is so obviously out of joint with the reality that it attempts to mould to its own particular purposes.

In this matter we can, following Fay and Moon, distinguish between the competence of an actor and his (or her) actual performance and, a fortiori, between competence and performative explanations (or theories).[107] They have described the significance of this distinction as follows:

> A theory of competence is designed to explain the competence of an actor, or more likely, the competence of an idealized actor who is perfectly rational, or has perfectly mastered the relevant rules. A theory of performance, on the other hand, while perhaps making use of it, or presupposing a theory of competence, is designed to explain what a person actually does, and so it would encompass all of the causal factors which bear upon behaviour.[108]

Now it is obvious that the former type of explanation is rational to its core, while the latter is rational only *qua* theory (which, hopefully, all our theories are) and not with reference to the type of explanation sought, which is causal and hence does not a priori presuppose or posit any idealized form of rational action on the part of the acting individual(s). Given this distinction and its implications, it should be obvious to the reader that, with regard to the concept of action, I am here engaged in the explication of a performative notion rather than a theory of competence. Indeed, in so far as competence explanations are quintessentially rationalistic (as distinguished from causal explanations), they constitute a model of explanation which is almost antithetical to the general theoretical stance presented here.

In having specified that the universe of cases to which our unit of analysis should properly belong is that of 'actions', we are of course still speaking about a unit which in no specific sense relates to what is normally thought of as 'foreign policy'. The first step towards achieving this more particular aim is to introduce the classificatory distinction between 'actions' which are also 'policies', and actions which are not; and obviously the species of 'action' which is appropriate here is the former rather than the latter.

This does not mean, however, that there have not been disagreements about the relevance or fruitfulness of using the concept of policy in referring to the political actions taking place across state boundaries. For although the term 'foreign policy' is ubiquitous in the literature, this should by no means lead us to assume that 'policies' as such have always been stressed, analysed or pinpointed in any specific manner. Rather, very often the term possesses merely a notational is distinct from a substantive function.[109]

In some instances this has been the result of a view of the international system which posits no clear distinctions between international relations, international politics and foreign policy; and in these cases 'foreign policy' has been used simply as shorthand for all the activities pertaining to what Stanley Hoffmann has called the 'Bergsonian drama' of politics on the international scene – a play in which 'foreign policy' locutions thus do not refer to anything distinguishable from the rest of the actions performed on this stage.[110] The obvious result, as K. J. Holsti has written, is that 'If the reader is confused over the use of the terms international relations, international politics, and foreign policy, he joins the company of most experts in the field.'[111] Charles Hermann puts the same sentiment even more succinctly when he notes that 'no agreement exists on the meaning of foreign policy.'[112] Thus it is not surprising that 'foreign policy' has been used interchangeably with these other terms to refer to anything that goes on outside the strict confines of the domestic political situation of states, and that as a result we can do almost anything we wish with it.

In other cases, however, 'policy' is conceptually distinguished from the rest of the activities taking place in the international system, but is nevertheless rejected as a fruitful concept for one reason or another. Thus Rosenau, for example, has written that 'policies have no fixed behavioural boundaries and are so variable, amorphous, and all-encompassing that the findings they yield obscure variance and defy cumulations.'[113] However, this is not a charge reserved to the area of foreign relations alone. In an overview of the field of comparative *public* policy Richard Rose has thus written:

> The term *policy* is perhaps best considered a generic symbol pointing toward a field of interest rather than a scientifically precise concept. This is because scholars have used the term with a very wide variety of meanings, some overlapping and some mutually exclusive. It can refer to a set of expectations and intentions, or to a series of actions and their consequences, or to all of these together. In colloquial English, we might say that a policy is 'what politics is about'. There is justification for defining politics as the study of policy, or *vice versa*.[114]

A more recent characterization is equally frank in its acceptance of the inherently unbounded nature of our concept.

> In brief, public policy as a focus of systematic comparative analysis is *more complex* than such phenomena as electoral votes, legislative roll calls, incidents of political violence, and elite ideologies ... Indeed, the appeal of public policy studies ... lies precisely in its richness. The complexity of the unit of analysis simply and appropriately reflects the fact that an action of government is rarely meaningful if conceived of as a discrete, disembodied event.[115]

Given these admissions, and the fact that 'policy anlaysis' today is a much more dominant approach among students of domestic rather than international politics, it is perhaps only to be expected that there exists so little agreement on 'policy' among the latter.

Another reason for the problematic nature of this concept is more specific to the area of foreign policy analysis itself. Since the term 'policy' has generically always been so closely associated with the name of this field of study as a whole, its meaning, in most of the literature, has tended to be implied rather than explicitly stated. As a consequence, it is commonly used to refer to anything from policy substances and policy processes to policy outcomes, i.e., to all activities covered by the broad label 'foreign policy'.[116] Obviously, however, this will not do if we are to avoid casting murky shadows of aspersion on the concept of policy itself.

In this matter I fully agree with those scholars who advocate that 'policy' should be defined with reference to *substance* alone, thus excluding both process and outcome.[117] What we need is a definition which pertains to the structure and contents of policies themselves, and therefore neither to the policy-making process (or policy determinants) nor to whatever functional, systemic, structural or other 'roles' they may serve, either as 'inputs' into the inter-national or domestic system, or as 'outputs' from a foreign policy system. In the analysis of these other matters 'foreign policy' functions as an independent variable; but here we are interested in foreign policy solely as the dependent variable. Thus policy determinants or processes, on the one hand, and policy effects or outcomes, on the other, must be clearly differentiated from the contents or substance of foreign policy as the explanandum – the phemonenon to be explained. On the face of it, this is to go back to some traditional concerns or modes of analysis in our field; and yet I feel confident that this is the best avenue to more fruitful research within it.

This stress on substance is particularly important in view of one of the main problems in the comparative analysis of foreign policy: the difficulty of finding theoretically relevant ways of identifying different kinds of foreign policies. In this matter Hermann has written:

> One can conceive of various intriguing relationships incorporating foreign policy as a salient variable, for example, the effect of elements both internal and external to a nation on it policies, or the consequences of different kinds of policies on various actors in the international system including those that originated the action, or the effects of policy on the processes by which it is formed.

However, he adds pointedly, the 'critical weakness lies in the absence of well defined foreign policy variables', i.e., variables explicated with reference to our need 'to establish meaningful ways of classifying different kinds of foreign policy'.[118] And the reason for this weakness is obvious: as long as we define policies in terms of the process of their emanation, or with reference to their outcomes, we cannot subsequently treat these as separate and independent variables explaining not only differences between various kinds of policies, but indeed policies *per se*. Or as Edward Morse has written, with particular reference to the former kind of definition, when 'process definitions of foreign policy are employed they tell us very little about foreign policy, but can help in the elucidation of a good deal about policy making ... No matter how much analysis is brought to bear on processes they can tell us very little about policies themselves and can hardly explain them.'[119] And the same applies to policies not defined independently of their outcomes or consequences.

Before proceeding to a somewhat more specific discussion of the meaning of 'policy', I would like at this point briefly to comment on a different though related concept which could conceivably take the place of 'policy' in the definition of our subject matter. Here I have in mind the concept of 'decision', which in recent years has been so successfully used by Michael Brecher in his extensive work on the foreign policies of Israel.[120] There is indeed much to be said for this subclassification of 'action' with reference to foreign policy analysis, since it would seem obvious that all foreign policy actions are in some way based on 'decisions' by relevant human actors.

However, the main problem with using 'decision' as the unit of analysis is that of observation, or what Patrick McGowan has called the 'unit-of-observation' problem in the comparative analysis of foreign policy.[121] Strictly speaking, decisions cannot be observed except by participants in, or those directly privy to, such actions; and while many decisions are proclaimed or published in one form or another, others clearly are not. And prima facie it is neither wise nor fruitful – especially when we are engaged in comparative analysis – to posit a unit of analysis which is of this nature. Brecher writes that a 'foreign policy decision may be defined as the selection, among perceived alternatives, of one leading to a course of action in the International System', and adds that since 'a decision is an explicit act of choice, which can be located precisely in time and space', it 'can be described and explained: that is, it is researchable.'[122] True, probably: but how true? I submit that although Brecher is right in principle, in practice we are faced with a different situation. Not all decisions are in fact 'open' and thus 'researchable'; and this pertains in particular to contemporary decisions, many of which have not yet become available, given the strict confines established by official secrets acts. 'Contrary to conventional wisdom or myth,' Brecher also writes, 'a decision is made by identifiable persons authorized by a state's political system to act within a prescribed sphere of external behaviour.'[123] In so far as this is a caveat aimed at holistic tendencies in the name of methodological individualism, I cannot agree more fully; nor do I disagree with this statement as a definition – or part of a definition – as to what a 'decision' constitutes (or, for that matter, a 'policy'). But it is no myth that it is often vexingly difficult to get at these decision-makers and their decisions, and to do so for comparative purposes (I once wasted more than a year – and lost my Africanist soul – in the hope of 'researching' such decisions in Africa).[124] Also, as Ole R. Holsti has pointed out, the distinction between decisions and actions is important for another reason as well: 'The literature on bureaucratic politics has illustrated the many potential sources of slippage between executive decisions and the implementation of policy in the form of foreign policy actions,' he notes in this connection.[125]

Furthermore – and this is most pertinent – I submit that those decisions which in actual fact are open and thus systematically researchable are precisely those which bear the imprint of 'policies'. Thus, in so far as policies necessarily imply decisions (but not vice versa), and in so far as the only systematically researchable decisions are those which are contained in the substance of policies, I feel that we have to reject Brecher's unit of analysis as a practicable option.

Indeed, I also submit that for precisely this reason there is great merit in McGowan's point that because 'of our need for reliability and hence for the possibility of replication, and because of the constraints imposed by our desire to examine the foreign policy behaviour of a number of polities at one time, we are forced to, and I for one would argue that we should, use only publicly available sources.'[126] Of course this poses great problems of bias, but at least this is a problem mainly of systematic bias, which can – at least to a considerable degree – be corrected by various means and techniques at our disposal. What we have here are in fact two choices facing us as dispassionate observers of foreign policy: on the one hand, to extract and rely on information based on the insider's 'how it really happened' omniscience (to quote Friedrich Ranke's celebrated phrase – and typical examples which spring to mind here are the various Watergate books, the Richard Crossman diaries, Henry Kissinger's memoirs, and so forth); or, on the other, to base our analysis on data culled from the public or semi-public record. Thus, in so far as the ideal conditions for Brecher's conceptualization would seem to imply the first choice, we have to reject it on principle as well, since it seems to me that only the latter practice ought to be permissible within the scholarly community. (We should not, however, forget Lewis Namier's dictum that 'A great many profound secrets are somewhere in print, but are most easily detected when one knows what to seek.'[127] The person who perhaps above everybody else – at least in the United States – has made this type of fact-seeking his particular métier is I. F. Stone, whose now defunct newsletter illustrates not only the appositeness of Namier's remark, but also the utter necessity of this type of relentless research in the face of governmental secrecy.) This restriction is one of the inevitable drawbacks with a field in which secrecy still plays – and, according to Kissinger's advice, ought to play – such an important role (and in which 'getting inside' is not really a solution at all).

As to the definition of 'policy', I see no reason for not accepting the one suggested by Morse, except on one point. He refers to 'policies' as 'courses of action' consisting of 'sets of directives' which are pursued individually or collectively in order to obtain a given goal or advantage; and to this he adds – still eliciting my full agreement – that obviously we are referring here to governmental actions performed on behalf of a sovereign body, and not to actions of private citizens or to actions of decision-makers when these are pursued outside their institutionalized roles or capacities.[128] But I think that he is unduly (or perhaps unwittingly) restrictive when he writes that those policies 'which are central to this context are characterized as "legitimate" and "authoritative" in so far as they are developed in terms of authoritative political institutions representing the whole society.'[129] This Weberian-sounding criterion may give the impression that 'legitimacy' must hold in a 'democratic' or 'representative' sense; and in so far as it does this it in fact excludes a plethora of 'policies' which are 'authoritative' in an 'official' sense, but whose perpetrators cannot be regarded as 'democratic' representatives of their respective societies. To my mind 'policies' are policies even if a Colonel Gadhafi (or a President Marcos or Pinochet, or, for that matter, a Politburo) 'autocratically' rather than 'legitimately' decrees them; and within the ambit of foreign policy studies we surely want to study them as bona fide policies irrespective of the type of rule that maybe involved. What counts here is not so much 'legitimacy' or 'authority' as *power*; and thus I submit that 'policies' are simply those directives which have been decreed or promulgated by those *in* power. This does not, of course, render the nature of this power empirically or normatively uninteresting; on the contrary, it allows us subsequently to use this concept to determine the role of different types of power structures in various forms of foreign policy.

One more aspect of 'policies' should be stressed and incorporated into the definition of our unit of analysis. This is the distinction between 'manifest' and 'latent' functions, a dichotomy first suggested by Robert Merton in his classic discussion on sociology.[130] To this distinction should be added a further one, introduced by Levy in his evaluation of Merton's position. This is the difference between 'unintended but recognized' and 'intended but unrecognized' functions – a set of distinctions which (once shorn of its functionalist terminology) bears directly upon the substance of policies.[131] As Steinbruner has written, some 'decisions actually have the effect or *outcome* intended; others do not. Some outcomes occur without any recognizable or reasonably imputed decisions to produce them.'[132] I agree here with the suggestion that we should consider only outcomes which are manifest in the sense that they are both *intended* and *recognized* as policies.[133] With reference to the first condition, the reason for this dictum is that, although the nature of policy actions may be perceived and interpreted by individuals in certain particular ways, they should not be so characterized if not so intended by the policy-maker in question. The danger in not stressing the manifest intention of policy actions is that the 'purposes' contained in them easily become confused with their 'effects', 'outcomes', 'functions' or 'roles', or with Popper's 'unintended consequences', all of which are easily imputed to the policies themselves. These concepts may provide criteria for evaluating policies, or can be analysed in terms of policies; but in such cases we are using 'policy' as an independent variable, which is not our intention here.[134]

With regard to the second condition, referring to policies which may have been intended but which remain unrecognized, the argument here is that they should be excluded for the simple reason that we have nothing to go by: the intention has never become an actuality *qua* recognizable policy. To start looking for intentions in an empirical policy vacuum is, in other words, a waste of time – even though they may in fact be there somewhere. Similarly, the phenomenon known as 'the rule of anticipated reactions' should be treated very gingerly in this context. This rule refers to situations in which 'one actor, B, shapes his behaviour to conform to what he believes are the desires of another actor, A, without having received explicit messages about A's wants or intentions from A or A's agents.'[135] As David A. Baldwin has noted in this connection, 'Some things "go without saying". Likewise, some influence attempts "go without making".'[136] However, such 'influences' *qua* putative 'actions' should not be 'said' to constitute *policy*-'making', irrespective of how powerful and palpable they may appear to be. Indeed, the feasibility of the method of imputation as such in the social sciences is a problem which, while not wholly intractable, deserves to be handled with utter caution, as Arthur Child already pointed out many years ago in a series of discussions on the problematic nature of this method in Mannheim's sociology of knowledge.[137] These caveats also stress, once again, why we should treat our unit of analysis as a species of action-like behaviour. For a central element of the meaning of action in the philosophy of the social sciences is precisely its manifest nature as against the wider meaning of the concept of behaviour.

It is in the light of these strictures that I feel that we have to reject the following proposal, made by Charles W. Kegley in his discussion of the need for a manifest unit of analysis. Noting, quite correctly, that people 'use the term foreign policy in different and often contradictory ways', and adding, quite correctly again, that such 'imprecision invites semantic confusion and encourages polemics rather than disciplined inquiry', he comes to a conclusion, however, which these insights do not support:

> To circumvent this problem, events researchers reasoned that foreign policy should not be defined in terms of motives or intentions of policy makers; such a definition would preclude observation of foreign policy, since it is impossible to 'get inside their heads' in order to discover what their true goals are. Instead, the assumption was made that foreign policy could most meaningfully be defined as overt state behaviour. While motives are not observable, actions are.[138]

I submit, on the contrary, that the analysis of motives and intentions is essential to the causal explanation of foreign policy *actions*; furthermore, that in principle these are observable when and if contained in *policies*; but that we should not try to seek for motives or intentions – 'true' or not – when they are not posited or recognizable in policy actions. 'Getting into their heads' has got nothing to do with the matter in hand; nor have attempts at trying to ferret out 'true' motives or intentions. Indeed, 'true' in this sense is one of the most slippery eels known to human discourse, and is best left to swim alone in its infinite regress waters. Thus to insist solely on 'overt state behaviour' in order to guarantee a manifest unit of analysis is, it seems to me, to throw the baby out with the bathwater; and this is precisely what Kegley does when a few pages later he writes that 'events' which tap 'overt and manifest behaviour . . . do not measure national goals, national interests, or the content of national policy orientations'.[139] Surely such 'events' – his unit of analysis – measure little at all in that case, and certainly not actions, even though he insists this to be the case.[140]

Once we have defined policies in the way suggested above, and only when this has been done, can we start differentiating between different kinds of policies – an essential step if we are going to be in a position to make potentially interesting and fruitful generalizations about our subject matter. Here I have in mind, for example, what Samuel Beer and Adam Ulam have called 'patterns of policies'; and to be able to delineate such patterns we must, needless to say, take a closer look at the nature and substance of policies, since they obviously vary immensely along different salient dimensions.[141] The same goes for the classification of policies in terms of 'policy arenas', in the sense that this notion is used by Theodore J. Lowi, or 'policy issue areas' as discussed by, e.g., Rosenau, William Zimmermann and, more recently, William C. Potter.[142] However, I will not pursue these aspects here, since before we can deal seriously with the substantive ramifications of foreign policy actions in their entirety, we first need to look at the classificatory implications of the third conceptual delimiter in our unit of analysis, that is, the meaning of 'foreign' in this context. Let us thus now turn to this last step in our ladder-descending exercise.

C 'FOREIGN' POLICY ACTIONS

The term 'foreign' commonly refers to characteristics which imply or assume a boundary between given entities. Foreign affairs scholars thus constantly refer to 'nations', 'nation–states', 'national actors', 'national states', 'national systems', 'states', 'state actors', 'political systems', and so forth, and are almost by definition committed to this practice. It also implies the concept of the 'international environment', which – from the vantage point of any of these entities – is usually considered to include all other such units in some configuration or other, in addition to the geographical expanses of the oceans (excluding certain parts defined in terms of sovereign jurisdiction), the ice-bound poles and even outer space. To these concrete spatial dimensions is usually added some form of analytic environment, commonly defined in juxtaposition to environed analytical systems. Now it is obvious, first of all, that some of these boundaries are at best ambiguous and thus not easily pinpointed; and secondly, that it is not unimportant for the comparative analysis of foreign policy actions that we particularize what form of boundaries (or 'foreignness') we are interested in, since it does make a difference which of these boundary phenomena we wish to incorporate into our definition of what constitutes a 'foreign' policy action.

Let me submit straight away that in my view we should dispense with any attributes referring to 'nation' in one form or another, despite the popularity of this term and its derivatives in the literature. There are several reasons for this dictum. First of all, it is clear that the concept 'nation' is different from the concept 'state', as is the concept 'nation–state' from 'state' or 'nation'. Thus to use the terms 'nation' or 'national' when we usually mean to express 'state' or speak in regard to it, is to be both semantically imprecise and lexically incorrect. For it is a fact that many independent states do not possess what is known and at least intuitively recognized as 'nationhood'; and the difference which this lack makes in both domestic and world politics is not to be slighted, either historically or analytically. Historically it betrays a sad lack of knowledge about political life during the past centuries and the past decades; and analytically, such a disregard can only be the result of what Sartori has pinpointed as 'conceptual stretching', that is, the attempt to cover an increasing array of world-wide phenomena – in our case, the 'lengthening spectrum of political systems' – by broadening the meaning of available concepts and hence their range of applicability.[143] And the indiscriminate use – on a world-wide, comparative basis – of the notions of 'nation', 'national', 'nation–state', 'national system' and 'national actor' is, in my view, a prime example of such stretching of the meaning of a characteristic (or cluster concept) to the extent that it retains little if any content or descriptive utility.

The fact is that, for better or worse, the connotations of the terms 'nation' and 'national' are historically, politically and spatially those which we commonly associate mainly with Western societies of the last two to three centuries. These are, more specifically, such traits and attributes as deep-rooted social cohesion or integration, the existence of strong loyalties and sentiments reposited in the 'nation', a common culture, language and religion (except for a few significant exceptions), coupled with a long-standing acceptance of the legitimacy of an 'own' political system – extant or not – tied to a certain territory, and so forth.[144] In short, they are the attributes associated with the traditional idea of what constitutes or should constitute a 'nation-state', an idea which evolved mainly in Europe following the demise of the secular powers of the Church, and which, expressed in terms of the Wilsonian principle of national self-determination, achieved orthodoxy in international relations theory – if not practice – following the end of the First World War.

It is my contention, in other words, that to apply a concept with these specific connotations indiscriminately to all entities in world politics which possess formal sovereignty and spatial reference, is to stretch and thereby obfuscate the meaning and fact-gathering worth of a prima facie fruitful term to the point that it no longer possesses any – or possesses only a small – linkable relationship to the essence of its original, and by no means obsolescent, meaning. Sartori is right, I believe, when he notes that the 'pre-1950 vocabulary of politics was not devised for world-wide, cross-area travelling', and that in the face of this we 'so far ... have followed (more or less unwittingly) the line of least resistance' by simply resorting to conceptual stretching.[145] The result, he enjoins, is that 'the very essence of comparing ... control ... is defeated, and we are left to swim in a sea of empirical and theoretical messiness.'[146] And I think that it is not unreasonable to claim that this indictment applies with the same force to the indiscriminate use of the terms 'nation' and 'national' as it does to the cluster of concepts which are exemplified in Sartori's argument.[147]

Secondly, to speak of 'national actors', etc., in this undifferentiated manner is to assume that the arena of world politics is populated by a collection of homogeneous entities possessing an array of common characteristics. However, this is obviously a fallacious assumption, since what we have is not an 'inter-*national*' universe of homogeneous actors but an empirical reality which is characterized above all by its wide variety of different and heterogeneous types of *states*. And while it is probably fair to suppose that at least part of the reason why the existence of 'national actors', etc., has been predicated as a common characteristic of this universe is to be found in the perceived need to alleviate the complex difficulties involved in world-wide comparative analyses, and while it is undoubtedly a fact of analytic life that all comparisons must of necessity involve some degree of simplification and hence distortion, it is nonetheless necessary to insist strongly on the debilitating effects of comparative endeavours based on concepts which are stretched to the point of being little more than vague, indefinite and undelimiting 'conceptual containers'. Such concepts lack almost totally the systematic import which is so vital to fruitful comparative analysis; and they do so precisely because they fail to achieve conceptual significance in the sense of constituting rich fact-gathering (or fact-differentiating) instruments in the comparative effort. The attributes of 'nationality' are certainly not unimportant; but they only become germane in a context in which we use them to characterize certain kinds of societies, not all members of the international community.

Thus, instead of speaking of 'national' as a boundary phenomenon which is significantly related to the notion of 'foreignness', we should reserve it for a different purpose and, I contend, in its stead posit the much stricter and more precise notion of 'state' boundaries. This concept is associated with a number of factors, the most important of which are the principle of territoriality and the notion of non-overlapping jurisdictions; the concepts of internal autonomy and external sovereignty; the dictum of the formal equality of states in international relations; and what Oran Young has referred to as 'functional congruence', i.e., 'the idea that a wide variety of human activities (both political and nonpolitical) can be defined spatially in terms of state boundaries.'[148] Thus, in contrast to the concept of nation, here we have a concept which is primarily legalistic and institutional in content, and which, furthermore, is also universally applicable, since it is based on the minimum requirements of the generally recognized canons of public international law. In addition, it refers to empirically identifiable – i.e., to 'natural' as distinguished from 'constructed' – entities in the international system, since we can determine their number and spatial location simply by consulting, under the rubric 'sovereign states', the latest edition of any standard yearbook on international affairs.

In this connection the distinction between what is usually called 'transnational' politics and 'foreign policy actions' should also be emphasized. The former concept is, needless to say, considerably more encompassing than the latter, enclosing under its umbrella not only 'foreign policies' but also the myriad activities, governmental and private, political and economic, which constantly impinge upon and cross state boundaries. These activities, it is claimed, have increased markedly during this century, leading to a growing state of interdependence between modernized societies. This, however, is still a controversial claim, and I shall not address myself to it here, aside from noting that I sometimes suspect that the 'myth' or 'reality' of interdependence (to allude to the title of one of a number of contributions to this discussion) is largely a matter either of Peter Pan's fairies – to wit, that the eye beholds what it wishes to behold – or a semantic muddle compounded by divisive methodological assumptions.[149]

Rather, I shall forthwith accept the proposition that whatever the merits of the case as a whole with regard to changes in the nature and volume of international transactions during this century, these changes have undoubtedly had political implications which, for better or worse, have brought the states and peoples of the world 'closer' to one another.[150] To this assumption I will immediately add a further, closely linked notion, namely the supposition that interdependence in the above sense is a consequence, above all, of the increased politicization of international economic affairs during the period in question.[151] This development is usually attributed to the international co-operation necessitated by an increased commitment to the production of collective economic goods, rather than to the pursuit of national security and other transcendental goals of one kind or another. In general, as Morse has written, these goods 'can be obtained by no society in isolation but require compatible efforts on the part of official and nonofficial groups in diverse societies'. They 'arise from growth in international trade and the concomitant necessity to regulate trade imbalance to produce additional liquidity, to finance trade, and to create all the other regulative devices which go along with trade practices, including agricultural, transportation, tax, labour, and development policies. ... All of these are further attenuated by the transnational mobility of capital.'[152] The importance of this phenomenon to us here lies in the fact that as a consequence of these developments, a number of political scientists (and economists) have been led to question the tenability of the analytical and disciplinary distinction between 'international' and 'national' politics in its traditional form.[153] They have claimed, instead, that the most salient features of international interaction pertain not so much to the maintenance of sovereign boundaries and the pursuit of national security goals defined in terms of these boundaries, as to the generation of wealth and welfare on a collective basis.[154]

In other words, we are dealing here not merely with the increasing interdependence between different domestic systems, but also with a

'process in which the traditional boundaries separating the nation–
state from the environing international system are becoming
increasingly obscured', as Wolfram Hanrieder noted some years
ago.[155] In addition to this erosion of state boundaries and the 'high
politics' associated with them, new international actors have arisen
which not only play a significant role in international interaction but
also have an autonomy of their own without either being primarily
political organizations or possessing concrete boundaries. They are
'transnational' in structure, and because of their scale and complexity sovereign states have found it increasingly difficult either to
control or to influence their far-reaching and diverse activities. The
result of these factors – and I have named but a few – is said to be a
crisis in sovereignty and boundary maintenance which, it is
maintained, makes the exclusive state perspective in international
relations theory increasingly obsolete.[156]

The question posed by this situation is how these developments
affect the definition of the subject matter of this discussion. The
answer is, I submit, that it is absolutely essential that we distinguish
clearly between the interactions and processes described above, and
foreign policy actions as our unit of analysis. For if the above claims
are valid as empirical propositions, they quite clearly constitute
extremely pertinent factors affecting the nature and course of foreign
policies; and for this very reason it is imperative that we define the
substance of foreign policy actions independently of these transnational factors.

This is particularly important in view of the fact that we are
talking about far-reaching and indeed profound claims, bearing on
the very essence of international relations as conventionally understood by the scholar and, one supposes, as practised by men of affairs
in high office; and as such they may even cast doubts on the utility of
pursuing the study of foreign policies *per se* in a world putatively
characterized by the erosion of the autonomy of governmental
decision-makers, by the blurring of the boundaries between
domestic and international politics, and by the obsolescence of the
state as the primary international actor. However, my assumption is
that before we can even begin to evaluate claims such as these, it is
incumbent upon us to acquire a clear notion of *what* is purportedly
being affected in each instance. That is to say, in order to pursue

these and similar types of queries it is necessary to focus on foreign policy actions and on the relationship holding between them and their consequences or outcomes, as well as on how these feed back into or constrain new foreign policy undertakings. For only then can we deal with statements such as, for example, that in 'the international system the significance of purposive action is declining relative to the part played by the apurposive and the inadvertent'; or the argument – submitted by Morse – that what is special 'about foreign policies conducted under modernized conditions, is the scale of the problem of control', which 'has affected the efficacy of government policy in all industrialized societies, thus creating a crisis in government authority and legitimacy which is fundamental to current debates concerning the future not simply of the nation–state, but of industrialized societies themselves'.[157] These are predications which obviously ought to be of great concern to both foreign policy decision-makers and to us as mere observers of their actions; and my point is that a serious discussion of them – and of all aspects attending international relations today – can become fruitful only after we have become fully cognizant of the kind of behaviour which is at issue when we are dealing with the foreign policies of states.

But let us once more return to our immediate topic here, that is, to the specification of 'foreign' in the definition of our unit of analysis. I submit that we now have a sufficiently clear notion of the meaning of 'foreign' policy actions, namely, those activities involved in some sense in the crossing of state boundaries. More particularly, given the obvious fact that we do not mean 'crossing' in a literal sense, we can specify such activities in terms of actions directed at, affecting, or responding to, individuals, groups, organizations, states or conditions situated outside a sovereign community and its geographical jurisdiction, i.e., actions which are directed toward the international environment (or rather, properly speaking, the 'inter-state' environment).

However, since we are for obvious reasons not interested in all such 'foreign' actions but only in a particular class of them, we have to exclude a number of these from our universe of cases. Thus, first of all, all actions across state boundaries are excluded which are not pursued by the properly designated government officials acting on behalf of their sovereign communities. As a consequence we here have two partially overlapping but independently identifiable circles of actions involved: the general class of boundary-crossing actions, and actions pursued by governmental agents acting in their official roles; and it is only the actions contained within the elliptical space formed by the overlap of the two that is of immediate interest to us here. In addition, of course, the strictures on what constitutes policies apply here, which gives us a third partially overlapping circle. Hence, 'policy actions' are also 'foreign' only if officials, acting on behalf of the state, direct such policies to recipients or conditions 'abroad'. In other words, we exclude from our universe of cases all boundary-traversing actions which are not policies, as well as those pursued by private individuals, groups or organizations, and government officials not acting in their official capacities. In addition, for the obvious reason that they do not emanate from 'within' any state, we should exclude all activities that have their origin in international organizations, both political and non-political.

The time has now come to conclude this discussion of our unit of analysis. On the basis of the considerations submitted above, I propose the following definition:

> 'Foreign policies' consist of those 'actions' which, expressed in the form of explicitly stated directives, and performed by governmental representatives acting on behalf of their sovereign communities, are manifestly directed toward objectives, conditions and actors – both governmental and non-governmental – which clearly lie beyond their sphere of territorial legitimacy.

This is, in my view, not only a sufficiently stringent classification of our unit of analysis, but also a conceptualization which, given its methodological and philosophical underpinnings, will be able to function well in all types of comparative and explanatory studies of foreign policy.

3

Comparative Analysis and Foreign Policy Explanations

If the conceptual exercise contained in the previous chapter has not been totally in vain, we should now be able– at least in principle – to recognize a foreign policy action when we see one. But 'knowing' a unit of analysis in this sense is not the same as understanding its empirical significance; it is merely a first step towards this larger but still somewhat distant goal. Furthermore, as J. Donald Moon has pointed out:

> political science, like economics, sociology, and anthropology, is not only concerned to understand particular events and traditions; it also aspires to compare and generalize about social phenomena. And though such generalizations must presuppose interpretative explanations of particulars, such explanation does not provide sufficient basis for the construction of more general comparisons and theories.[1]

In this chapter I shall first briefly discuss the method and role of comparative analysis itself in relation to these generalizing, explanatory ambitions; and then, in a more substantial section, present a framework in terms of which this comparative method can be applied.

A   THE NATURE OF COMPARATIVE ANALYSIS

'In the last resort,' a student of foreign policy has advised us, 'comparative method is a valuable form of intellectual therapy.'[2] Certainly one therapeutic effect pertinent here – though probably not the one this particular scholar had in mind – is the sobering (and hence salubrious if exasperating) experience, when confronted with the term 'comparative method' and its synonyms, of having to acknowledge, once more, that we are not dealing with something that is cut and dried and therefore easily pinned down and dissected.

Some years ago David Apter, in a short introductory essay to a collection of papers on comparative methods in sociology, thus felt impelled 'to remark on the curious quality of the word "comparison".' He goes on to explain:

> To have substance its emphasis must first of all be a methodological one. But as surely as there is no one comparative method or even a good set of rules to which we can all subscribe, such an emphasis is insufficient. Theoretical models and general scientific paradigms must also be considered for their influence on comparative research. Nor is it a matter of one theory, or of one scientific logic. The contemporary situation, after all, is one distinguished by methodological pluralism, with many open-minded initiatives and a corresponding diversity of priorities concerning research goals and techniques of analysis.[3]

It is certainly not difficult to document this 'curiousness' of our concept, nor to exemplify Harry Eckstein's more succinct judgement, made more than two decades ago – in what perhaps still remains one of the most authoritative readers on comparative politics – that the 'field is today characterized by nothing so much as variety, eclecticism, and disagreement.'[4] Typical of one polar position in this matter is, e.g., Guy E. Swanson's assertion that the words 'comparative studies ... erroneously imply that some research is not comparative. That is an error because all behaviour and, consequently, all research entails comparison.'[5] Or as he notes elsewhere, 'thinking without comparisons is unthinkable. And in the absence of comparisons, so is all scientific thought and all scientific research.'[6] Oscar Lewis, in an anthropological collection, goes even further in his forthright assertion that 'comparison is a genetic aspect of human thought rather than a special method', which also seems to be W. J. M. Mackenzie's view when he refers to a 'general agreement that one cannot not compare'.[7]

As against this neo-Cartesian position ('I think, therefore I compare') R. M. Marsh, for example, typifies a radically different view when he insists that comparative sociology should be regarded as a distinct field because its data and goals are different from analysis limited to single societies.[8] D. P. Warwick and S. Osherson, in their introduction to still another anthology on this topic, take yet a different tack when they argue that the 'difference between the comparative and the non-comparative wings of the social science discipline . . . lies more in the range of variation considered than in a distinctive methodology', adding that comparison 'in its broadest sense is the process of discovering similarities and differences between phenomena'.[9] This perspective seems to be inspired by both the 'cognitive' position outlined above and Émile Durkheim's dictum, undoubtedly still influential today, that 'Comparative sociology is not a particular branch of sociology; it is sociology itself, in so far as it ceases to be purely descriptive and aspires to account for facts.'[10]

The situation is no different in the foreign policy literature. This is well described by Patrick McGowan in the following passage, excerpted from a collection of essays on the comparative analysis of foreign policy:

> As a method of inquiry, comparison can be applied in a variety of ways to achieve a diversity of goals. There is no agreement on the definition of the comparative method . . . Some scholars view comparison as a form of measurement; others view it as a technique for clarifying the meaning and empirical referents of concepts; still other social scientists regard comparison as being synonymous with the logic of scientific analysis in general; some see comparison as a particular type of research design; finally some scholars view the comparative method as a solution to the problems of valid cross-cultural measurement and explanation. And there are yet more subtle distinctions that can be drawn among the views of writers on this subject.[11]

To this list we should also add all those analysts – and they are many and of all nationalities – who have chosen to view these matters in a somewhat more ethnocentrically straightforward light: 'a political investigation is often said to be comparative,' one scholar thus reports laconically, 'if the political scientist is American but his subject is France or Russia'.[12] This is a usage of the term which is also typified by the common subdisciplinary distinction between, on the one hand, 'Comparative Politics' and, on the other, 'American (or Swedish, or British) Politics'. Despite the curious dovetailing of form and content – of method and substance – which this usage exemplifies, it is also the way the eminent editors of the *American Political Science Review* have, once again, preferred to classify their book reviews.

Even more interesting, however, is the fact that, while all the views that we have considered hitherto have at least one aspect in common, namely, that doing social science in some sense or other involves the use of comparative analysis, there is also a widespread opinion that does not consider it part of the social sciences at all. Hence it is not surprising that Evert Vedung feels compelled to note that, given 'an international controversy about the problems of comparative research', it is the 'more surprising . . . to discover that a great many renowned methodological works do not present even the slightest attempt to single out any specific comparative method.'[13] Indeed, some of these works do not even mention the word itself, or in any case (which is no less telling) do not list it in their indexes.

In the face of these various and conflicting standpoints, at least one thing seems immediately clear to me, namely, that we should forthwith dispense with all purely cognitive preoccupations regarding the meaning of 'comparison', and in their stead focus on the methodological aspects of comparative analysis, particularly those linking comparison and explanation. Obviously we all perforce think comparatively most of the time; to claim otherwise would be as silly as to maintain – even though more than a few eminent historiographers have done precisely this – that a historical fact is 'unique' without thereby *pari passu* inferring or invoking certain 'generalizing' (or, for that matter, 'comparative') criteria. However, these common-sense notions are not germane in the present context; they are taken for granted just as one takes for granted that the statement 'Xamantha is the most beautiful girl in the world' is a comparative statement at the same time as it expresses uniqueness. But in terms of our explantory aims a claim such as this has little value, even though comparatively one may be able to prove one's case by showing that nobody else possesses the abundance of delectable attributes defining Xamantha's physiognomy (operationally a Miss Universe pageant would, presumably, do the trick more or less adequately). In this matter Morris Zelditch has, I believe, made some trenchant and pertinent remarks in his essay on 'Intelligible Comparisons'.

In it he notes, first of all, that one important use to which we may put comparisons is in descriptive investigations of one kind or another. Thus a comparison can provide a simple but necessary frame of reference in terms of which nominal quantities may be interpreted, for example, in a statement such as 'In comparison with B, A is rich, but in comparison with C, A is really little more than a pauper' (or 'Xamantha might to the pageant judges be the most beautiful girl in the world, but in comparison with my Yolantha, she is very plain indeed' – to which, not inconceivably, a superannuated Oxonian would retort: 'Zuleika still beats them all!').[14] However, as against this basically descriptive usage – and the trivial examples are of course mine solely – Zelditch notes the following:

> An investigation has an explanatory purpose if it yields or tests one or more general explanatory sentences. A sentence is *general* if all its terms are general. Its terms are general if they are not proper names and do not imply proper names. Thus,
>
> 1 Great Britain is a democracy, is not a general sentence, but
> 2 A democracy is stable if its wealth is equally distributed, is a general sentence.
>
> A sentence is *explanatory* if it asserts a relation between two or more variables. Therefore (2) is not only general, it is also explanatory . . .[15]

Having established these distinctions, Zelditch then proceeds to make the important point that 'Not every comparative study is explanatory and generalizing, but every explanatory generalizing study is comparative', and then adds that a study is comparative 'only if two or more units are compared with respect to the same concept', while comparability is determined by the following rule: 'Let 1, 2, 3, *n* be units in each of which the process Ø takes place. Then 1 is comparable to 2, 3, *n* if and only if (a) there exists a variable V common to each of them and (b) the meaning of V is the same for all of them.'[16] What we have here are thus two different dimensions of the comparative approach in social analysis, that is to say, *descriptive comparisons* and *explanatory comparisons*. Also, it is clear that the latter dimension presupposes the former but not vice versa;

and that we can hence engage in comparative analysis without necessarily having to proceed to the higher, general level of explanation.

Furthermore, the discussion above has emphasized the importance of the notion of *comparability*, a point which, however elementary it may seem, nevertheless needs to be particularly stressed. The fact is that it is not entirely uncommon for scholars to dispense with this requirement altogether when discussing the comparative method. Thus we find, e.g., that 'comparative method' is used to refer to 'social scientific analyses involving observations in more than one social system, or in the same social system at more than one point in time'.[17] Against this preoccupation with the 'number of N' problem we need to juxtapose Zelditch's dictum that 'a study is not comparative if there are not at least two units being compared: but more than this is required', namely, that the 'two or more units are compared *with respect to the same concepts*.'[18] Or as Eckstein has put it, 'comparative study is ... the study of numerous cases ... with a view to reporting and interpreting numerous measures *on the same variables* of different "individuals".'[19] To establish such conceptual comparability is also the whole point of Arthur Kalleberg's discussion in his essay on the logic of comparison, in which he stresses the need for properly defined comparative concepts which will 'make it possible for specific states, within a class, to be ranked along *various common* dimensions'.[20] It should be added, however, that he does not (as some of his commentators seem to imply) consider this procedure to constitute the comparative method as such; rather, he quite explicitly refers to it as a prime logical requirement underlying or permitting adequate comparative analysis.[21]

With regard to our unit of analysis it can now be stated that comparability holds as long as 'foreign policy actions' can comply with (a) and (b) as posited by Zelditch above; and that we are involved in explanatory comparisons when these are couched in general terms. Furthermore, it is my belief that our unit of analysis is indeed viable in terms of these two comparability conditions; and that it is in principle also amenable to comparative explanations in terms of the generality requirement, i.e., in terms which do not rely on proper names.

However, to this it should immediately be added that while explanatory comparisons in this sense ought to remain the *telos* motivating the comparative analysis of foreign policy, this ambition should not lead us to denigrate the worth of descriptive comparisons, or the seemingly pedestrian activities involved in their establishment. Nor should the significance of the generality criterion be overemphasized. Indeed, in a critical self-evaluation of the field of comparative foreign policy, Charles W. Kegley has come to the conclusion that the level of generality in this area should be considerably reduced. His argument runs:

> Patterns in foreign policy behaviour valid through time and across space have not been forthcoming. CFP [comparative foreign policy] data speak loudly and clearly: the world of foreign policy is more complicated and idiosyncratic than initially suspected (hoped). Looking for similarities, CFP research has (re)discovered differences; searching for cross-national commonalities, cross-national variations have been found. Generalized statements about foreign policy phenomena have not emerged. In fact, the history of CFP research is cluttered with disproven claims regarding universal features of foreign policy. Covering laws have not covered . . . Nomological or 'law-like' statements have not been found. Instead, indeterminate, multiple, and relative ones have. Uncertainty and distrust of generalization have been the most important products of empirical research.[22]

However, he adds that this pessimism (and the advice to lower the level of generality by pursuing middle-range, contextually bounded generalizations) 'does *not* require sacrifice of comparative methodology . . . To pursue generalizations that are meaningful and falsifiable at this level requires that controlled comparisons be made.'[23] In view of the unfulfilled promises connected with the various comparative foreign policy projects of the 1970s to which Kegley refers, his point is well taken.

This leads us directly to the role of case studies in comparative foreign policy analysis. As with definitions of the comparative method in the social sciences, there is no general agreement on what case study may be said to be, how it differs from comparative analysis or whether, indeed, it constitutes an essentially different methodological approach or not.

One common assumption is, of course, that case studies are

entirely different things from comparative studies, with regard both to their methodological nature and to their analytical function. Thus it is held, e.g., that case study is not even a method but merely a genre – and a very common and popular one, to boot. 'It is not much of an exaggeration to say,' one eminent political scientist thus notes of his own discipline, 'that the case study literature in the field comes close to being coterminous with its literature as such.'[24] Case studies in this sense can refer to analyses on the most microcosmic to the most macrocosmic levels of political phenomena; and their methods and the types of questions posed run the gamut from psycho-historical examinations of prominent politicians or statesmen to case studies of transnational integration or the systemic transformation of world politics. Since this range encompasses just about everything under the sun worth calling politics, it is not surprising that studies of this kind are so prominent and numerous in our field.

On the other hand, as Eckstein has also pointed out, this 'plenitude of case studies is not associated with any perception that they are a particularly useful means of arriving at a theoretical understanding of the subject matter of political study.'[25] It is when we come to this juncture, i.e., to the relationship between case study and more 'general' (or 'generalizing') studies, and hence to the link between the two, that real differences of opinion emerge – not only about this link in itself, but also with respect to the 'essential' nature of the case study method. One can refer to two general views on this relationship, the one antithetical (and negative) and the other decidedly more positive and non-dichotomous. I shall concentrate here on the second, leaving the first aside, except to note that proponents of this view usually subscribe to the proposition that case studies are essentially 'particularistic' in nature, and hence in all important respects – and not merely with regard to scope or technique – different from the type of 'generalizing' (or experi- mental) model underlying the comparative approach. In political science the 'behavioural revolution' is often held to constitute a watershed in the establishment of both this dichotomy and the subsequent bifurcation of the discipline into two entirely different scholarly crafts.

The second merits more attention – which it has indeed received.

Arend Lijphart reflects the general tenor of this view when (in a widely quoted essay on our topic) he asserts that 'the case study method can and should be closely connected with the comparative method', and that 'certain types of case studies can even be considered implicit parts of the comparative method.'[26] Neil J. Smelser, writing of what he calls 'isolated clinical case analysis', similarly avers that 'in so far as the study is couched in a general conceptual framework and related to other general findings . . . it becomes explicitly a comparative study.'[27] Lijphart expands on his claim by differentiating between six ideal types of case studies, of which two (atheoretical and interpretative case studies) have no implications of a theoretical kind, in that they are pursued entirely for their own sake *qua* unique cases; while the other four (hypothesis-generating, theory-confirming, theory-infirming and deviant case studies) do have such implications in one way or another, inasmuch as they 'are all selected for the purpose of theory-building'.[28] Of these the last three come closest to being comparative; and they do so because they 'focus on a particular case which is singled out for analysis from a relatively large number of cases and which is analyzed within the theoretical and empirical context of this set of cases'.[28] Eckstein, in a long essay on 'Case Study and Theory in Political Science', has even more emphatically defended and expounded upon the close relationship between certain kinds of case studies and the generalizing (or theoretical) animus underlying the comparative method. At the same time he presents a somewhat different list of types of case studies, namely, (1) configurative-idiographic, (2) disciplined–configurative, (3) the heuristic case, (4) plausibility probes and (5) the crucial case. These can, in turn, be linked to different options regarding the relationship between case studies and comparative analysis, ranging from the first view referred to briefly in the previous paragraph (that case studies are wholly unequal to comparative studies) to the other extreme, that is, that case studies are superior to comparative analysis with regard to the testing of theories or hypotheses. Between these poles he lists four other options: (1) these two modes of inquiry, while remaining highly unequal, are nevertheless not totally – or as some would say, 'paradigmatically' – segregated; (2) case studies can function as a hypothesis-generating handmaiden to comparative analysis; (3) case studies are important as plausibility probes; and (4) in the process of validation, case studies and comparative studies are separate but equal means to the same end.[30]

The question that has to be posed here is not in the first instance how one should sort out and classify different types of case studies, but whether case study as a method of analysis is suitable for the scholar engaged in the comparative study of foreign policy. And the answer must surely be in the affirmative. The next question then becomes How?; and here the response is perhaps somewhat less unequivocal. It is clear, however, that for comparative purposes neither Lijphart's nor Eckstein's first two species are to be recommended. They (and particularly the first type in each instance) in fact constitute precisely those kinds of studies which for so long have been pointed to by the comparativist as telling illustrations against the theoretical value of idiographic studies. It is of them – but only of them – that it can still be claimed that 'case study and theory are at polar opposites, linked only by the fortuitous operations of serendipity.'[31] As to the rest, the thrust of the argument here is that in so far as comparative studies aim to establish empirical generalizations, none of these is unimportant, while some undoubtedly will give us more mileage than others. Eckstein, for example, thus recommends crucial case studies in the first instance, while Lijphart opts for hypothesis-generating and deviant case studies. Obviously, however, one's choice to a large extent depends on the type of questions posed and the type of explanations sought, as well as on the empirical characteristics and accessibility of the phenomena in question. Thus, for instance, the use of plausibility probes is certainly to be recommended for avoiding what otherwise may turn out to be expensive comparative wild goose chases. Similarly, heuristic case studies may prove to be fruitful for generating hypotheses which in turn can be pursued via plausibility probes or crucial case studies. In any event, the use of case studies as explicated here is not to be viewed as antithetical to the comparative endeavour. Rather, as Eckstein in particular has so persuasively argued, the intelligent use of such studies is always to the advantage of comparative analysis.

B FOREIGN POLICY EXPLANATIONS: A CONCEPTUAL FRAMEWORK

If case studies are to benefit comparative investigation in any of the various ways suggested above, the two approaches will have to be concatenated by means of a common conceptual framework. In the remainder of this chapter I will suggest and discuss an analytical structure for explaining foreign policy actions which, it is claimed, will be equally fruitful *qua* framework for both of these investigatory purposes.

Before doing so, however, it may be useful as a preliminary step to distinguish between two methodological dimensions which are relevant to the study of both foreign policy in particular and politics in general. The first of these refers to the *level of generality*, and the second to the *level of analysis*. Although some aspects of these dimensions have been discussed on the preceding pages, they have not been treated *per se* and in relation to each other. Here my aim is to bring them together not only to clarify a few fundamental distinctions regarding various approaches to the study of international politics, but also, on the basis of these, to demarcate the particular approach which will be recommended below.

As posited here, the level of generality is logically identical in form to the ladder of abstraction which was discussed (and utilized) in conjunction with the unfolding of our unit of analysis. However, here its function will be somewhat different, inasmuch as it will be used to characterize the significant properties of various analytical approaches rather than classifying the particular empirical entities which we propose to investigate. For our modest purposes three such levels of generality will be postulated here: high, middle and low. This is obviously to simplify both our thinking and the objects of our thought; but for the logical purpose of distinguishing broadly between types of approaches, this is quite sufficient. Or as Giovanni Sartori has noted:

> Clearly, there is no hard and fast dividing line between levels of abstraction. Borders can only be drawn very loosely; and the number of slices into which the ladder is divided largely depends on how fine one's analysis needs to be. Three slices are sufficient, however, for the purposes of logical analysis.[32]

As we shall see immediately, the same arguments do not hold for our other dimension, which logically bears no resemblance whatsoever to any kind of ladder.

Although it is perhaps tempting to conflate the level of generality and the level of analysis, the latter will here refer to something quite different, that is, to the micro/macro dimension, sometimes also explicated in terms of the molecular/molar distinction. J. David Singer, in his famous article on 'The Level-of-Analysis Problem in International Relations', has suggestively evoked this distinction in terms of a choice between 'the flowers or the garden, the rocks or the quarry, the trees or the forest, the houses or the neighbourhood, the cars or the traffic jam, the delinquents or the gang, the legislators or the legislative, and so on'.[33] In other words, macro entities are 'wholes', consisting of a host of lesser elements which for purposes of analysis have been aggregated and transposed into macro units. On the micro level no such aggregation of parts into wholes occurs. Instead, each component is dealt with as a discrete and irreducible datum, about which one can generalize but which cannot, *qua* object of analysis, be transubstantiated into a larger ontological whole.

Contrary to what is often thought to be the case, the choice of level of analysis does not in and by itself determine the analytical approach of an investigation. It does, however, put methodological and epistemological restrictions on both the kinds of questions that can be posed and pursued and the types of empirical entities – i.e., units of analysis – that can be used for these purposes. In other words, the level of analysis crucially determines the kind of primary data that is feasible; but it does not in itself imply *how* these data will be utilized, i.e., entail the selection of a particular methodological approach, framework or explanatory mode. Such implications are obtained, however, once we conjoin our two dimensions to generate a matrix consisting of six different combinations, as shown in figure 1.

On the basis of figure 1 it now becomes clear why the micro–macro dimension by itself is insufficient for characterizing existing approaches to the study of international relations. For as this matrix illustrates, both the micro and the macro level of analysis can – both substantively and logically – involve approaches differing significantly in terms of their level of abstraction. This is very important to

| | | Level of analysis | |
		Micro	Macro
	High	1	2
Level of generality	Middle	3	4
	Low	5	6

Figure 1 Analytical approaches to the study of foreign policy

note, since these two levels of analysis are frequently compared in terms of levels of generality which are not strictly comparable. Singer's article is, I suggest, a case in point.

Generally speaking, when Singer refers to the macro type of analysis, he has in mind approaches belonging to cell 2 in our matrix, while his micro-level examples are typically defined in terms of the characteristics of cell 3, or sometimes (although this is not always obvious), by those of cell 5. This easily gives the impression that macro studies as a whole are inherently more 'scientific' in the sense that they tend to be more abstractly theoretical or generalizing. But such an assumption is surely not warranted, either logically or empirically. As figure 1 illustrates, a 'whole' can in fact be situated very low on a ladder of abstraction. A particular flower in a garden is no less general than the garden as a whole (so to speak) in which it is rooted. Of course, the garden is more complex, but that is another matter; for it is still a specific garden, situated on a very particular spot. And although it is true, on the one hand (as Oran Young has noted), that conceptually 'systemic perspectives are oriented toward high levels of abstraction and macro-analysis', it is equally clear that most of the literature on, e.g., realism and the balance of power belongs to cell 4, while much of the traditional work on American or Soviet foreign policy can easily be placed in cell 6 (it is also here, incidentally, where most sins of reification are committed).[34] On the other hand, while Singer hardly (if at all) refers to studies belonging to cell 1, this is by no means an empty box but, on the contrary, characterizes precisely the type of approach – often reaching high levels of generality – to which the comparative foreign policy movement of the past decade and a half has paid such ostensive tribute.

However, my intention here is not to pick a quarrel with Singer's argumentation but, instead, to situate more precisely the type of explanatory framework that I intend to posit below. (But I do agree with Young that Singer's article is mistitled in so far as his aim really is to discuss the pros and cons of two approaches or perspectives rather than two levels of analysis.)[35] And obviously the overall thrust of my previous discussion is to propel us toward cell 3 in the matrix, i.e., toward the pursuit of what can be called *comparable case studies* of *foreign policy actions*. In other words, it is my contention that we should concentrate our efforts on a level of generality that is neither too abstract nor too particularistic, and that our investigations should be couched wholly in terms of the micro-analytical study of foreign policies *qua* specific classes of action. Or as Moon has written: 'In addition to the analysis of particular cases . . . the social scientist must deal with the general regularities resulting from particular kinds of actions.'[36] What this means more specifically will, it is hoped, become somewhat clearer as we turn to the final topic of this chapter, namely, the delineation and explication of a conceptual framework which, it is claimed, will make the types of analysis discussed above both feasible and meaningful.

The framework that will be discussed below is based on the claim that the analysis of foreign policy is best pursued in terms of a tripartite approach consisting of an *intentional*, a *dispositional* and a *situational* dimension of explanation. Although each dimension can lead a semi-independent existence, they are all nevertheless closely linked in the sense that they can be conjoined in specific ways to render increasingly exhaustive explanations of political actions. The procedure adopted here will be to unfold each dimension in turn and in such a manner that our framework as a whole will emerge in the form of a step-by-step process of conceptual augmentation.

(i)   *The intentional dimension*

The *intentional* dimension embraces two conceptual categories which, it is claimed here, are essential to all explanations of foreign policy actions. In barest outline, I will propose that such explanations must in principle always embrace a determination of (1) the particular *choice(s)* implicated in a policy, and (2) the *motivation* underlying its pursuit. Let me briefly comment on these two concepts, as well as on their relationship to each other and to the type of explanation which figure 2 illustrates.

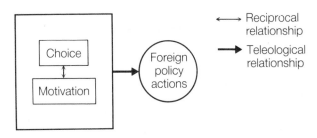

Figure 2   Intentional explanations of foreign policy actions

Generally, when speaking of the reason why a particular policy is pursued, we have in mind the aim, the goal or the objective which the policy in question is intended to accomplish. However, on closer inspection this type of query often turns out to be considerably more complex than may initially appear to be the case. A major reason for this is that in ordinary usage these terms tend to refer inter-changeably to both ends and means, and sometimes to both at the same time. Often the two are also conflated, usually in the sense that ends are used – consciously or not – to legitimize or rationalize means in one way or another. This is the case, for example, when a decision such as that of bombing Hanoi is defended by referring exclusively to the need for vouchsafing American security, an explanation (long favoured by Henry Kissinger) which surely assumes something that is by no means obvious: that the policy of bombing Hanoi was directly linked – and hence necessary – to American security or, indeed, that it was in this sense *zweckrational* at all. In order not to beg questions of this kind, we are, in other words, impelled to distinguish between the choices involved in taking particular actions, and the motivation underlying these actions. Or as Martin Hollis has written, 'the actor . . . needs to be found good reasons for his choice of goals. The enquirer looks for further goals to which the immediate goals are a means.'[37] Thus, although the concern for American security (however ill conceived) most probably was involved in the policy of bombing Hanoi, it could at best only have been implicated as a motivating reason for the particular choice involved in pursuing this specific action (i.e. forcing, or, in the parlance of the time, 'bombing' the North Vietnamese to the negotiating table), not as the goal itself. Indeed, the choice of *not* bombing Hanoi could conceivably have had the same or – as many have maintained – an even better effect. Thus there is no reason, with respect to this example, even to assume that the particular choice made was in fact the best one, given the motivation behind it, namely, winning the war.

Conversely, when we inquire as to the underlying reason for some purposive behaviour, we will probably not be satisfied if reference is made solely to the immediate goal(s) contained in it. The murderer who is asked why he poisoned his wife (a 'domestic' example fully equivalent in dignity to the previous, *realpolitische* one) may in all honesty reply that poison happened to be the handiest and least suspicious means around for killing her, since his greenhouse had been stocked with the stuff for years. This does not, of course, explain why he killed her, but merely why he happened to poison her. However, once it becomes evident that the reason why he did away with his wife was his desire to be rid of her while retaining her money (a view, in the Vietnam context, often espoused by New Left critics), we know the motive behind the whole sad business. A similar distinction can be found in game-theoretical analyses of decisions, in which it is usually expressed in terms of choices and preferences.[38] It is also intimated by Martin Seliger when he discusses the differences between the operative and fundamental levels of discourse in the formulation and pursuit of policies.[39]

There is, however, an important additional aspect to this distinction, which should not be confused with the above notion of a strict means–end link in purposive behaviour. This aspect refers to actions which, while purposed by a 'motivation' in the sense discussed above, also involve 'choices' which in themselves are unrelated to, or independent of, this larger purpose, but which at the same time are necessarily tied to the pursuit of the larger purpose which motivates the action in the first place. As an illustration of this type of contingent linkage between 'motivations' and particular 'choices' we can look briefly at figure 3, which purports to represent a map of four possible routes (R_1, R_2, R_3 and R_4) leading from town T to the respective destinations D_1, D_2, D_3 and D_4.

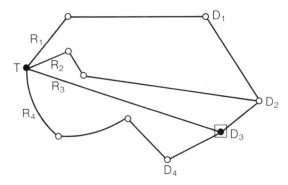

Figure 3   Choices in the pursuit of an intention

Let us assume that three actors (A, B and C) wish to reach D_3 – Nirvana, say – and that they all know that the quickest, shortest and in all ways most comfortable route is R_3. Nevertheless, A chooses to take R_4, and in response to our bewilderment explains that he always prefers to take the most scenic route (or, in his own words, that his aim is 'never to travel quickly but always pleasurably'). Similarly, traveller B (whose filial piety is well attested) chooses R_2, explaining that his mother lives in D_2 and that he has promised to visit her *en route*; while traveller-cum-angler C, mindful of the excellent fishing at D_1, chooses R_1. In each instance here we are given the reason for the particular traveller's choice – his immediate goal, so to speak – but not the purpose behind the trip itself, i.e., the motivation guiding the venture as a whole: reaching D_3 (or achieving Nirvana). And the reason for this is of course the fact that the particular choice which is made in each case does not pertain to this ultimate destination – which is common to all (and known to us) – but to something subsidiary or secondary. Nevertheless, the choice itself is provided by, and in this sense dependent on, the objective of reaching D_3; for without it there would be no choice to be made in the first place. On the other hand, the case with regard to R_3 is different, since here we have a typical example of a direct means–end link between the objective of reaching D_3 and the reason for choosing R_3: for (as both we and our actor already know) the latter is, after all, the quickest, shortest and in all ways most comfortable route to D_3.

The point of this discussion is, in other words, to argue for the necessity in the analysis of foreign policies of distinguishing between *two* types of choices, the first of which is coupled directly in a consciously rational manner with the motivation underlying the action, while the second, although contingently part of this action, is not linked to such an explicit means–end chain. For the sake of simplicity I shall, *faute de mieux*, refer to these as *primary* and *secondary* choices.

Furthermore, although I have not specifically argued for such a differentiation above, it is in my view also fruitful to make a distinction between *instrumental* and *consummatory* motivations with regard to the pursuit of foreign policies. The difference between these two concepts is that while an instrumental motivation (e.g., the achievement of a balance of payments in international trade) can always be viewed as a means (or 'instrument') towards a further state of affairs *qua* ultimate end (e.g., safeguarding a country's economic and military security), this does not hold for consummatory motivations. These are, essentially, ends in themselves (like achieving Nirvana), and are thus usually justified in terms of transcendental values of one kind or another.

On the basis of this discussion the following specification of the nature of, and distinction between, these two dimensions can now be given. 'Choices' will refer here to the reasons for an actor's decision in the face of a particular choice situation, while 'motivation' points to a condition or state of affairs which an actor intends either to change or to maintain. In other words, 'choice' indicates why an actor opts for a particular course of action in the pursuit of an intended state of affairs, while 'motivation' describes this intention itself. (Why an actor intends one rather than another state of affairs is a question which, given this framework, can only be answered in terms of the dispositional dimension of explanation, which will be discussed below.) This difference can also be expressed as follows: a particular action is motivated by some purpose or other, which in turn implicates a choice (or a series of choices) with respect to its pursuit. And while one therefore cannot intend a choice, choice itself is always intentional, even though (as G. H. von Wright has pointed out) it may be entirely fortuitous.[40]

Hence the difference, in intentional explanations, between primary and secondary aims, on the one hand, and instrumental and consummatory motivations, on the other, is that the former refers to the type of choice that is implicated, while the latter refers to the type of intention *qua* desired state of affairs that is involved in the pursuit of the particular action. Motivation, in this (but not in a dispositional) type of explanation, is thus a given factor, while the range of possible choices is limited by it. Furthermore, this is a reciprocal relationship in the general sense – which also applies to the function of this term below – that these two factors are viewed as both mutually dependent and analytically distinct (a relationship which will be taken for granted without further discussion or justification).

For purposes of simplifying the present analysis, and in order, perhaps, to forestall at least some of the problems – usually of a viciously regressive kind – attending both the means–end division and the choice–motivation linkage, the above distinction can also be expressed in the following manner. Let us define 'choices' as all the *operational objectives* – *zweckrational* or not – of foreign policy actions, and 'motivation' as the *interests* (both instrumental and consumma-tory) involved in their pursuit. At this point it is immaterial what particular interests – for example, statist, governmental, societal or organizational – are implicated, or if they are 'real' or spurious. The assumption on which this stipulation rests is the simple notion that foreign policies are always motivated by some interest or other, be they instrumental or consummatory; and that the question as to whose, or what kind of, interests are involved is empirical and should hence not be settled stipulatively or a priori. I am thus eschewing both classical realist assumptions – that the will to power (in some sense or other) is the motivating force behind all foreign policies – and the more sophisticated game-theoretical premises espoused, for example, by William H. Riker and (if to a lesser degree) Thomas C. Schelling, namely, the centrality, in the actions of rational political man, of the urge to win (or at least to form winning coalitions). Furthermore, and for similar reasons, I do not accept as fruitful in this connection the revisionist historians' view of the crucial significance of economic determinism in the definition and pursuit of the 'national interest'.

In my view the above constitutes, in a most skeletal fashion, the basic conceptual framework for an intentional explanation. In many instances this teleological model also comprises a sufficiently self-contained and viable framework *per se* for the analysis of foreign policy actions. Thus, if one wishes to analyse the foreign policy doctrine of a government, or its conception of the national interest, it is in terms of this dimension that such an examination must proceed. The same applies to the study of all explicit policy statements, whether they have the function of stating a decision, defending or rationalizing it, or in general influencing the minds of others, be they foreign governments or entire adult populations. It should therefore be emphasized that although the intentional dimension is only designed to yield *ex post facto descriptive explanations* of this kind, it nevertheless constitutes a central analytical dimension in the study of foreign policy.

(ii)   *The dispositional dimension*

This leads us to our second explanatory level, which for lack of a better term will be referred to as the *dispositional* dimension of explanation. As I shall try to argue below, this is also the level on which we have to operate if we wish to augment our purely descriptive, teleological explanations with *causal* explanations.

Something of the nature of this dimension is intimated in the following passage by Alexander George and Robert Keohane, dealing with the notion of the national interest in particular and the role of values generally in the formulation of foreign policies. They argue that interests 'can be seen as applications of values in context: values applied in the light of situations as they appear to people involved in them. As used by the policy-makers, the phrase "national interest" implies a choice among values standing behind these interests.'[41] Their point is that 'values' can in a crucial sense be seen as determining foreign policy interests (as expressed by policy-makers), either in the sense that such interests are essentially the form that values take in this context, or because values 'stand behind' such interests. The thrust of this type of notion is, in other words, the claim that the factors characterizing the intentional dimension can themselves be further explored in terms of concepts belonging to a different explanatory dimension. More specifically, it is suggested that the particular motivations and choices describing the reason(s) why a particular policy was pursued can in turn be explored in order to answer a type of question that the intentional framework itself cannot accommodate, that is to say, why these particular motivations and choices were implicated in the first place. In short, it allows us to pursue the query why a decision-maker was (or is) *cognitively disposed* towards a particular intention rather than towards some other state of affairs (hence the 'dispositional' locution here). One can also describe the distinction between these two levels in terms of an 'in order to' and a 'because of' – or a teleological and a causal – dimension, the former referring to the intentional sphere itself as discussed above, while the latter constitutes the link between this intention and the *having of it*; how a particular *intention* has come to be a particular *actor's* intention. In my view there are *two* broad conceptual categories which are essential to a causal analysis of this kind, namely, *values* (including the *norms* which they underwrite) and *perceptions* (see figure 4).

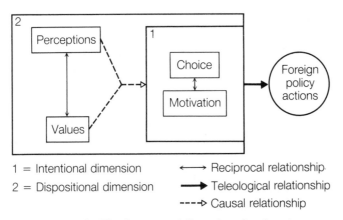

1 = Intentional dimension   ⟷ Reciprocal relationship

2 = Dispositional dimension   ⟶ Teleological relationship

                                      ---⟶ Causal relationship

Figure 4   The dispositional dimension of explanation

Philosophically, these two categories parallel a pair of concepts made famous by Donald Davidson in his discussion of the causal nature of reasons. He has written that 'whenever someone does something for a reason ... he can be characterized as (a) having some sort of pro attitude toward actions of a certain kind, and (b) believing (or knowing, perceiving, noticing, remembering) that his action is of that kind.'[42] He then adds that this pair can together be called the *primary reason* why an agent performs an action, and that it is *this* reason which is the cause of that action. With this view I fully concur. The same also applies to his argument that 'if we are intelligibly to attribute attitudes and beliefs ... we are committed to finding, in the pattern of behaviour, belief and desire, a large degree of rationality and consistency.'[43] However, while Davidson seems to imply that knowledge of the 'pro attitudes' and cognitive 'beliefs' which have caused an action is sufficient in itself to explain that action in full, the framework presented here is based on the notion that such primary reasons refer only to the *causal factor* or link in the performance of an action, not to the intention itself, which necessarily implicates a teleological description of an action. Somewhat contrary to Davidson, I thus distinguish between a primary reason *for* an action, and the intention *of* that action. This, however, in no way contradicts his contention, but merely augments it with a dimension that is not crucial to the outcome of his particular argument as such. One can also consider the distinction between an intentional and a dispositional dimension to be an acknowledgement that, while the proponents of the so-called logical connection argument (such as von Wright) are correct in so far as they insist that intentional explanations *per se* cannot be causal, they are in error (and Davidson right) if they wish to make a similar claim for the kinds of primary reasons that are posited here.[44]

With respect to the study of foreign policy, these two dispositional categories are in no way strangers but, on the contrary, figure in various capacities in most of the pertinent literature. Hence there is here no need as such to justify the assumption that, in one way or another, perceptions and values are crucially important factors in the process of foreign policy decision making. What does call for some justification and discussion, however, is the manner in which these factors are treated in the present framework, especially since my conception of their role here will be central to the discussion, in the next two chapters, of the conceptual utility of 'ideology' in the analysis of foreign policy.

We will turn first to the normative category – that of *values* and *norms* – and briefly consider the implications of positing it as a dispositional conception rather than in terms of the intentionalist – and presumably equally normative – concepts of motivation and choice. What does it mean to refer to values as a causal notion, and why distinguish between causal and teleological normative concepts?

Let us consider the following three instances from the literature regarding the role of values – and particularly competing values – in the analysis of decision making. The first is provided by John D. Steinbruner, whose discussion and critique of the 'analytic paradigm' – of which Graham T. Allison's Rational Actor perhaps continues to be the most representative (or at least most quoted) model – is particularly pertinent here. He has described the characteristics of this approach as follows: 'A given process of decision is analytic if upon examination one can find evidence that there was at least limited value-integration, that alternative outcomes were analyzed and evaluated, and that new information regarding central variables of the problem did produce plausibly appropriate subjective adjustments.'[45] However, and this is a signal contribution on his part to this whole literature, Steinbruner has been able to show that in many types of situations this model is contradicted by the available cognitive evidence. He thus notes that

> in analyzing higher-order cognitive operations under uncertainty, cognitive theory directly contradicts the assumption of value integration advanced by the analytic paradigm ... Cognitive principles ... suggest the contrary *assumption of value separation.* According to this assumption, the two values of a complex problem will not be related to one another in the mind of the decision maker, but divided and pursued separately, as if they were independent considerations. The information-processing operations of the human mind strain to set up single-value decision problems.[46]

George, in his discussion of psychological constraints on rational decision making, and particularly of the problems of 'value-complexity' and 'uncertainty' in this connection, takes a somewhat different and broader tack when he analyses the tendency towards 'malaise' on the part of decision-makers when faced with difficult value trade-off problems. More specifically, and with particular reference to the solution of the value-complexity problem (we shall return to 'uncertainty' when discussing the role of 'perceptions'), he first of all notes that 'as decision theorists have emphasized, there are analytical ways of dealing with value-complexity in choice situations in order to strive for as "efficient" and acceptable a solution to such problems as possible.' However, he adds almost immediately, 'Such analytical techniques may be relevant in principle but, for various reasons, difficult to apply in practice in the settings in which foreign policy decisions are made.'[47] In its stead he proffers the following analysis and recommendation:

> It is useful to distinguish three different ways in which a policy maker may attempt to deal with the malaise associated with value-complexity. First, he may *resolve* the value conflict, at least in his own mind, by devising a course of action that constitutes either a genuinely creative analytical solution to the problem or a spurious or illusory resolution that may also be psychologically comforting even though analytically defective. A second way is to *accept* the value conflict as unavoidable and to face up to the need to make the difficult trade-off choice as part of one's role requirements as a decision maker . . . Finally, the decision maker may seek to *avoid* a value conflict by denying its existence or playing down its importance.[48]

Our third example comes from I. M. Destler's analysis of *Presidents, Bureaucrats, and Foreign Policy*, in which the author writes:

> Rational policy making may be salutary as an ideal, and reasoned analysis may be able to improve policy making at many points. But there is no way for reason alone to overcome the diversity of goals and means that are inevitable among participants in foreign policy making. Goals are based on value preferences as well as rational analysis . . . Thus it is unrealistic to hope men would reason their separate ways to common policy conclusions even if they approached the problems from the same vantage point and possessed the same information. But they don't.[49]

In this connection he refers in particular to the norms and values created by organizational subcultures and their various parochial perspectives and priorities (a theme to which we shall have reason to return below).[50]

My reason for citing these scholars is that all three, in their discussion of the nature and effect of values in decisions, refer to activities of the mind which are not, and cannot be, intentional in the sense that this concept has been used here. Instead, their conclusions indicate that values belong – both logically and empirically – to a different and antecedent dimension in the decision-making process. For while in the intentional dimension motives and the range of available choices are *given*, in the sense that they are *per se* normatively unproblematic descriptions of actual intentions, this does not hold for the nature of values as discussed above. On the contrary, as both Steinbruner and George have shown, conflicts between these have to be resolved in the mind of the actor *before* he can intend the action which the intentional dimension in our framework is designed to describe. In Steinbruner's terminology, intentions refer to 'single-value decisions', not to the choice between various motivations in a situation of value-complexity.

Furthermore, once we conceive of values in this causal manner, we can also explore the determinants of particular motives and choices, as well as the reasons for possible incompatibilities between them; for these can then be analysed as consequences of values (and norms), that is, as '*values applied* in the light of situations as they appear to people involved in them'.[51] From this it also follows that if and when there is a conflict or a contradiction between motivation and a particular choice – which may often be the case without the actor even being aware of it – that is the result of a prior condition of value-complexity; and as we have seen above, such conflicts can only be resolved cognitively in the manner suggested by George. The same must be said for the case where conflicts of this kind remain unresolved: in such instances the 'blame' ultimately rests on incompatible values, not on incongruous motives and choices.

One is also able, on the basis of this distinction between two normative dimensions, to define particular motivations and choices in terms of values without getting trapped by – often pernicious – circles of definition and/or interpretation. It thus allows us, for example, to define the concept of the 'national interest' in terms of the particular utility calculations, on the part of the pertinent actor(s), between values of various magnitude and complexity. Or as

George and Keohane have written, 'in so far as the concept of national interest is to be useful as a criterion for policy, it must specify some means by which leaders can determine which values and therefore which interests are to be included, and which excluded, from the set of national interests.'[52] When viewed in this way, the often maligned notion of the 'national interest' is anything but a hollow concept.

The role of *perceptions* in foreign policy decisions is a topic which deserves to be treated much more extensively than either space or time affords here, particularly since it can be argued that perceptions as a broad cognitive–psychological category are the prime causal factor in all such decisions. 'Fact, analysis, idea, and misinformation,' Charles E. Lindblom has written, 'achieve their effects even when influence is unintended, simply because all of us constantly react to our perceptions of the world around us.'[53] Or as Robert K. Merton has noted in his classic analysis of the self-fulfilling prophecy, 'men respond not only to the objective features of a situation, but also, and at times primarily, to the meaning this situation has for them. And once they have assigned some meaning to the situation, their consequent behaviour and some of the consequences of that behaviour are determined by the ascribed meaning.'[54] In the same vein, but with particular reference to international politics, Anatol Rapoport writes that the 'seat of international relations (as of all politics) is in the minds of men. Hence international relations are what they are because the people who speak about them and people who design and execute foreign policies think they are what they are.'[55] In view of the recent extensive work which has gone into the analysis of this aspect of foreign policy, I shall only briefly consider here some of the ramifications of treating the perceptions of decision-makers as a dispositional factor in terms of which intentions – and hence actions – can be explained.

Since the main theme of this work on the role of perceptions in decision-making is the prevalence of various psychological and cognitive departures from the so-called 'analytic paradigm', let me specify in somewhat more detail the conception of rationality that is being put to task in this literature. Before doing so, however, it should be added that while this questioning of the utility of a rational choice model has been an ongoing concern for a considerable period, the model itself continues to be used and advocated on a broad front, both in theory and in practice. As two reviewers of this topic – Donald R. Kinder and Janet A. Weiss – have noted, this reflects a 'curious disjuncture': for

> [while] much contemporary literature on decision making is careful to finesse empirical claims to rationality ... rational models of choice continue to dominate popular and scholarly analyses of political events ... Decision makers-in-training continue to be taught techniques to maximize rationality. In spite of a veneer of skepticism, prevailing conceptions of political decision making still honour the idea of rational choice in important ways.[56]

This of course makes a clarification of the type of rationality that is being challenged in this literature all the more necessary, particularly since this scepticism pertains not to a conception of rationality in terms of a pure or perfect rational choice model (which hardly exists at all in empirical social science today), but, rather, to a conception of this model that has already been qualified in important respects. Here I have in mind the introduction to this vocabulary of such modifying concepts as 'satisficing', 'muddling through', 'bounded rationality', and so forth.[57]

Steinbruner, in the passage on 'value-complexity' to which I have already referred, writes the following in further clarification of the 'analytic' model, and particularly of the rationality assumptions underlying it:

> The analytic paradigm is defined as a set of assumptions about how the decision process operates in relation to the complex decision problem. A given process of decision is analytic if upon examination one can find evidence that there was at least limited value integration, that alternative outcomes were analyzed and evaluated, and that new information regarding central variables of the problem did produce plausibly appropriate subjective adjustments. In following the process through a sequence of decision points, it can be found analytic if one can observe a causal learning process; that is, an explicit set of calculations which evolve in such a way that higher, more general conceptions of decision objectives came to be included (upward expansion), as well as critical environmental interactions which were previously excluded (lateral expansion).[58]

Clearly, this is not in any sense a rigid conception of the nature of 'rationality' or 'rational choice' in decision making: on the contrary, as pointed out by Kinder and Weiss, this is a common – indeed, a commonsensical – approach to political decision making. And yet, as they immediately add, the fact remains that there is considerable evidence to suggest that people are 'incapable of carrying out the mental operations required by these assumptions'.[59] Steinbruner, for his part, claims that while this is the case, such evidence will not by itself topple the popularity of this model; nevertheless, it is *de facto* slowly being replaced by models which make more sense of the cognitive reality of decision making. This, in turn, necessitates at least a brief discussion of these post-'analytic' contributions to this area of research, as well as a specification, given these alternative claims and frameworks, of the manner in which 'perceptions' as a dispositional factor can be said to affect the intentions – and hence actions – of foreign policy actors.

For the sake of simplicity, and following Robert A. Abelson, let us distinguish here between (1) claims regarding distortions – broadly speaking – in the decision-maker's *view of reality*, and (2) various cognitive and psychological limitations characterizing the *information processes* of decision making in such a way that they tend to follow '"psycho-logic" rather than formal logic'.[60] These are obviously overlapping categories, but nevertheless they serve the purpose of differentiating between two general types of implicit or explicit propositions in this literature.

A representative example of current research pertaining to the first type is the 'cognitive mapping' approach as developed by Robert Axelrod, G. Matthew Bonham, Michael Shapiro and others.[61] Essentially, this technique outlines a procedure for giving a systematized, pictorial representation of the causal assertions and claims which decision-makers make with regard to a specific problem, issue or policy, which can then in turn be analysed for purposes of comparing these cognitive maps with the reality which they purport to represent. One of the main conclusions of this work is that 'Decision makers create causal maps that misrepresent the dynamics of the decision problem. They tend to forget about the possibilities of feedback or reciprocal causation. Although in reality policies have complicated, unpredictable, and unintended consequences, they are seen to have only simple, straightforward consequences.'[62] George has also dwelt on this aspect, noting, for example, that:

> In the effort to capture the perspective of their adversary, policy-makers often 'overrationalize' the actions and behaviour of the opposing government. That is, they slip into the highly questionable assumption that everything the other side does is the result of unified planning and highly centralized calculation. The other government is reified; its actions are viewed as the product of rational calculations by a superordinate individual. Moreover, personalization of other governments is often accompanied by stereotyping them as friend or foe.[63]

In other words, these studies indicate that what the decision-maker perceives is not necessarily the 'objective features of the situation' but, rather, an 'assigned' or 'ascribed' meaning; and that these imputations – on the bases of which decisions are made – constitute a distortion of reality.

The second type of cognitive constraint on the perceptions of decision-makers – that which pertains to the information process itself as distinguished from their constructions of reality – has received even more attention in the literature. Robert Jervis, in particular, has discussed it extensively in his book on *Perception and Misperception in International Politics*.[64] There he focuses on the manner in which the intentions of adversaries are assessed by foreign policy actors, and emphasized how these intentions – being in themselves necessarily ambiguous, and hence easily subject to differing and indeed contradictory interpretations – are prone to be misperceived, leading to responses based on mistaken 'images' rather than on an accurate ascertainment of the particular intention underlying the action in question. The core of his analysis accordingly consists of descriptions of how these mistaken 'images' guide the processing within the decision-maker's mind of all incoming information, and particularly of how they persist in the face of contradictory information.

Kinder and Weiss have amplified further the notion of the power of the principle of irrational cognitive consistency, in terms of three major mechanisms which influence the decision process: (1) 'the uncritical assimilation of new information to decision-makers' established beliefs, expectations, and preferences'; (2) 'post-decisional rationalization', i.e., 'evidence that the chosen alternative is imperfect – that it may have some negative consequences – is reinterpreted, discounted, or forgotten, because it is inconsistent with the decision-makers' behaviour'; and (3) 'the failure to perceive trade-off relationships, the failure to recognize that the choice of one alternative obtains a greater return to some values only at the cost of losses in some other respects.'[65] They also add that decision-makers tend to perceive more order and certainty than the objective facts warrant; that in 'their construction of stable, internally consistent belief systems, decision makers fashion pictures of the world that are much more regular and orderly than is reality itself.'[66] The cognitive consequence of this practice is that new ideas do not get much – if any – scope for growth, while its political effects are essentially conservative. The combined thrust of this principle is illustrated by Dean Acheson's laconic description of Arthur Vandenberg's characteristic stand in the face of policies that he opposed: 'He declared the end unattainable, the means hairbrained, and the costs staggering.'[67] It should be added, however, that it has recently been called into question whether misperceptions of this kind really matter all that much in reality. Thus Arthur A. Stein has concluded not only that misperceptions affect choice and outcome only in a narrow range of circumstances, but also that they can lead to conflict as well as to co-operation.[68]

George follows a similar track as Jervis in his discussion of the policy-maker as 'consistency seeker'. At the same time, however, he wants to emphasize that the 'pronounced tendency toward consistency striving is inherent in human behaviour. Thus, perception and interpretation of new information would hardly be possible unless it were filtered through existing beliefs and frames of reference. One must be careful,' he therefore enjoins, 'not to apply the lables of "close-mindedness", "cognitive distortion", and "irrationality" in too facile a manner.'[69] Nevertheless, he agrees that consistency seeking is often genuinely problematic, citing as an example the fact that 'many historians believe that distorted information processing of this kind contribute to the exacerbation of the Cold War'.[70] He also refers the reader to Ole Holsti's study of

John Foster Dulles, in which it is shown how the latter, on numerous and momentous occasions, interpreted Soviet actions in a manner which was obviously more finely attuned to his own vivid imagery of the Soviet leaders as implacably hostile foes than to the available facts themselves (at least as interpreted by most other knowledgeable observers).[71]

However, George has also gone beyond an analysis of the nature and problematic aspects of consistency seeking in the information processes of decision-makers. He thus notes that a 'shift has occurred away from the fundamental premise of earlier cognitive balance theories that viewed man as a "consistency seeker", to the different premise of recent attribution theory (and other psychological theories as well), which views man as a "problem solver".'[72] This new emphasis draws attention to three types of activities in which man *qua* decision-maker-cum-problem-solver engages: (1) discerning the attributes of other actors and social phenomena (hence 'attribution' theory); (2) inferring the causes of important events (*vide* 'cognitive mapping' above); and (3) predicting historical trends and other actors' behaviour. The composite picture which emerges from this is of the decision-maker as a serious person trying most earnestly to be an applied scientist in his approach to the job of making decisions. In this literature we are also once again confronted with various types of cognitive flaws – or, as he also calls them, attributional biases – in the information-processing systems of policy-makers. Typical of these are the following: the tendency to overemphasize situational variables when explaining one's own behaviour, while emphasizing dispositional variables when describing other people's behaviour, particularly if one dislikes them (Daniel Heradstveit's studies of Arab and Israeli opinion leaders come to mind here); the propensity to overlook the evidentiary value of non-occurrences when explaining situations or making inferences about the behaviour of others (a tendency which, as George reminds us, Sherlock Holmes did *not* suffer from when he perceived the significance of the dog which did not bark); and the inclination, in predictions, to employ a limited stock of 'heuristics' or 'rules of thumb', which, moreover, often deviate considerably from what would seem to be scientifically (or statistically) appropriate.[73]

We need not for our specific purposes delve deeper into these various aspects of the discussion regarding the role of values and perceptions in the explanation of foreign policy, except to note that it is most difficult not to view these two factors as so closely interrelated that it is well nigh impossible to speak of the one without implicating the other. Values (and norms) obviously colour our perceptions (even when we are not aware of it), while – if perhaps in a somewhat less obvious fashion – our perceptions fashion and reinforce our normative premises and pursuits. Or as four scholars of foreign policy behaviour have recently put it, commenting on the importance of Milton Rokeach's work in this area:

> A decision maker's values may be expected to shape his or her reactions and perceptions as a believer, perceiver, information processor, strategist, and learner ... values constitute a significant part of the *content* of a belief system and play a central role in determining the *structure* of such a system. Basic values can obviously shape the definition of situations and contribute to the process of selective perception. In the information-processing stage, values function as screens and thereby produce selective exposure.[74]

Nevertheless, for analytical purposes it is both necessary and feasible to treat them as separate causal factors in explaining motivations and the various choices that we make in the pursuit of intentions. On the whole, this is also in line with the way that these factors have been treated in the pertinent literature.

However, before turning to our third and final explanatory dimension, one additional aspect of the dispositional dimension should be touched upon briefly, since it pertains directly to our subsequent discussion of the role of ideology in the analysis of foreign policy. I have in mind the status of the various types of 'belief systems' in the framework discussed here. The question is how the notion of a belief system – such as George's 'operational code' – is to be regarded in relation to our two explanatory dimensions (and their constitutive variables).

First of all, it should be emphasized – even though it is probably self-evident – that the notion of a belief system as an analytical construct belongs to the dispositional rather than to the intentional dimension. A person does not intend his beliefs; but beliefs, however defined, certainly underlie and inform intentions, and can in that sense be viewed as causal factors in their explanation. Secondly, the notion of a belief system is to be regarded here in terms of our two basic dispositional categories, not as an explanatory variable in its own right. Hence, since belief systems are constituted by perceptions and values *qua* analytical entities, they also have all the hallmarks of a construct of the second degree. Thus I cannot fully agree with George when he writes of operational codes that

> beliefs of this kind serve as a prism or filter that influences the actor's perception and diagnosis of political situations and that provides norms and standards to guide and channel his choices of action in specific situations. The function of an operational code belief system . . . is to provide the actor with 'diagnostic propensities' and 'choice propensities'.[75]

Rather, in my view constructs such as 'belief systems' or 'operational codes' serve merely as concepts for referring to the cognitive characteristics, operations and interplay of the mind with regard to perception and valuation. It is the perceiving and evaluating *actor* who 'causes' the pursuit of intentions, not second-degree analytical constructs such as the operational code of a person. Despite the reificatory overtones in the passage above, this is also, I suggest, what George is really saying.

Thirdly, it should be made clear that the sources of the decision-maker's values and perceptions – and hence of his belief system – are exogenous variables in this framework, and are for this reason excluded from it. If one is engaged in the comparative analysis of foreign policies, then the question of the origin of personality traits should remain unposed (which does not mean that it is unimportant). The germane question here is not how values and perceptions have arisen, but what their effects on the pursuit of given policies are. On the other hand, if one is interested in answering the psychological question of how beliefs are formed, then obviously our independent variable is no longer policies but beliefs.[76]

Fourthly, and despite these stipulations, we are now able to speak of our two dimensions in the following prototypical manner:

> The reason for government A's actions in this matter is explicable in terms of its stated foreign policy doctrine (or set of principles); and it, in turn, can be viewed as a consequence of, or caused by, the

prevailing belief systems (or operational codes) of its foreign policy decision-makers.

Furthermore, and as long as we remain fully cognizant of the basic concepts which constitute these broad cognitive notions, as well as of the relations characterizing the links between foreign policy actions and our two dimensions, we can now posit the following preliminary *special version* of our general framework as hitherto discussed (see figure 5).

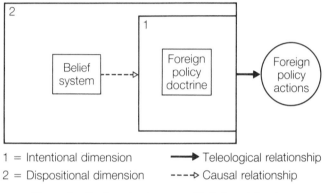

1 = Intentional dimension ⟶ Teleological relationship
2 = Dispositional dimension --→ Causal relationship

Figure 5   Explanation in terms of beliefs and doctrines

It shows, in a most elementary fashion, the suggested role of various ideational notions in the explanation of foreign policies. More to the point, it represents the following two fundamental methodological claims: (1) that we should regard all the various *doctrinal* aspects of foreign policies as intentional in nature and hence as teleological in thrust; while (2) all psychological–cognitive notions such as *belief systems* should be viewed as dispositional factors and hence as causal in relation to both doctrines in particular and foreign policy actions in general.

(iii)   *The situational dimension*

Although the third and final explanatory level will be described somewhat more briefly than the first two, this does not mean that the *situational* dimension is in any sense negligible in the analysis of foreign policy. On the contrary, I fully subscribe to the view that 'situational forces exert powerful influences upon a decision-maker's ability to perform' all the complex processing tasks involved in the pursuit of foreign policy, as well as to the conclusion that there exists a 'frail or nonexistent understanding of situational charac-teristics themselves'.[77] Indeed, one of the criticisms levelled – somewhat unfairly, in my view – against Jervis, Axelrod and others writing in this tradition is that 'None offers an analysis systemati-cally informed by an understanding of the external, situational constraints that affect individual choice.'[78] Thus, although this dimension too will get less than the full treatment that it deserves, I shall nevertheless try to remedy – at least partially – the lacunae intimated in this charge. It is my aim, in particular, to situate this dimension in relation to the first two in such a manner that the framework acquires a systematic wholeness, despite the semi-autonomy of its constituent dimensions.

As I have already argued in the previous chapter, the type of analytical model which is being discussed here – in which the concept of action is the crucial explanandum – must necessarily posit all situational factors as indirect and cognitively mediated rather than in the form of directly causal variables. As we have already noted (quoting the Sprouts once more):

> environmental factors (both nonhuman and human) can affect human activities in only two ways. Such factors can be perceived, reacted to, and taken into account by the human individual or individuals . . . in this sense alone can . . . environmental factors . . . be said to 'influence', 'condition', or otherwise 'affect' human values and preferences, moods and attitudes, choices and decisions . . . Secondly, environmental factors may be conceived as a sort of matrix . . . which limits the execution of undertakings.[79]

Hence, although Jon Elster's conception of the 'rational actor' approach to the study of human behaviour is very close in some important respects to the notions underlying the present framework, it is also somewhat different in regard at least to the particular point being made here:

> Any single piece of human behaviour [Elster writes], may be seen as the end product of two successive filtering devices. The first is defined

by the set of structural constraints which cuts down upon the set of abstractly possible courses of action and reduces it to the (much smaller) subset of feasible actions. The second filter is the mechanism that singles out which member of the feasible set shall be realized.[80]

For while his second filter corresponds closely to my dispositional dimension (he, too assigns 'values' to it), his first filter is somewhat too 'rational' for our purposes, as the preceding discussion has tried to argue. Instead, the point here is precisely that his subset of feasible actions is still too encompassing, since the actor may – and often does – fail to perceive (and thus to act upon) the whole of this subset. (Of course, he may also 'perceive' options which in fact are not feasible; this is indeed a common occurrence which, however, does not affect my argument here.)

In other words, however important situational–environmental factors are as constraints, their significance here lies solely in how they in fact affect the actors on the foreign policy scene, be they single individuals (like Dulles) or groups of individuals acting as a body (such as the National Security Council). This relationship can be illustrated in the simple manner shown in figure 6.

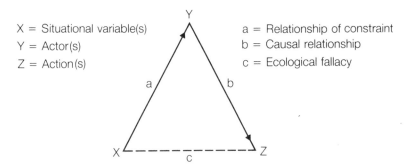

X = Situational variable(s)	a = Relationship of constraint
Y = Actor(s)	b = Causal relationship
Z = Action(s)	c = Ecological fallacy

Figure 6   The relationship between situational variables, actors and actions

In this view any direct explanatory linkage which is posited between X and Z will necessarily suffer from the ecological fallacy, except when in the form of a shorthand for a + b. Typical examples of the latter, legitimate kind of claim would be most types of hypotheses linking, e.g., smallness of size, or the geopolitical situation, of a state to a particular type of policy. What these propositions usually imply

– when it is not explicitly stated – is that the foreign policy decision-makers of a given state are in some sense or other cognitively constrained by factors of this kind, inasmuch as it is the apperception of these which affects their foreign policy actions. The ecological fallacy is usually a consequence of adducing factors such as class, the economic system or geopolitical aspects as *independent* structural variables in foreign policy analysis. In this connection we can, with Elster, distinguish between the following two types of ecological explanations: 'In an extreme version this could mean that the constraints jointly have the effect of narrowing down the feasible set to a single point: in a weaker and more plausible version that the constraints define a set which is so small that formal freedom of choice within the set really does not amount to much.'[81] In my view, the above fallacy pertains to both of these forms, i.e., even when an analysis would show that no other than the observed action was really possible.[82]

Having emphasized this cognitively mediated character of all situational and environmental factors, we can now proceed to place this dimension within our framework as a whole. I shall do this in terms of two concepts, which are intended jointly to encompass all the crucial situational factors in foreign policy decision making. These two will be called *objective conditions* and the *organizational setting* (see figure 7).

I do not think that there is much point in dwelling long on the meaning and significance of the *objective conditions* characterizing the situation within which the foreign policy-maker is placed to act. It suffices here to note that these conditions know no international or domestic boundaries, and that their pervasiveness is such that neither rich nor poor country can escape their steady and enduring grip. Still, this grip itself has many forms and degrees of intransigence; the extent and effects of poverty in Chad are, for obvious 'objective' reasons, markedly different from those in either Czechoslovakia or Canada. Being both socio-economic and physically concrete, these conditions are as much man-made – though often unintended – as a product of natural history and other seemingly implacable forces. They pertain equally, for example, to the supply of colonizable land during the heyday of the imperialist scramble, to the economic conditions of the Great Depression, and to the

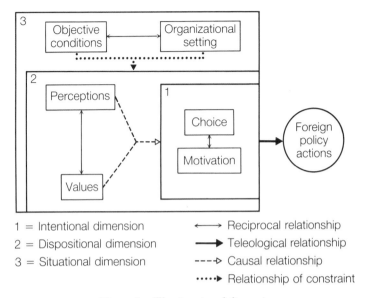

1 = Intentional dimension   ⟷ Reciprocal relationship
2 = Dispositional dimension   ⟶ Teleological relationship
3 = Situational dimension   ---⟿ Causal relationship
                                   ·····⟿ Relationship of constraint

Figure 7   The situational dimension

geographic and market vagaries of the oil supply today.[83] At the same time, when an appeal is made to their significance, the thrust of the argument is often to infer some fundamental philosophical implication – such as determinism against the freedom of will, or historical materialism *contra* idealistic voluntarism – which prima facie appears to bear little or no resemblance to reality itself. In other words, this is a category that embraces such a host of phenomena that it would be silly to attempt discussing it further and more seriously in the present context. It must nevertheless be emphasized that although the putative effects of objective conditions can be over-stressed, we should never allow them to be underestimated or ignored in the study of foreign policy.

Although the *organizational setting* of the foreign policy process is a somewhat more containable cup of tea than the above category, at the same time it raises the Janus head – or, in the view of some, the spectre – of bureaucratic politics. It also introduces the notion of 'structural constraints' to our discussion, allowing us to pinpoint the specific meaning of this concept for purposes of the present analysis. Let us briefly look at this latter, more general notion before turning to the more specific aspects of the decision-maker's bureaucratic and organizational beholdenness.

While the concept of 'objective conditions' refers to the concrete givens of a situation, be they geographical, geopolitical, economic, demographic, technological, and so forth, the type of constraints emanating from the organizational setting are viewed here as *structural* for the reason that this is not a material but a different and wholly abstract type of notion. That is to say, although both factors act as constraints on foreign policy actions, their constraining propensities differ fundamentally in so far as the first refers to the multitude of materially objective elements characterizing the situation of a state (or society) in the international system, while the second relates to an abstract notion that is used to characterize the decision-making situation of particular actors. It is also akin to the usage of the term by social anthropologists, who have appropriated it for many decades to refer to the systemic, holistic aspects of societies as distinguished from their constitutive elements or interacting units. This has meant, of course, as Meyer Fortes wrote many years ago, that 'we discern structure in the "concrete reality" of social events only by virtue of having first established structure by abstraction from "concrete reality".'[84] In our case the abstraction involved refers to the decision-making system, not to societies as a whole; i.e., we are interested solely in the effects of the structural practices of the organization *qua* system on its output of foreign policy actions. Or as Kenneth N. Waltz has put it:

> in defining structures, anthropologists do not ask about the habits and the values of the chiefs and the Indians; economists do not ask about the organization and the efficiency of particular firms and the exchanges among them; and political scientists do not ask about the personalities and the interests of the individuals occupying various offices. They leave aside the qualities, motives, and the interactions of the actors, not because those matters are uninteresting or unimportant, but because they want to know how the qualities, the motives, and the interactions of tribal units are affected by tribal structure, how decisions of firms are influenced by their market, *and how people's behaviour is molded by the offices they hold.*[85]

The point of emphasizing this type of constraint is contained in the fundamental premise that the way decision-makers behave is closely linked to the type of structure, or, to use a Marxist term, the *praxis*, characterizing the decision-making system within which they are placed to produce foreign policy actions.[86] This supposition will be examined briefly as we now take a quick look at some of the recent literature on the organizational and bureaucratic aspects of foreign policy decision making.

The fundamental feature of current foreign policy making consists of the fact, an American scholar has written, that it 'is a shared prerogative of a great number of individuals and organizations standing in uncertain relationship to each other. Policy making can thus be viewed as a complicated process by which these actors work with and against each other to evolve and carry out proposed courses of action.'[87] Or as Steinbruner has expressed the same notion, the 'point of departure is the existence of a number of actors, each with some power to affect the other actors and thus the ultimate decision. For the decision process as a whole, this means that there is a dispersion of power to affect the outcome – one of the identified characteristics of complexity.'[88] This probably holds for most other Western countries as well, even though the above observation – and much of the current literature in this area – is based on American experiences and case studies. It is the uncertainty and complexity of the relationships holding between various decision-makers – both individual and collective – as well as the multiplicity and amorphousness of the organizational and bureaucratic boundaries (and sub-boundaries) of the system as a whole, that make it imperative that we look at the organizational setting not in terms of neat organizational charts or formally defined offices and hierarchies, but in terms of the various factors – formal and informal – structuring the decision-making system. As William Bacchus has written, 'participants in the policy-making process do not inhabit a neatly defined and regularized world, although much of what they do is determined and channelled by bureaucratic norms and operating patterns.' Rather, the 'characteristics of this complex and untidy process define the context in which each participant functions.'[89] This picture is, of course, in marked contrast to earlier expectations regarding the functioning of complex organizations. George has commented on this optimistic and 'scientific' approach as follows:

It was hoped and expected that division of labour and specialization within the organization, coupled with central direction and co-ordination, would enable the modern executive to achieve the ideal of 'rationality' in policymaking. Worth recalling in this connexion is that many years ago the concept of 'bureaucracy' was synonymous with 'rationality'. Needless to say, that was before experience with complex bureaucracies gave the term its present invidious connotation.[90]

Without lamenting further, let us consider some aspects of the organizational setting which are relevant to the present discussion.

On the basis of recent literature on this topic, the organizational setting can be characterized structurally in terms of two broad types of decision-making systems. The first of these has a dynamic import, while the second constitutes a conservative process sustaining – wittingly or not – the status quo. Although 'paradigmatic' (in Robert Merton's rather than Thomas Kuhn's sense), both types can probably be said to have empirical reference to most organizational settings, while the mix in each particular case undoubtedly shows great variation both over time and across different settings. We will now look very briefly at each of these.

Destler has characterized the first type of decisional setting as follows:

> [Foreign policy] is the 'outcome' of the political process, the governmental actions resulting from all the arguments, the building of coalitions and countercoalitions, and the decisions by high officials and compromises among them. Often it may be a 'policy' that no participant fully favours, when 'different groups pulling in different directions yield a resultant distinct from what anyone intended.'[91]

Allison's description is in terms of a game, the particular victor of which is neither determinable before the fact, nor always easily recognizable after the fact; indeed, it is not always clear if there is such a victor at all:

> Following Wittgenstein's employment of the concept of a 'game', behaviour in international affairs can be conceived of as something that emerges from intricate and subtle, simultaneous, overlapping games among players located in positions in a government ... The moves, sequences of moves, and games of chess are thus to be

explained in terms of the bargaining among players with separate and unequal power over particular pieces, and with separable objectives in distinguishable subgames.[92]

Roger Hilsman has described the result of this type of 'pulling and hauling' (a favourite machismo phrase in this literature) in terms of the following dynamic pattern: 'policy changes seem to come through a series of slight modifications of existing policy, with the new policy emerging slowly and haltingly by small and usually tentative steps, a process of trial and error in which policy zigs and zags, reverses itself, and then moves forward in a series of incremental steps.'[93] It should perhaps be added that although in Lindblom's celebrated description of 'incrementalism' this type of decisional procedure may in fact constitute the most rational type of policymaking in view of present-day organizational and political realities, its presence in bureaucratic politics 'reflects more the internal dynamics of decision making than any conscious design to maximize our ability to cope with an unruly world', as Destler has written.[94]

If the dynamic view of the organizational setting stresses the notion of a tough game with high stakes and powerful players (and hence uncertain outcomes), the static or conservative model quite openly plays down the active role of rival players and instead emphasizes the impact of the organizational factor *per se* on the structural character of the decisional setting. Here the central notion is not that of the game but of standing operating procedures, which have become crucial to governmental activities inasmuch as the latter have pre-eminently come to consist of the co-ordination of a large number of quasi-independent organizations, each with its own tasks and responsibilities. As Allison has put it, to 'perform complex routines, the behaviour of large numbers of individuals must be coordinated. Coordination requires standard operating procedures: rules according to which things are done. Reliable performance of action that depends upon the behaviour of hundreds of persons requires established programs.'[95] In other words, this model views governmental action as organizational output rather than the outcome resulting from the political pulling and hauling between a number of more or less powerful players. Such output can be characterized in terms of two structural properties which are relevant here, the first defined with reference to the *types of activity* – the *modi vivendi*, so to speak – that organizations foster, the second with reference to the *normative structures* that such procedures create and develop.

The theoretical backbone for analysing the first structural property is provided by contemporary organizational theory, particularly the work which builds on Herbert Simon's seminal contributions, as well as on the writings of Richard Cyert, James G. March and their various collaborators.[96]The essence of these departures from traditional economic theory on organizational behaviour lies in their emphasis on the effect of organizational structure and practice – rather than of market factors – not only on the development of goals and expectations, but also on the execution of choice. Allison, in his elaboration of the organizational process model of foreign policy analysis, has extended these notions in terms of the following basic propositions: (1) foreign policies are to be viewed as organizational outputs; (2) the range of effective choice in foreign policy is limited by organizational routines; and (3) the situation constraining the range of possible decisions on the part of leaders is structured by organizational outputs.[97] His further discussion and empirical application of these basic notions is too well known and finely elaborated to deserve the inevitable simplification of a brief summary here.[98]

The normative structures which are highlighted in this literature on the organizational setting of the decision-maker are usually defined in terms of the role which bureaucratic subcultures and norms play in the production of organizational outputs. It is in this connection that the famous maxim 'Where you stand depends on where you sit' has been coined, referring to the solipsistic claim that 'men in positions tend to see issues in terms of their positions.' Or as Destler has put it, 'While officials' views and actions are not predetermined by the positions they hold, they are greatly influenced by them ... Thus each views a problem from his own particular "perspective".'[99] This leads not only to the development of organizational subcultures with their own 'rules of the game', norms and intra-bureaucratic loyalties, but also to the kind of parochialism which Anthony Downs has described in terms of the concept of 'bureau territoriality'.[100] Or as Waltz has noted laconically, 'Organizations have at least two aims: to get something done and to maintain themselves as organizations. Many of their activities are directed toward the second purpose.'[101] In extreme cases this can lead to the phenomenon of 'bureaucratic free enterprise' (analysed in particular by Gordon Tullock) and its almost total fragmentation of the organizational system as a whole.[102] In Stanley Hoffmann's description, when this occurs administrative politics have come to replace foreign policy.[103] However, a less extreme and more central thrust of the literature on normative structures is that 'organizations develop relatively stable propensities concerning operational priorities, perceptions, and issues', to cite Allison's version of this proposition.[104] It is also this notion – that 'the office makes the man' – which is most pertinent to our present concerns; therefore I shall end this chapter by linking it to the previous discussion of the dispositional dimension in general and the concept of belief systems in particular.

In view of the basic theme of this analysis, namely, the role of cognitive and normative factors in the explanation of foreign policies, and the function, more specifically, of the concept of ideology in such undertakings, it is now finally possible to tie the various ideational elements of the framework together. First of all, it follows from our discussion that the above structural–normative propensities should be clearly differentiated from the role of normative concepts in either the dispositional or intentional dimension. This point is illustrated in figure 8, which also constitutes the *final* sketch of the *special version* of our framework. Since I have already commented on the meaning and role of 'belief system' and 'foreign policy doctrine' in this framework, it will suffice to say a few brief words about the 'organizational subculture' and its function in this elementary conceptualization. This term represents the various structural propensities inherent in the decision-makers' organizational situation, and which, in the sense discussed above, constitute the constraining factors which cognitively impinge on the decision-maker in his or her pursuit of foreign policy.

This means, secondly, that this concept does *not* refer to a causal factor in the analysis of foreign policy, in the sense that 'subcultural' structures can be said to 'cause' anything in the dispositional or

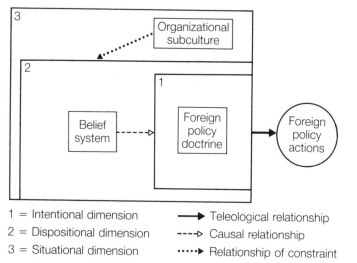

Figure 8   Explanation in terms of subcultural socialization, beliefs and doctrines

intentional dimensions of our framework. Rather, the relationship is one of constraint, limitation or intervention; and it is in this sense that we speak of these structures as intervening variables, i.e., in terms of the notion that under certain structural conditions certain types of belief systems are fostered (or present) while other types are suppressed (or absent). Or as Steinbruner has put it, 'If stable features of the mind encounter stable features of organizational settings, it should produce coherent, recurring patterns of behaviour in the organizational decision process, other things being equal.'[105] The crucial predication here – it should be stressed – is that 'mind encounters organizational settings', not the other way round. From this it follows that I cannot accept the notion that the 'conduct of actors in society is treated as the outcome of a conjunction of social and psychological determinants, in which the former dominates the latter through the key influence attributed to normative elements.'[106] The voluntarism represented in the framework discussed here is thus not reconcilable with either Émile Durkheim's structuralism or Talcott Parsons's functionalism, both of which accord priority to the situational dimension over the dispositional dimension. It does, however, try to respond to the claim, suibmitted by Anthony Giddens, that 'the analytic philosophy of action lacks a theorization of institutions.'[107] Viewed in our situational terms, it seems entirely sensible to connect agency – or action – with a conception of structural constraints, without being forced into a position in which subject is controlled by object (to use a hallowed Marxian locution). It is in this sense, and in this sense alone, that structural analysis enters into our framework.

It is also in these terms that Steinbruner posits his three 'modes of thinking . . . each of which seems clearly associated with a certain kind of organizational situation'.[108] These three 'cognitive syndromes' – 'grooved', 'uncommitted' and 'theoretical' thinking – are 'structures of the mind' which are formed under given organizational conditions, and which, once they become established in the individual decision-maker, lead him to impose certain characteristic patterns on the immediate policy issues confronting him. Translated into George's terms, the claim here is that the 'operational code' of the decision-maker takes its specific form as a consequence of how his perceptions and values are moulded by his particular organizational setting. We are now thus able to ask why certain people have the belief systems or operational codes that they have, without either having to implicate any reificatory notions about norms or subcultures as causal agents, or being forced to dispense with these concepts altogether because of their structural rather than purposive nature.

In summary, we can now posit the following prototypical link between foreign policy actions and our three explanatory dimensions:

> The reason for government A's actions in this matter is explicable in terms of its stated foreign policy doctrine (or set of principles); and it, in turn, can be viewed as a consequence of, or caused by, the prevailing belief systems (or operational codes) of its foreign policy decision-makers; and these have been formed within the particular foreign policy organization and decisional environment of the state in question.

This form of explanation is sufficiently exhaustive for most purposes, especially since – as I have implied above – it can easily be put to serve both case studies and the comparative analysis of foreign policy.

4

The Concept of Ideology

The latter-day restitution of the concept of ideology is coeval with the growing manifestation of cognitive, perceptual, normative and related factors in the analysis of political behaviour. As one of the core concepts most often appropriated to denote these various ideational phenomena, 'ideology' is conceived to possess not only wide applicability, ranging from individual behaviour to collective action, but also the ability to link together many of the central – but not always easily concatenated – concepts of political analysis. Furthermore, being abstract and theoretical at the same time as referring to causal relations between actors and their actions, it is often ascribed considerable explanatory power with respect to a host of phenomena in various discourses. And since 'ideology' by most accounts has travelled both widely and well, it has not only acquired an enviable comparative reputation across interpersonal, societal, international and other boundaries, but also found easy access to a variety of other disciplines within both the social sciences and the more genteel confines of the humane arts in general. All in all, therefore, the popularity of our concept seems in most key respects to be eminently justified.

And yet, despite the general soundness of the criteria for scientific fruitfulness which are implied in the above characterization, this concept continues to remain deeply problematic as a descriptive and explanatory tool in political inquiry. How is this annoying discrepancy to be explained? The problem, I submit, does not lie in the actual ambition of adopting the concept for the above reasons, but in the exceedingly slipshod way that, although encumbered and compromised by decades of political defamation and philosophical partisanship, it has been conceptually rehabilitated for these purposes. This development is, in turn, but one of many examples of an endemic shortcoming in our discipline as a whole, namely, that most of the time we do not really know how to define our concepts in such a manner that they *can* be made to serve the analytical purposes for which they have ostensibly been created. Hence, before we can examine 'ideology' itself, it will be necessary first to tackle head-on a fundamental issue which hitherto has only had its surface lightly scratched: the methodological question of how to handle the metalinguistic and semantic problems attending the concepts of our disciplinary vocabulary. On this front there is both good news and bad news to be reported.

A   PROBLEMS AND ISSUES OF CONCEPTUALIZATION

The pursuit of queries relating to the semantics of conceptualization and political analysis is, I am happy to report, particularly active at the present time. This is the good news. The bad news – though, frankly, it could be much worse – is that this, too, is an area characterized less by received tradition and an authoritative corpus than by the apparent urge, most commendable in itself, to approach the problem from as ecumenical a point of view as possible. However, if this does not sound too pessimistic it is because at the present time I find the good news far more important than the bad.

One important consequences of this growing interest among political scientists in terminological and conceptual issues is a fuller appreciation not only of the fundamental semantic problems caused by the fact that the language of our discipline coincides with the language of everyday discourse, but also of the methodological necessity, in the face of this situation, of distinguishing clearly between the two. Giovanni Sartori, in his most recent contribution to this discussion (which he has also had a great part in fostering), puts this point in his characteristically forceful manner:

> One of the celebrated dictums of Wittgenstein is that 'the meaning of a word is its use in the language.' The dictum is easily extended to concepts. If so, it cannot be left at that . . . Whatever else 'science' may be, its necessary, preliminary condition resides in the formulation of a

special and specialized language (not to be confused with a calculus or a formalized language) whose distinctive characteristic is precisely to correct the defects of ordinary language.[1]

Similarly Felix Oppenheim, an equally active participant in this ongoing debate, has noted in his book on *Political Concepts*: 'The method I have applied is based on the conviction that ordinary language is in general too blunt a tool to be of use for scientific investigation and that the language used in political life (and in most political writings) is especially ill suited for the purposes of political inquiry.'[2] As previously indicated, this no-nonsense conclusion is one which I find intellectually both congenial and persuasive.

Conversely, it is not equally easy to accept some of the more extreme semantic consequences of the argument which Michael Shapiro has submitted in his book on *Language and Political Understanding*. 'The position to be presented and elaborated throughout this analysis,' he writes, 'is that language is not *about* objects and experience, it is *constitutive* of objects and experience.'[3] For although the constitutive capabilities of language – emanating from the 'discursive practices' which suffuse the intestines of social life – cannot be denied, this should not be taken to imply that language therefore possesses no fundamental significatory function or reference in either daily life or the conduct of inquiry. Being essentially different things, the one attribute does not – nor should be made to – exclude the other. Or, given the terms of a central notion in Michel Foucault's thinking that has inspired Shapiro's book, that is, the claim that language *is* power, not *about* power, the position that I defend is based on the claim that language is necessarily and obviously both (and much more besides); and that it is precisely because of this complex, multiple function of language that one must insist on the continuing necessity of distinguishing between the discourse(s) of ordinary usage and the essentially referential language of scientific analysis. Indeed, it is only in terms of the latter that we can, for better or worse, speak meaningfully – and perhaps even powerfully – about discursive practices at all (which, I should add, is precisely what Shapiro does). Thus, while I am inherently sympathetic towards his 'literary readings of the non-literary', I would be most unhappy to see this type of semiological project becoming the cornerstone of *conceptualization* in the social sciences.

In any case, it would do us all much good to be periodically reminded of the appositeness of Karl Popper's famous remark that although 'we are prisoners caught in the framework of ... our language ... we are prisoners in a Pickwickian sense: if we try, we can break out of our framework at any time.'[4] This assurance goes a long way towards redeeming us from some of the harsher implications that can be drawn from Shapiro's Foucaultian premises.

It is due in part to this functional complexity of language that so many of the terms of social and political analysis are in such dire need of clarificatory explication before they can begin to function properly as analytical tools. As I have previously suggested, this does not mean that we should start from scratch, eschewing ordinary usage and viewing the technical language of the natural sciences as our sole model for this task of semantic correction. On the contrary, most scholars today who worry about these matters would probably agree with the following recommendation, submitted by Carl Hempel some three decades ago:

> Taking its departure from the customary meanings of the terms, explication aims at reducing the limitations, ambiguities, and inconsistencies of their ordinary usage by propounding a reinterpretation intended to enhance the clarity and precision of their meanings as well as their ability to function in hypotheses and theories with explanatory and predictive force.[5]

However, in the absence of a well-articulated consensus on how to go about achieving the goals posited in Hempel's prescription, it will be necessary first of all to discuss some of the more controversial issues attending these problems, before attempting to submit a more constructive contribution to their solution.

The first of these concerns the elementary difference between, and relative importance of, *words* and *concepts* with regard to the methodological issues and problems which we are discussing here. For our purposes 'words' will be regarded as linguistic expressions, either single terms or sets of terms, such as 'cat' or 'to be a nincompoop'; and we usually understand their meaning(s) through their established usage(s), which often vary but which nevertheless are held together by the interrelated features – or clusters of properties – which we tend to attribute to the given expression. (It is in this sense that Wittgenstein spoke of a 'family of meanings' or 'family resemblance'.) They are the product of linguistic needs and habits, and acquire their meanings more or less willy-nilly as they are used in the various discourses and discursive practices characterizing social life. It is about 'words' in this sense that most so-called linguistic philosophers have spoken when emphasizing the crucial role of ordinary usage as the semantic crucible of linguistic development.

Concepts, on the other hand, are not linguistic expressions but abstract constructions labelled by words or expressions. For example, as Hempel has put it, the expression 'soluble in alcohol' conveys the concept of 'solubility in alcohol', which constitutes an abstract property shared by some substances but – luckily, I may add – not by others.[6] It is also in this sense that an eminent scientist has spoken of concepts as 'ideas which receive names', thus *pari passu* comprising the core units of the scientific process.[7] But although concepts are abstract constructions of the mind, this should not lead us to assume that the meanings of words, or their 'conceptions', as they have also been called, are mere psychological attributes while concepts are abstract entities exclusively populating the more abstruse regions of Platonic ideation. Rather, concepts are invariably rooted in conceptions (Abraham Kaplan, echoing Wittgenstein, thus speaks of the former as 'families of conceptions'); and hence all conceptual change is necessarily a concomitant of changes in the conceptions which enter into these abstract constructions.[8] In other words, the process of conceptualization – as an example of cogitative activity *par excellence* – is one in which words and concepts constantly interact with each other, giving meaning not only to specific phenomena but also to the relationships connecting them.

In view of these differences, it is surely obvious that *qua* social or political scientists – rather than, say, linguistic philosophers – our first concern should be with concepts rather than words. That is to say, our primary focus ought to be on conceptualization rather than on the definition of words. What does this mean? It means, for example, that I am in disagreement with the general stance of Evert Vedung's claim that the 'most important tool for concept formation is definition', i.e., 'specification of meaning'.[9] Since definitions are a dime a dozen (for reasons which have made Humpty Dumpty justly famous in wide philosophical circles), I instead subscribe to Brian Barry's recommendation that 'it is useful to see the *implications* of the *alternative definitions* and to notice the way in which the *choice of a definition is affected by what it is that we want to explain.*'[10] That is to say, it is not the *semantic* aspect – what Vedung calls the 'celebrated problem: What is the meaning of meaning?' – which is pre-eminent but, rather, the *conceptual* task of constructing a 'special and specialized language . . . whose distinctive characteristic is precisely to correct the defects of ordinary usage' (to quote Sartori once more).[11] And such correction, I submit, is *not* in the first instance a matter of defining words; instead, it involves the submission of our core concepts to the type of explication hinted at by Hempel above and expounded more recently and fully by Oppenheim. Let us briefly consider some of the more specific reasons in favour of stressing the crucial role of conceptual explication and hence for de-emphasizing the importance of pure linguistic concerns in present-day political science.

When Oppenheim writes that he is 'concerned with the analysis of concepts, not with the definition of words', he has in view the following type of enterprise: 'To adapt ordinary discourse for scientific purposes, one must make explicit the rules governing the use of concepts, sharpen the criteria of their application, reduce their vagueness and eliminate their ambiguity, and hence sometimes modify their meaning.'[12] He gives three reasons why this should be seen to comprise a conceptual rather than a linguistic analysis.[13]

1 Because of the common semantic problems associated with synonymy and homonymy – i.e., respectively, that a single concept can be labelled by several words, and that the same word is often used to express two or more concepts – it is more feasible and analytically appropriate to concentrate on concepts rather than on words. For example, the *word* 'freedom' applies (in Oppenheim's view) to at least five *concepts* of 'freedom'; hence, if one were to focus primarily on the word, this would tend to obscure rather than reveal the very real differences between these various concepts. We would then get either a very vague definition, building on the principle of the lowest common semantic denominator; or we would arbitrarily have to scuttle some of the concepts (or notions) to which the word

refers. Both of these consequences are exceedingly common within our discipline.

2 Words tend to acquire their meaning(s) not in isolation, but as part of expressions in which they typically occur. This semantic fact, added to that of homonymy, necessitates the analysis of various expressions rather than a single word in order for us to be able to pinpoint the different concepts which may be implicated. Words such as 'influence' are thus not fully meaningful by themselves, since they need to be placed within characteristic phrases (or sentences) in order to become fully comprehensible. The conceptions that they convey are not, so to speak, meaningfully contained in the single words themselves. John Lyons has discussed this aspect in terms of referring and predicative expressions, a distinction which he describes as follows: 'there are certain linguistic units whose function it is to refer ... and certain linguistic units ... whose function it is to be predicated, or predicable, of entities that are referred to.'[14] As we shall see below, this is a distinction which will become fundamental when discussing the attributes of entities.

3 Many of the core terms of our discipline (such as 'power', 'equality', 'interest' and, I may add in anticipation, 'ideology') function as *nouns* in everyday speech, while at the same time they are meant to refer to *properties* in the social sciences. This semantic characteristic of everyday usage can have unfortunate methodological implications, particularly in the form of the fallacy of reification, which occurs when such 'abstract nouns are treated as though they were proper names and denoted abstract entities ... in much the same way as proper names denote individuals.'[15] Words often have semantic characteristics which, if transferred to the concepts of the social sciences, will tend to obscure rather than enlighten the scholar's analysis of social reality. It is in this light – of trying forcefully to counteract such conceptual guilt by lingusitic association – that we have to appreciate the harshness of Sartori's injunction that 'a soft social science that bows to Wittgenstein's dictum negates the very possibility of its ever becoming a science.'[16] Indeed, the connection between the later Wittgenstein's claim in favour of the primacy of everyday usage and the emphasis here away from words towards concepts is very close; for it is precisely the

problematic nature of the linguistic implications of everyday words that impels us to opt for a conceptual language which is more suitably conceived for scientific communication and analysis. In short, the arguments against 'words' are little more than an extension of the arguments against 'ordinary usage'.

A second semantic–conceptual issue which in recent years has enticed a group of scholars into an open – if gentlemanly – fray must be dealt with more briefly than it perhaps deserves. This issue, which to my knowledge was by name first raised in a lecture given to the august Aristotelian Society by W. B. Gallie in the 1950s, but which has much older roots and other offshoots (most notably in Karl Mannheim's sociology of knowledge), rests on the claim that the meanings of at least some political and social concepts are 'essentially contested'. Gallie himself has put this proposition as follows: 'there are disputes, centred on . . . concepts . . . which are perfectly genuine: which, although not resolvable by argument of any kind, are nevertheless sustained by perfectly respectable arguments and evidence.'[17] In a more recent review of this debate, John Gray has distinguished between three different conceptions of this general claim. The first and weakest of these merely refers to the fact that the meanings of concepts are continually being contested for various historical, cultural and other empirical reasons. The second – and a stronger and more interesting – version claims that in so far as debates about which criteria are properly applicable to a concept can be shown to be rationally inconclusive, there are philosophical reasons for predicating the disputability of the correct use of such a concept: 'no logically coercive reasons for privileging one set of candidate criteria over all others' can be found.[18] The third and strongest variant refers to the nature of the dispute itself, since it asserts that a concept is essentially variable because its 'subject matter is in its nature such that there are always good reasons for disputing the propriety of any of its uses.'[19] Obviously, the first of these claims is trivially true and hence of little interest here, since the conclusion that a concept is contested because of its contestedness is in no way to adduce evidence for the essentiality of this characteristic. As Barry Clarke has noted, this notion of contestedness is not sufficient for distinguishing between 'an essentially contested concept and different concepts which share the same word'.[20] In other words, it does not allow us to distinguish between a case of homonymy and a case of an essentially contested concept. Nor does it, as Ernest Gellner has pointed out, help us to separate concepts which may have an essentially disputabled character from concepts which are simply (or radically) confused.[21]

The two stronger versions, on the other hand, constitute serious philosophical attempts to argue for the view that all conceptual frameworks are *per se* 'ineradically value-dependent', as Steven Lukes has put it; and hence, that it is impossible to privilege any particular one over another in rationally persuasive terms.[22] In Martin Landau's memorable phrase, such frameworks 'plagiarize the *Zeitgeist*', and are therefore as variable as this ephemeral conception itself.[23] The difference between them is that the second version is couched in terms of the rational unsettlability of disputes regarding the applicability of rival conceptual criteria, whereas the third posits such a claim with respect to the nature of conceptual disputes themselves. The former thus constitutes a variant of the proposition that the social sciences are inescapably non-objective – i.e., normative – because of the essential value-dependence of their constitutive elements, while the latter and more radical version asserts that rival frameworks, theories, *Weltanschauungen*, etc., are in a fundamental sense rationally incommensurable. K. I. Macdonald has made a similar distinction when, in an exchange with Lukes, he speaks of the difference between disputes about 'power' which arise as a consequence of contending perspectives and values, and disputes which arise from 'within' the concept itself.[24]

In my view, neither of these variants of the essential contestedness thesis is persuasive. With regard to the weaker claim, it follows logically that if one accepts the principle of the essential contestedness of the meaning of concepts, then one must *ipso facto* draw the conclusion that there is no rational way to argue for the superiority of any one over the other(s). In short, by accepting the validity of this thesis, one is also compelled to endorse conceptual relativism, the epistemological principle which claims that since 'Truth is made to depend on concepts, and as concepts are relative to "forms of life", truth must be as well.'[25] Furthermore, as Clarke has argued, the position taken by Lukes with respect to 'power' – i.e., that contests over concepts are essentially disagreements resulting from different evaluative perspectives, and hence that conceptual disputes reflect social disputes, inasmuch as our perspectives are always socially determined – necessarily leads to the conclusion that whoever wins such an argument does it not by dint of intellectual persuasion but simply by virtue of having won a socio-structural contest. Or as he puts it, the 'criterion of the truth of a statement would on this analysis be merely that the statement prevailed; that it was the necessary and sole victor of an "essential contest".'[26] Thus the significance of this thesis does not relate to any essential conceptual properties, but to the essentiality of contests. Conceptual disagreements would, in this view, merely be the outcome rather than the source of the dispute(s) in question.

However, it is obvious that these are not the types of philosophical conclusions that, for example, either Lukes or Gallie draws – or would wish to draw – from their premises. The former quite explicitly argues for the theoretical superiority of his three-dimensional conception of 'power' over other, less 'radical' views of this purportedly 'essentially contested' concept, thereby rendering his own argument highly contestable. And Gallie delivers an encomium of the hoped-for felicitous consequences of his thesis which, given the strict logic of his argument, is surely destined to continue remaining little more than a wishful desideratum. Given the particular claim that we are discussing here, there is no reason to assume that 'one desirable consequence of the required recognition in any proper instance of essential contestedness might therefore be a marked raising in the quality of arguments in the disputes of the contestant parties.'[27] Desirable? Certainly. But probable or possible? No.

The radical variant of this thesis can be viewed as an example *par excellence* of the 'paradigmatic' notions fostered by the unfortunate induction into the social sciences of Thomas Kuhn's enormously successful monograph on *The Structure of Scientific Revolutions*. As I have suggested elsewhere, the main theme of this debate is little more than a resuscitated version of some of the more epistemologically radical claims of Karl Mannheim's sociology of knowledge, and particularly of his arguments against the fallaciousness of the doctrine of the genetic fallacy.[28] The predication of the rational incommensurability of competing conceptual frameworks thus coincides with Kuhn's notion that once a 'paradigmatic' impasse has been reached, i.e., when two proponents possessing different points of view 'discover that they differ about the meaning or application of stipulated rules . . . then their prior agreement provides no sufficient basis for proof . . . and the debate continues in the form it inevitably takes during scientific revolutions.'[29] That is to say, they then speak 'from what I have called incommensurable viewpoints', as Kuhn writes.[30] When this is the case, the only type of argumentation that remains available is the supra-theoretical instrument of persuasion (presumably excluding physical suasion), which leads either to a 'conversion' (or '*Gestalt* switch') on the part of one of the disputants, or to a recalcitrant adherence on the part of both to two incommensurable viewpoints. 'Good reasons', in the scientific, the philosophical or the commonsense meaning of the phrase, do not function in such conversions. Indeed, not even the translation of terms across these types of 'paradigmatic' barriers is possible, since adherents of two such different frameworks speak two totally different languages – even when and if the terminology is the same.

It is for this reason that proponents of this position have been called 'radical meaning variance' theorists, since they hold, in one way or another, that 'translations from one scientific tradition to another force radical changes in what is observed, in the meanings of the terms employed, and in the metastandards involved.' They 'claim [Carl Kordig continues] that total replacement, or reduction, is what does and should occur during scientific revolutions.'[31] This position, as that of any incommensurability viewpoint in general, is even less tenable than the weaker version discussed above. Ironically, the basic argument against it is known – quite unfairly, I should add – as the Mannheimian Paradox, or the so-called self-referential problem.[32] For when the radical claim is maintained that no two conceptual frameworks are commensurable, this also entails the general proposition that no invariant standards *per se* exist. But this constitutes a contradiction, since if this claim is put forward in all seriousness as credible, it *ipso facto* purports to be a claim necessarily presupposing the notion of objective validity; but if so, it itself is false. Such classical vicious circles, emanating from the innate radical relativism of all these types of claims, are inevitable as long as we do not accept the logical necessity of both first-order and second-order invariance, i.e., invariance with respect to both the meaning of the concepts and the metatheoretical standards which we employ in the scientific enterprise itself as a whole.[33]

A third and related aspect which needs to be considered briefly at this point concerns the role of values in conceptualization. In the ensuing analysis of 'ideology' I shall proceed on the assumption that a fruitful explanatory concept is in principle always a normatively (or morally, or ethically) neutral concept; and therefore, that the explication and reconstruction of such a concept both can and is meant to be an equally value-neutral intellectual enterprise. Hence I reject the view that political concepts necessarily 'describe from a moral point of view or, less restrictively, from a normative point of view', and that they do this 'while conveying the commitments of those who share them', as William Connolly has written.[34] The concept of ideology itself, having long endured the fate of both deep disapprobation and high esteem from all sides – and often from the same side – of the politico-normative spectrum, is in particular need of deliverance from this type of loose talk. The mere existence – and, indeed, wholesale acceptance and approval – of the delightful argument that proffered definitions of 'ideology' are either acceptable or unacceptable because of their 'ideological' nature, is surely reason enough for insisting strongly on the continued observance of the Weberian tradition hallowing the separability of 'facts' and 'values'.[35] This applies both to those who, like H. D. Aiken, in the extensive debate for and against the thesis of the 'decline of ideology' in contemporary politics, have inveighed against its proponents because they represent an 'anti-ideological ideology', and to Joseph LaPalombara's type of open espousal (in the same exceedingly confused debate) of the notion that his own counter-arguments 'may be in part – and quite properly – identified as ideological'.[36] Here, once again, the distinction made by Ernest Nagel between 'appraising' and 'characterizing' concepts continues to retain its relevance; and so does the dichotomy between both Arthur Kalleberg's first-degree and second-degree constructs, and Abraham Kaplan's notions of act meaning and action meaning (both of which we have discussed in a previous chapter).[37] In other words, I am claiming that 'ideology', or 'power', 'interest', etc., as characterizing, second-degree concepts defined in terms of an action meaning framework are prima facie as value-independent as, e.g., 'Swiss cheese' or a bottle of '*premier cru* claret'. The separability thesis defended here is thus in no way compromised by the espousal of an intentional framework premised on the concept of action as the primary unit of analysis. For the fact that 'actions must be characterized by reference to the actor's purposes and preferences is no obstacle, since assertions about an actor's valuations (e.g., about his welfare preferences in connection with his self-interest) are descriptive, not evaluative.'[38] In other words, the distinction between facts and values in no way hinders the assertion of facts *about* values. However, this does not imply that political science is 'value-free'; that value judgements are 'meaningless'; that political ethics is 'fact-free'; or that political science should rid itself of ethics.[39] The fact that a piece of 'Emmental' or a bottle of 'Château Margaux' are neutral, descriptive terms does not mean that one cannot feel very strongly for or against – or perhaps even be indifferent to – their gustatory referents, either in general or in specific instances.

However, since the claim that the normative and descriptive aspects of scholarly discourse and concepts are essentially insepar-able is a variant of the second essential contestability thesis (and, incidentally, their proponents usually the same people), there is no need here to dabble further in this hornet's nest. I merely wish to add that if, as Connolly writes with respect to the concept of power, 'a neutral, operational definition acceptable to all investigators regard-less of their ideological "preference" is not forthcoming', then (1) the most effective refutation of this claim would be to construct precisely such a definition of our concept; and (2), in attempting to do this I do not – à la LaPalombara – contemplate either the submission or the admission of 'ideological' preferences of any kind whatsoever.[40] On the other hand, given the 'public character' (in Popper's sense) of our disciplinary dispensation, I obviously cannot posit the type of authoritatively allocated – i.e., state-sanctioned – definition which is enjoyed both by *echt* Swiss cheeses and *premier cru* clarets.[41] For this liberal-pluralist dispensation we should, on the other hand, remain continually grateful.

The final and most important aspect of the analysis of the language of political science that will be considered here concerns the means for achieving the kind of conceptualization that has been discussed above. In this connection I shall concentrate on two recent but different prescriptions for achieving the same conceptual cure. On the one hand, Sartori has proposed that the rules which govern the reconstruction or formation of concepts are interpretative rules contingent upon semantic fields. Hence, as the first step in conceptualization, 'we are peremptorily required to master the *meaning function* of words – that is, semantics.'[42] Thus, while he endorses the notion that 'it is our thinking that monitors our language', he nevertheless makes the word his basic unit of analysis, a decision which, in turn, is premised on the claim – long made famous by St John – that 'in the beginning is the word.'[43] Oppenheim, on the other hand, pointing to the 'similarity between constructing good explicative definitions and good scientific theories', and hence to the need for bearing in mind this close affinity when reconstructing the basic concepts of our discipline, posits a procedure which on decisive points differs from the method advocated by Sartori.[44] He thus writes that 'Clarifying the language of political inquiry consists . . . in constructing an adequate scientific language out of elements of ordinary discourse. This task involves explicating the basic concepts, analyzing the logical structure of the statements, and investigating the logical relationship between these statements.'[45] Elsewhere he also refers the reader to Hempel's description of this method, cited earlier in this chapter.[46] In other words, priority is here given to the desiderata of the scientific process rather than to those pertaining to the analysis of the semantic fields of concepts.

Clearly, the semantic inductivism recommended by Sartori forces him to traverse a considerably longer and more circuitous route than Oppenheim towards their common aim of reconstituting political concepts (and, a fortiori, of ridding political science of the more nugatory effects of its dalliance with neo-Wittgensteinian semantics). It involves a process of sifting through all the diverse attributes of a word, constructing matrices of these charcteristics, and then ordering them in terms of their disciplinary and theoretical applicability. It is only after these extensive classificatory steps have been taken that the proper process of concept formation – or reconceptualization – can take place. Oppenheim begins from the other end, so to speak, and is hence able to get to the heart of the matter with far greater dispatch. He thus starts by immediately analysing concepts with reference, broadly speaking, to their logico-theoretical import; and in principle he never leaves this context, not even when he compares his reconstructions with other inter-pretations of the concept. This is unquestionably a more parsimo-nious method of examining the suitability of concepts for political or social inquiry.

Consequently, if one's prime purpose is to conceptualize for pre-established theoretical purposes – such as the comparative analysis of policies – then I, for one, am not convinced that choosing Sartori's longer, semantic route is really worth the candle: particularly not if the end product is envisaged to be very similar. The catch-all method advanced by Sartori will most certainly produce a richer and better organized semantic yield than would Oppenheim's less even-handed approach; but this semantic ecumenism does not seem to add anything significant to the conceptual end of such an exercise. Thus if, as Oppenheim writes, a 'scientific study of political actions, thoughts, and institutions in their variations in time and space requires the construction of a solid and general conceptual scheme by which to express such comparisons', then at least on this score – and here Oppenheim has neatly pinpointed the *raison d'être* of the present study as a whole – I would place my bets on the logic of the 'scientific' rather than the 'semantic' mode of conceptual recon-struction.[47] But this bet is also buttressed by a few additional arguments which in my view help to qualify it further.

The first of these refers to the supposition that the central objective of such a reconstruction is the establishment of explana-tory rather than mere descriptive concepts; and as such it is little more than a short elaboration on a previous theme. For present purposes, the important aspect of this desideratum refers to conceptual scope or, as Hempel has put it, to the systematic import or value of a concept: the capacity of a scientific concept to generate valid statements about its purported subject matter other than those that state the contents of the concept itself.[48] Thus the meaning of a concept may in all respects be admirably transparent and yet remain sterile or artificial, which is the case when we cannot do more with it than we first intended. This type of conceptual anaemia has – I need not add – all too often afflicted the classificatory schemas or typologies of our discipline. A concept which does not suffer from this barrenness is sometimes referred to as expressive of a 'natural' classification, its naturalness consisting 'in this, that the attributes it chooses as the basis of classification are significantly related to the attributes conceptualized elsewhere in our thinking.'[49] In other words, concepts are not fruitful merely because they have a clear meaning and empirical referents: for they must also, and primarily, be attuned to generating valid propositions, i.e., to the explanation of phenomena and not merely to their description.[50] It is with regard to this point that the interdependence between concept formation and theory formation is most clearly perceived; and why, I would claim, the reconstructive, explicative method is more germane to our specific needs than a semantic approach which in the first instance is geared toward descriptive (or empirical) adequacy rather than explanatory significance in the sense outlined here.

A further contributory argument in favour of this choice is equally abstract but has implications which are sufficiently substantive to warrant particular attention. Fred M. Frohock, in a discussion of that most fundamental of concepts in our discipline, that is, 'politics' itself, has taken notice of, and attempted to respond to, an aspect of the neo-Wittgensteinian penetration of political science that we have not explicitly considered yet: the claim that taxonomical definitions of political concepts are chronically unable to stipulate the common properties which have constituted the hallmark of the logic of classification ever since Aristotle; and that this condition reflects the semantic fact that ordinary language does not support the fundamental taxonomic notion that things that are describable with a common term must share at least one common property. In short, it is proposed that 'common names need not denote a class property, but only a grouping of properties no one of which is found in all of the things which the word describes.'[51] As we have already noted above, this semantic characteristic is usually referred to in terms of the 'family resemblance' of words, and has in the eyes of some philosophers been viewed as a powerful tool in resolving many linguistic–philosophic conundrums. It has also led to the claim that since the taxonomic method itself is fundamentally deficient, we should in its stead posit the so-called cluster theory of reference.

This theory denies 'that any single property can be isolated to identify the reference of a name, for no one property can be viewed as essential for successful reference.'[52] For example, the word 'democracy' variously refers to the distribution of power, economic equality, participation in politics, unhampered access to power, a free press, a politically responsive system, civil rights and liberties, and so forth.[53] Thus any political system which possesses *all* of these attributes is unquestionably regarded as a democracy. But so is also, on most accounts, a system which has many (or some) of them but not all, though – and this is the crux of the matter – it has been impossible to achieve a consensus on which of these properties are absolutely essential and which are merely contingent. (This problem, incidentally, is closely linked to the second essential contestedness claim previously discussed.) It is this condition – the lack of decisive, necessary attributes, and hence the admission of heterogeneity to the meaning of the concept – which makes it into a typical cluster concept. In other words, it is maintained that the *extension* of a term such as 'democracy' is so variable that it cannot have a homogeneous intension, i.e., a definable, common property or characteristic which is shared by all the entities belonging to the class of 'democracy'.

Assuming that this indeed constitutes a problem, how is it dealt with by the two approaches to conceptualization that we are considering here? To Sartori's immediate advantage speaks his recognition of this issue, at least in the sense that he is very occupied with the intensional characteristics of terms, and particularly with the various types of configurations (or clusters) which these can be seen to form. Indeed, he is so cognizant of the problematic nature of the link between an intensional pool of heterogeneous characteristics and the extensional task – in his graphic phrase – of 'seizing' the object, that he calls this the '*sine qua non* problem' of conceptualization.[54] However, in addressing himself to the issue of how to establish the 'essential' (or 'defining') properties of a concept, and how to distinguish these from 'contingent' characteristics, he introduces a distinction between 'pure science' and 'applied science' which, in my view, tends to fudge rather than to clarify the problem facing us here. He thus writes that in 'pure science precedence is given to the *theoretical fertility* of a concept, whereas the applied science must give precedence to the *empirical usefulness* of a concept, that is, to its extensional or denotational adequacy.'[55] Having established this distinction, he then poses the following leading question and immediately offers us his own view: 'how do we decide which characteristics belong to the defining properties? With respect to empirical knowledge (not in other domains and respects) ... The *defining properties are those that bound the concept extensionally*.'[56] But this is surely not sufficient for purposes of political analysis, inasmuch as it really begs the question with respect to many of the central concepts of our discipline.

This Sartori also admits when, referring to the above distinction, he explicitly acknowledges the following shortcoming of his approach:

> Clearly, the rule satisfies the requirement of empirical adequacy, not the requirement of theoretical fertility. With respect to the latter, I must leave the argument by noting that after a conceptual reconstruction we are likely to be far better equipped than otherwise for looking into the characteristics that serve the advance of the 'pure science'.[57]

But obviously, when speaking about such concepts as 'democracy', 'politics', 'equality', 'interest', 'liberty', 'ideology', and so forth, we have in mind concepts which refer to both 'theory' *and* 'concrete reality', and which thus possess, if they are to function effectively as analytical instruments, both theoretical fertility *and* empirical usefulness. This was indeed the point of my previous argument in favour of the type of analysis recommended by Oppenheim. Hence, in so far as Sartori's approach is geared primarily towards the latter aspect, it does not resolve (though it recognizes) the problem that Frohock has highlighted. In any case, it is precisely our 'working back' *from* the referent (the term's extension) *to* the pool of intensional characteristics which putatively raises the issue of intensional heterogeneity in the first place; therefore it is not entirely credible that this process will at the same time lend itself to solving the very problem that is occasioned by it.

Oppenheim, on his part, does not discuss this issue in these terms at all, nor does he use the intensional/extensional frame of reference which is so central to both Sartori and Frohock (but particularly to the former). As we have already noted above, his reason for this is the claim that this type of analysis pertains solely to 'property' concepts, and therefore not to empirical referents of the kind which Sartori has in mind when he speaks of the extension of terms. In other words (but using Sartori's terminology), he limits himself quite consciously to the analysis of the intensional aspects of concepts; and hence the process of conceptual explication and reconstruction that he advocates is one that does not include the extensional attributes of concepts. Although this may seem to speak against Oppenheim in regard to the issue raised by Frohock, I would argue that the opposite is in fact the case. Let me briefly expand on this claim.

Lyons, referring to a common view stretching from Rudolf Carnap back to John Stuart Mill, has described the difference between the meaning of 'extension' and 'intension' as follows: 'the extension of "red" is the class of all red objects and ... its "intension" is the property of being red.'[58] This specification makes it clear that (1) the terms 'intension' and 'extension' are logically interdependent and (2) that the concept of 'property' is logically prior to that of 'class'. Or, as Sartori himself has put it (quoting M. R. Cohen and Ernest Nagel), 'the denotation of a term clearly depends upon its connotation.'[59] (The paired terms 'extension'/'denotation' and 'intension'/ 'connotation' are here, as in most of the literature, used synonymously.) It is in view of this perspective – of the cognitive pre-eminence of intensional characteristics with respect to ascertaining the constitutive properties of the crucial terms of our discipline – that we should understand Oppenheim's exclusion of purely extensional considerations in the process of conceptual reconstruction. This also explains why he has chosen an explicative, logical approach to the task of determining the essential properties of such terms as 'power', 'freedom', 'egalitarianism' and 'interest'.

With regard to the issue raised by Frohock's discussion, this viewpoint has the following implications. It means, first of all, that he is not confronted with the various problems attending the semantic intension/extension dichotomy which complicate Sartori's analysis, leading the latter – at least in effect – to raise his hands in considerable exasperation. And secondly, this viewpoint allows Oppenheim, if he so desires, to address himself to the implications of the cluster theory in a sufficiently effective manner.

His argument would, surmisably, be similar to Frohock's case against the proponents of the cluster theory of reference. Essentially, the latter's approach is to posit the notion that if 'core' attributes of concepts can be determined, then the cluster theory can be shown to be deficient. Three conditions specify whether such core elements can be said to be present: '(1) they are constant with variation in all, or most, other properties of the term. (2) When they change, all, or most, other properties of the term change as well. (3) A change in core terms ordinarily produces a change in the sense, or meaning, of the term.'[60] Frohock then claims – on the basis of a series of arguments to which I refer the diligent reader – that such core properties can in fact be determined for terms such as 'democracy' and 'politics'; and hence, that this provides a strong case against the claims of the proponents of the cluster theory. In my interpretation, this is also the type of logical explication of the constitutive properties of concepts that Oppenheim's method is quintessentially intended to serve. Consequently, in so far as his method of analysis scores considerably better in this respect than Sartori's, we have here an additional reason for preferring to base our bets on the former.

This approach also has the following consequences with respect to the issue discussed here.

1 Since the type of logical, explicative analysis that is advocated here pertains solely to the intension of a term, this means that its extension can legitimately continue to remain heterogeneous despite the establishment of intensional core attributes. For example, even though the term 'democracy' can be shown to possess a core meaning (say, 'popular sovereignty'), it can nevertheless continue to denote a series of surprisingly different bona fide democratic polities (such as, e.g., both Sweden and Switzerland). Or as Frohock has put it, 'a heterogeneous extension is still consistent with a homogeneous core.'[61] One important implication of this is therefore that it continues to be imperative that we distinguish clearly between necessary and contingent attributes of concepts.

2 Although the extensional heterogeneity of a term does not *per se* affect the core meaning of a concept, this does not mean that the extension of a term is unimportant in this process. It means, rather,

that our conceptual interest in the extensional aspects of terminology is one of consequence, not genesis. If we posit x and y as the core (or 'necessary', 'essential' or 'definitional') properties of a concept P, what effect will this have on the classification of all the things which go by the name of 'P'? This, and not the reverse, is the logic underlying the approach discussed here. This is also one implication of Oppenheim's caveat that although ordinary language is a very blunt instrument, it nevertheless must remain an essential part of conceptual explication.

3 Since the intension/extension dichotomy seems to be more trouble than it is worth, I suggest that it be set aside until its value for conceptualization – as distinguished from semantic or linguistic analysis – has been better certified. Sartori himself admits that there is not general agreement on its meaning; and I am not at all persuaded that Vedung's subsequent reformulation and extension of Sartori's conception of this dichotomy has improved the situation.[62]

B   THE EXPLICATION AND CONCEPTUALIZATION OF IDEOLOGY

(i)   *Introduction: The historical dimension*

Conceptual disputes owe much of their quarrelsomeness and acrimonious tone to the historical roots of words, and particularly to their subsequent profluence within the history of ideas. This is especially true for terms of which this *Bedeutungswandel* is tied to the major political, social and intellectual upheavals of the most recent centuries, and which as a consequence are burdened with a heavy if not always venerable historical ballast. Given this historical dimension of language, it may seem attractive simply to jettison such semantic dead-weight altogether and to proceed to the reconstruction of a term without regard to its genesis and historial development.

This, however, is a temptation which must be resisted at all costs. For as Sartori has reminded us, 'meanings are not arbitrary stipulations but *reminders of historical experience and experimentation* . . . Terms such as power, authority, violence, coercion, law, constitution, liberty, etc . . . reflect experiences, behavioural patterns, and perceptions resulting from historical learning; they are, so to speak, *existential reminders*.'[63] In view of this, it is my conviction that, in the pursuit of political inquiry, the process of explication and conceptual reconstruction must instead be intimately linked to an historical understanding not only of the imputed *raison d'être*, but also of the substantive application and analytical justification, of a concept. In other words, the germane question here is not in the first instance what semantic meaning the usage of a term has acquired, but rather: why were certain concepts formed when they were formed, and for what purpose are they still being used today? Or as Quentin Skinner has put it (while chiding us for generally misperceiving the interpretative nature of the history of ideas), 'what we still cannot seem to learn – to cite Collingwood's very important point – is *what* questions the use of the expression was thought to answer, and so what reasons there were for continuing to employ it.'[64] H. L. A. Hart makes a similar observation when, before proceeding with his classic analysis of the concept of law, he posits the following starting-point for his discussion:

> Plainly the best course is to defer giving an answer to the query 'What is law?' until we have found out what it is about law that has puzzled those who have asked or attempted to answer it, even though their familiarity with the law and their ability to recognize examples are beyond question. What more do they want to know and why do they want to know it?[65]

It is these types of interpretative, historically cognizant queries – as distinguished from questions pertaining to mere linguistic usage and semantic practice – that we need to pose and to pursue at this juncture if there is to be any chance for our term of achieving conceptual redemption from its present desiccated condition.

Abraham Kaplan has implied a similar point when he distinguishes between 'notational' and 'substantive' terms, of which the former are essentially interchangeable with other terms without any loss of descriptive content, while the latter are distinctive in the sense that no other term (or set of terms) adequately reflects the substantive content subsumed by each.[66] Clearly, notational terms are not puzzling in the sense adumbrated by Hart, since their meanings are easily established by referring to lexigraphically equivalent terms or expressions. Substantive terms, on the other hand, have no semantically equivalent 'notations' (or synonyms); and they are puzzling when – which is the case with most historically evolved political terms – their substance is such as to invite queries of the kind that we have been forced to pursue here.

In an article on 'The Idea of Political Development', Harry Eckstein has provided us with a most suggestive introduction to the kind of historical approach that I have in mind here. Since it is my contention – which I shall amplify below – that the ideological phenomenon itself is a concomitant of political development as discussed and conceptualized by him, let us briefly consider the premises and ramifications of his analysis.

In order to do this it is not necessary to go into the details of Eckstein's exposition of the nature of 'developmental' thinking itself. Instead, a crucial quote from Émile Durkheim (in Eckstein's view, the 'quintessential developmental theorist') will help to give the gist of this approach:

> Every time we explain something human, taken at a given moment in history . . . it is necessary to go back to its primitive and simple form, to try to account for the characterization by which it was marked at that time, and then to show how it developed and became complicated little by little, and how it became that which it is at the moment in question.[67]

What are the implications of this 'developmental' view of political history? In Eckstein's opinion, they include at least the following notions: change is inherent in society, and hence it is necessary to think in terms of some conception of 'social time' if we are to be able to apprehend this factor; such change flows along a continuous dimension, and must therefore be conceptualized in dimensional terms (exemplified by, e.g., Ferdinand Tönnies's polar types *Gemeinschaft/Gesellschaft*, or Durkheim's organic and mechanical modes of social solidarity, or the traditional and rational systems of action as described by Weber); dimensional changes involve changes in degree with critical thresholds (here, again, the above dichotomies provide excellent examples); and, finally, it implies a conception of rule-governed, necessary change – of an underlying moving force, in terms of which the animus of development can be explained.[68] Given these considerations, Eckstein then asks himself the crucial question of how one is to characterize a 'continuum of political time' which corresponds to the above requirements; and he comes to the conclusion

> that the most serviceable way to characterize such a continuum is also the simplest: *what grows in political development is politics as such* – the political domain of society. Through political history, political authority and competition for politically allocated values have continually increased. Using Durkheim's terminology, we might regard this as growth in 'political density,' perhaps as a special aspect of a growing 'moral density.' More and more political interactions occur, overall and in place of nonpolitical interactions.[69]

This growth of the political sphere can also be couched in terms of the ancient distinction first made by Aristotle and latterly revived by Hannah Arendt and Jürgen Habermas, between the 'private' and 'public' realms of social life.[70]

Eckstein posits six stages in the history of politics which describe the trajectory of 'politicalization' – his term – from simple to highly advanced politics (or from 'social polities' to 'political societies', as he also calls the poles of political development). Of these only the last two, occurring during the timespan in Western history which roughly corresponds to the past two centuries, are of interest here. In his view, this period is inaugurated by the politics of *incorporation*, which is characterized pre-eminently by the pervasiveness of the theme of democratization, and hence by the entry into politics of increasingly large numbers of new participants. But once these demands for access have been sufficiently satisfied, political life can be seen to evolve into the politics of *incumbency*, geared above all towards the retention and consolidation of power, which today consists mainly of achieving and maintaining the support of mass publics via – but by no means exclusively via – the polling booth. The reason for our interest in these two stages is that it can be argued, both historically and logically, that it is not until we arrive at this stage in Western history that political ideas and doctrines come into their own as large-scale and potent *causal* factors in political life. In other words, I am suggesting here that it is only when the 'density' of politics – i.e., the 'politicization' of society – starts moving rapidly towards its maximal pole that the role of the ideational realm in political life starts achieving its prominent contours and becomes increasingly central as, initially, an instrument for gaining entrance to political (or 'public') membership and, subsequently, as a heavily utilized – and also, I should add, well financed – means for obtaining and retaining political incumbency.

Nor is it difficult to perceive why this should necessarily be the case. For it is obvious, on the one hand, that the politics of both incorporation and incumbency have intrinsically depended on the mobilization of large groups of people; and to achieve this the role of 'publicly' oriented ideas and doctrines have been – and remain – crucial. On the other hand, neither of these stipulations is relevant to the stage immediately preceding the period that we are considering here. In Eckstein's analysis, politics during this earlier era consisted in the main of the interplay of interests, i.e., as a marketplace for the distribution of influence and spoils. Such interests could not be – and were not – pursued by activating society (or even segments of it); on the contrary, this was an age typified by privileged groups jockeying amongst themselves 'as placemen and as purveyors and receivers of favours'.[71] It is thus a very significant step in European history from this 'extraordinary politics of interests' among a small group of select personages (and their retinues), to the transformation achieved by outside challengers who 'have resources of their own that can be effectively mobilized – such as strikes, violence, and the like'.[72] And it is most difficult to conceive how, without the introduction into political life of ideas and doctrines as purposively mobilizing political levers, this step would ever have been feasible in the first place.

Equally significant, this is also the period which saw not only the entrée – in the writings of the French *philosophe*, Antoine Destutt de Tracy, in 1796 – of the world 'ideology' into the European republic of letters, but also its apotheosis, during the first decades of this century, into a cardinal Leninist principle of mass politicization and revolutionary action: a feat on Lenin's part which was all the more notable in view of the fact that he was able to accomplish it despite the massive resistance of his revolutionary comrades to this dignification of a term and a notion which both Marx and Engels had done so much to vilify. It is in this concomitant development of new forms of political life *and* the growth and fruition of the mobilizing potential of ideational activism that we find, I submit, the significance of the ideological factor as a modern political phenomenon. This is also a conclusion that is emphasized by John Herz when he writes that 'Ideology thus seems to have emerged when, in an age of modernization and the spread of literacy, masses were being mobilized for the support of movements and policies – that is, in Europe, approximately with the French Revolution.'[73] Anthony Giddens, discussing Habermas's conception of ideology, adds that according to the latter it 'did not just come into being with the rise of bourgeois society; it is actually only relevant to the conditions of public debate forged by that society.'[74] Without an understanding of this historical anchorage, the concept will continue to remain a more or less insignificant notational convenience rather than a substantive and analytically fruitful notion.

Given this genesis and development of the concept, it is not difficult to perceive why it continues to puzzle and exasperate students of contemporary political development. For it is clear that the differences between the French *idéologues* and Lenin's ideologists could hardly have been more pronounced, despite their common acceptance of the intimate bond between the ideational realm and public life. For, obviously, this link was perceived very differently by the two groups. In the case of the former, *idéologie* as a *science des idées* was posited as the blueprint from which could be deduced the optimal patterns of socio-political interaction, i.e., the rational basis for an activist programme of societal reform and political reconstitution. This is an intellectualist's argument *par excellence*. The Leninist ideologist, on the other hand, is admonished in no uncertain terms (particularly in *What Is to Be Done?*) to view ideology as a manipulative instrument for collective action in history – as a vehicle, in the hands of the dedicated avant-garde, for arousing and channelling the potential revolutionary consciousness of the oppressed masses. Thus whereas the *idéologues*, true to their Enlightenment roots, wished above all to let unprejudiced ideas speak for *themselves*, the Leninist ideologists certainly did not give much for the worth – and even less for the positive function – of an independent ideational realm. But Lenin certainly believed fiercely in the *use* of ideas, as long as it is informed by the 'right' theory and remains solidly in the hands of an effectively organized and cognizant elite of Marxist–Leninist revolutionaries. 'In the struggle for power,' he thus intoned, 'the proletariat can become, and inevitably will become, an invincible force only when its ideological unification by the principles of Marxism is consolidated by the material unity of an organization which will weld millions of toilers into an army of the working class.'[75] This anti-intellectual stance is a far cry from the notion – and here I cite George Lichtheim's description of the thrust of the *idéologues'* beliefs – that 'Once human nature is properly understood, society will at last be able to arrange itself in a harmonious fashion ... Reason progressively discloses a true picture of humanity which constitutes the foundation of civic virtue.'[76] Nevertheless, I submit that the concept of ideology must be viewed in terms of *both* of these polar traditions, particularly since – as I shall argue below – they continue to exist as two separate strands of the 'ideological' phenomenon in contemporary politics.

However, if it is granted that ideology in the above sense constitutes an inherent aspect of the process of politicization that has marked the development of Western societies since the French Revolution, are we not then ignoring what perhaps remains the most important historical datum about the concept: its indisputable beholdenness to the Marxian legacy? In Sartori's phrase, the term still – if anything – constitutes an 'existential reminder' of the fact that, were it not for Marx's appropriation of it (particularly in *The German Ideology*) for a scathing critique of certain specific 'ideological' notions as well as of the functional role of ideas in society in general, the term might have no history at all to speak of or appeal to. However, as I have argued elsewhere, Marx's use of the concept is not empirical or political but essentially epistemological and philosophical; and hence, whatever influence his *Ideologiekritik* may have had on intellectual history in general – which, to say the least, has been neither negligible nor consistently enlightening – its impact on modern politics cannot be considered especially profound.[77] The most telling proof of this conclusion is the fact that in the Marxist tradition itself it has been the Leninist rather than the Marxian usage of 'ideology' that has left its mark on contemporary political life. The same goes for Karl Mannheim's epistemological extension of the Marxian analysis to the sociology of knowledge (with which the concept is also often associated). He, too, added considerably to the historiography of philosophical speculation but, sooth to say, little to the conceptualization of political reality itself.[78]

(ii)   *The expression to be defined*

As we have previously noted, most of the important concepts of political science refer to properties in one form or another, i.e., to whatever 'can be asserted or predicated of individual entities of some particular kind'.[79] The conceptualization of these properties is thus the main object of explication; and, following Oppenheim, I shall pursue this aim by giving the definiendum a grammatical form which stresses this aspect of our disciplinary language. Oppenheim has exemplified this procedure as follows:

> To define the concept of democracy is to say what property it is that we attribute to an organization when we call it democratic. Not 'democracy' but 'x is democratic' (or 'x is a democracy') is the expression to be introduced into the language of political science (and later to be defined). Once 'x is democratic' has been defined, we can say that the noun 'democracy' refers to the property x has when x is democratic.[80]

This logical structure of the definiendum is fundamental to the explication and conceptualization of 'ideology' that will be pursued here, at the same time as it departs from most typical ways of presenting and discussing definitions. But I am convinced that any initial misgivings or inconvenience caused by this unconventional – and perhaps somewhat cumbersome – way of expressing the definiendum will be compensated for by the subsequent conceptual pay-off.

When discussing the concept of ideology here I will thus have in mind the property or properties which a given entity must have in order that it will be conceptually feasible to refer to it as 'ideological'. But expressing the definiendum in this grammatical form – 'x is ideological' – should not be understood to imply that only the adjective 'ideological' will be defined here, thus somehow rendering the noun 'ideology' otiose by stipulative fiat. For it is clear that in so far as we are able to define the meaning of 'x is ideological', we are also able to say that 'ideology' refers to the property which x has when x is ideological. In short, the meaning of the concept of ideology *qua* attribute is not as such determined by the grammatical form that its definition takes. But in the explication of its meaning there is a distinct advantage in constantly being reminded – if only grammatically – that we are dealing here not with a *thing* called 'ideology', but with a *property* which can be attributed to some entities but not to others. Hence the expediency of expressing the definiendum in this manner.

But before proceeding to a discussion of the defining characteristics (or definiens) of our concept, it will be necessary already at this stage to settle a substantive question regarding the proposed definiendum. This query pertains to the nature of the variable x in the expression 'x is ideological.' Why is this deemed necessary at this point? Because we obviously have to know, before we can even start considering possible properties, what type of entity we have in mind when proposing to attribute characteristics to it. When referring to the concept of democracy above, Oppenheim thus makes it clear that this property can only be properly predicated of human organizations, even though he has not in any sense attempted to define 'democracy' itself. By positing a conceptual starting-point in this way, this procedure not only makes the task of defining the concept immediately more manageable, but also precludes a priori the types of definiens which would be logically or otherwise inappropriate in characterizing the entity (or variable) in question. This type of determination thus constitutes one of the very first – and also, it should be added, most effective – steps in the explication of a concept. This applies as much to 'ideology' as it does to the various concepts which Oppenheim has reconstructed in his book.

However, it is obvious that already in the attempt at specifying the single variable of our definiendum we run into difficulties of major proportions. This is also one of the prime reasons why our concept is more problematic than most: for there is no agreement even on the type of *entity* of which one can predicate the property of being ideological. ('Democracy' seems in comparison to be easy as pie; hence we shall continue to keep it in sight as a handy conceptual exemplar.) Nevertheless, here I shall briefly argue in favour of the claim that 'ideology' can properly be viewed only as an attribute of *ideational entities*, and hence not of actors or agents of any kind (which is the most common alternative). Nor should it be construed to constitute a characteristic of psychological, social, cultural, structural, systemic or other such non-ideational variables, even though all figure prominently in this capacity in the literature. Let me address myself first of all to the question of why ideology cannot credibly be predicated of actors, after which we will consider the inappropriateness of the other types of variables.

At first sight it seems quite natural to speak of an agent in 'ideological' terms, in the sense that the expression 'P is ideological' seems to have the same logical implications as 'P is powerful', where P is an actor, be it a single individual or a collectivity. There is, however, a fundamental difference between these two expressions, inasmuch as 'ideological' and 'powerful' can be shown logically to constitute two essentially different types of concept. On the one hand, Oppenheim has argued that 'power' necessarily entails a relationship between two actors, as a consequence of which it is a quintessentially *relational* concept. In his view, the term refers either to P's having power over Q (another actor) with respect to x, or to P's exercising power over Q with respect to x; and in this sense 'powerful' must be conceived as an attribute of such a relationship, and hence presupposes two actors if it is to be predicable at all. In barest outline, this is a view that we also find in Robert Dahl's influential discussion of the power concept, as well as in the non-pluralist tradition fostered by P. Bachrach, M. S. Baratz and their various associates.[81] Against this view it has been argued (e.g., by Hanna Pitkin) that someone 'may have power to do something all by himself, and that type of power is not relational at all.'[82] However, Oppenheim's answer to this is that it too constitutes a relational concept, albeit – in distinction to his own definition – one which instead of three variables expresses a two-term relation:' "power" functions in a relational sense as referring to someone's ability either to do something by himself or to control activities of others.'[83] But however we look at 'power' – either as presupposing Robinson Crusoe cum Friday or in splendid isolation – it is undeniably a concept which would be more or less meaningless in the social sciences if defined without reference to a relational property of at least one actor.

'P is ideological', on the other hand, does not refer to a relational concept but invokes, like 'democracy', a *property* concept. Thus when we say that 'P is democratic', we are, logically speaking, claiming something entirely different from when we say that 'P is powerful.' For although we may in everyday usage attribute 'democratic' characteristics or propensities to people, we do not *define* 'democracy' in terms of people or their behaviour *per se* but with reference to organizational structure in some sense or other. In other words, whereas the definienda of 'power' take the logical form of 'P has power over Q with respect to x' or 'P has the power to do x', or something along such lines, the definiendum of 'democracy' would be expressed simply as 'x is democratic' – i.e., without any actor variable. The expression 'P is democratic' would thus be acceptable only elliptically as an empirical claim in respect of P's organizational behaviour (which is either true or false), but not as the definiendum of the concept of democracy itself. The same applies to 'ideology'; and it does so for exactly the same logical reasons. Thus although 'P is powerful', 'P is democratic' and 'P is ideological' may seem to have the same logical structure, their explication makes it clear that ordinary usage would lead us astray if we were to conclude that the conceptual implications of these grammatically similar expressions are logically identical. Only the last two – expressing prototypical empirical claims rather than definienda – can be described in those terms.

But if the variable x in the definiendum of ideology cannot be construed to refer to an actor, does this also exclude the notion of a psychological entity? For it is conceivable that the expression 'x is ideological' can be interpreted to refer to certain psychological properties purportedly characterizing the behaviour of given actors, rather than to the actor himself. If this is so, why should the variable in our definition not be posited as a psychological factor? Once again, a comparison with the concept of democracy will help to clarify why this would be a most unfortunate delimitation of the potential explanatory utility of 'ideology'. For the expression 'x is democratic' can also be interpreted in a similar way to refer to psychological propensities in the behaviour of an actor. But we do not make this interpretation, for the simple reason that although some of us would perhaps want to claim, for example, that certain types of actors tend dispositionally to be more (or less) democratic than other types, to do this by definition would be to foreclose any means of testing it as an empirical hypothesis. Similarly, to view the variable in our definiendum as some kind of psychological entity would be to squash effectively one of the perennial issues in the analysis of putative ideological phenomena: the question whether they can be shown to covary with particular types of psychological dispositions, syndromes or clusters. Thus we should strongly resist any temptation to view the variable in our definiendum in terms of psychological 'types', 'mentalities', 'consciousness' or similar entities.

Sartori's decision to disregard this issue and its implications flaws in a fundamental sense what otherwise was a most timely article on our concept. For when he speaks of the 'ideological mentality' and of 'open' and 'closed' minds, and of the importance of 'how one believes' when specifying the *meaning* of ideology, he is – as more than one critic has pointed out – begging a question which should be settled by empirical rather than conceptual determination.[84] Precisely the same logical argument applies to predicating 'ideology' in terms of cultural, social, structural, systemic and other such strictly non-ideational entities. To do so is in each instance to posit a priori an answer to the query whether ideology actually constitutes – in some sense or other: examples abound – a cultural, social, structural or systemic phenomenon. If we are going to be able to take and pursue such claims seriously, it thus behoves us to resist all inclination to substantiate them by definition.

However, this argument does not apply when we postulate this variable as an *ideational* entity. That is to say, in so far as we are obliged to foreclose some particular class of variables from empirical determination – all definitions must of necessity do this – then in my view we have here the most obvious (and least counter-intuitive) candidate. Indeed, my argument is that it would *not* be controversial in the above sense to maintain that 'ideological' is 'by definition' an ideational property; and that this proposition pertains equally to ordinary usage and to scholarly discourse. Even more important, this interpretation accords best with the historical development of the concept as sketched above. None of the classic contributors to our concept – from Destutt de Tracy to Mannheim – spoke of it in a non-ideational sense. Indeed, to Marx this ideational characteristic of ideology also constituted the very reason why he so vehemently denigrated the so-called German ideologists: precisely because they put their trust in ideas (and bad ones at that) instead of in revolutionary praxis. Rather, what clearly *is* controversial is the *kind* of ideational property or properties that our concept can be claimed to represent. With this in view, let us now turn to a consideration of the defining characteristics of the concept of ideology.

(iii)   *The proposed definition and its defining characteristics*

In a previous and extensive study I have discussed and critically analysed some of the central classical conceptions of ideology. The book in question concludes somewhat wearily by suggesting that the only dimensions of the concept which seem salvageable pertain, broadly speaking, to three aspects of putative ideologies: their *cognitive*, *affective* and *action-oriented* characteristics.[85] This elliptical, slightly peremptory but – I continue to believe – a propos conclusion was in no way meant to be a definition of the concept, but merely an indication of the conceptual elements which had survived a sustained methodological attempt to give these conceptions a good (and long) run for their money. It was perhaps also intended as a promissory note suggestive of further conceptual elaboration on a suitable future occasion. If so, that time is now upon us, and hence I shall forthwith face up to the task of translating and extending this vague conclusion into a proper definition.

Given 'x is ideological' as our definiendum, in which x refers to ideational entities, i.e., to ideas for short, this undertaking requires that we now transform the elements in the above conclusion into definitional characteristics (or definiens) referring explicitly to the properties which ideas must have if they are properly to be characterized as 'ideological'. For clearly it will not do simply to proceed by stipulating as ideological all ideas which in some way or other are 'cognitive', 'affective' and 'action-oriented'. Were we to do so, we would have to agree, for example, not only that the Ten Commandments are eminently ideological, but also – and obviously no reflection on either Moses or Yahveh is intended here – that the same goes for most *idées fixes*, chronic phobias and similar cognitive–behavioural aberrations. Rather, following (if only in this instance) Habermas's suggestion of treating 'ideology . . . as a specific form of idea-system, characteristic of modern politics', I shall posit the following definition of ideology, and then discuss – in an explicative fashion – the three defining characteristics which, in my view, constitute the core of the concept.[86]

> *Definition*: x is ideological when x is a political doctrine which purports to motivate an actor P to do y (or not to do z) for the sake of the collective interest of Q.

The three definiens which I have in mind and shall discuss below are 'political doctrine', 'motivational purport' and 'collective interest'. However, before doing so, let us very briefly consider the elements of this definition which do not *per se* comprise defining characteristics.

First of all, 'actor P' in our definiens is intended to refer both to individual human actors and to collectivities consisting of such individuals. This specification thus in no way undermines the methodological individualism which was defended in our discussion of the concept of social action. As was noted there, reference to collective actors (or terms) is fully feasible as long as they are conceptualized as properties of sets (or series) of individuals. When we speak of somebody (or something) – e.g., Winston Churchill's speeches during the Second World War – as motivating a whole nation to act together for a concerted purpose, we do not mean that the British people acted as one collective entity, but rather as a nation of sentient people mobilized individually by Churchill's eloquence to act in consort for a common purpose. In other words, his speeches can be said to have had an effect both on individual citizens and, in the sense outlined above, on the nation as a whole. The latter effect is, however, contingent on the former. Similarly, we can speak of ideologies in both of these senses without compromising the principle of methodological individualism.

The phrase 'to do y (or not to do z)' merely indicates that here we have in mind purposive behaviour, i.e., the concept of action as discussed in chapter 2. It thus excludes (by definition, so to speak) all types of behaviour which cannot be defined in these terms (such as, e.g., mere cogitation, or walking – or talking – in one's sleep). Since action itself can be defined both in terms of commission and of omission, it has been necessary to include both a positive and a negative form of this predication.

Finally, 'for the sake of . . . Q' is meant to denote an exclusively collective entity, and thus never individuals (except when, in the traditional figurative sense, they – e.g., queens – have been placed to represent such collective entities). The most common Qs in this connection have been states, nations, nationalities and classes. However, to limit ideologies to these specific types of entities would, in my view, be both unhistorical and conceptually counterproductive. In short, any collective political entity can, in principle, be invoked in an ideology.

(a) *Political doctrines*

Lenin, Nicholas Berdyaev once wrote, 'had no philosophical culture', but instead

> fought all his life for that integrated totalitarian view of life, which was necessary for the struggle and for the focusing of revolutionary energy . . . He fought for wholeness and consistency in the conflict. The latter was impossible without an integrated dogmatic outlook, without a dogmatic confession of faith, without orthodoxy. He demanded deliberate thought and discipline in the struggle against everything elemental; this was his basic theme.[87]

Despite a contrast which could hardly be greater, Lichtheim's characterization of the original *idéologues* has a similar thrust:

> the 'Science des idées' is to yield true knowledge of human nature, and therewith the means for defining the general laws of sociability. The reduction of individual 'ideas' to generally held notions is intended to lay bare the common ground of human needs and aspirations, thus providing the lawgiver with the means of furthering the common good . . . Once human nature is properly understood, society will at last be able to arrange itself in a harmonious fashion. As with Condorcet, Destutt's aim is pedagogical: it is to lay bare the guiding principles of republican citizenship.[88]

Clearly, what these two polar dimensions in the history of our concept have in common is their emphasis on the doctrinal nature of political systems of thought *qua* ideologies: the notion that in order to be successful, political actions – be they 'revolutionary' or 'republican' – must be based on a body of explicit principles, precepts, tenets, commitments and similar authoritative predications. This is also a dimension which, whatever the subsequent vicissitudes of the concept during this century, has been retained in most of its contemporary usages. Thus *Webster's Dictionary* speaks of ideologies as 'the integrated assertions, theories, and aims that constitute a sociopolitical programme', while particular scholars speak variously of 'comprehensive patterns of cognitive and moral beliefs', 'patterns of beliefs and concepts ... which purport to explain complex social phenomena', 'systematic factual assertions about society', 'reasonably coherent bodies of ideas', 'general system of beliefs', 'the more or less coherent and consistent sum total of ideas and views on life and the world', and so forth, almost *ad infinitum*.[89] Or in Plamenatz's more prosaic terms, 'Ideology, to many people, means above all the doctrines that political parties and other organizations are committed to.'[90] As a general if vague connotation of the term, this usage is so common that there is little need either to belabour further its constant occurrence in the literature, or to justify its central role as a defining characteristic of our concept.

However, there is a need to examine in somewhat more detail the following implications of the meaning of 'doctrine' in this connection. First of all, 'doctrine' as a definitional characteristic is here not to be confused (or conflated) with two of its more wayward and contumelious cousins, namely, 'indoctrinate' and 'doctrinaire'. For while these latter terms have often – and perhaps for good reasons – been associated with our concept, the meaning of 'doctrine' by no means implicates them. On the contrary, doctrines need not at all be doctrinaire; nor are they necessarily designed to function solely or even mainly for purposes of indoctrination. Just as we often speak about philosophical, economic, psychological, literary, theological and other such doctrines without in any sense implying the above connotations, we can also refer to political doctrines in an entirely unprejudiced (and unprejudicial) fashion. One important consequence of this stipulation is that as a defining characteristic 'doctrine' therefore does not distingush between what Sartori has called 'ideological' and 'pragmatic' belief systems, or between any of their constitutive aspects (such as 'open' or 'closed' cognitive structure, 'empirical' or 'rational' cultural matrices, and so forth).[91]

Secondly, it should be stressed that 'doctrine' not only fails to differentiate between these – and similar – types of belief systems, but that it is *meant* to fail altogether in referring to such systems. For inasmuch as 'doctrine' is intended to characterize not '*how* one believes' but *what* is to be believed (or not believed), or what is worthy of belief (or not worthy of belief), it must be clearly differentiated from the psychological question of how that which is believed is believed, as well as from the 'cultural' question (in Sartori's terminology), of *why* one believes that which one believes.[92] In short, the notion of 'doctrine' that is discussed here is wholly neutral with respect to the response which it – as a purely ideational characteristic – may (and often does) create among potential 'believers'.[93] Indeed, in view of my previous emphasis on the non-psychological nature of our definiendum itself, this is logically a most obvious standpoint. At the same time it also implicates the view that the concept of ideology should forthwith be set free from its long-standing semantic involvement – bordering on forced marriage – with the whole socio-psychological tradition surrounding the notion of belief system.[94] It is only when 'doctrines' *qua* ideological ideas are implemented – e.g., in political socialization or mobilization – that queries relating to the structural constitution and functional requisites of belief systems potentially arise.

At such a point 'ideology' has, however, moved on to being an empirical rather than a conceptual issue. In other words, and speaking in terms of the distinction between what Vedung calls 'content-oriented' and 'function-oriented' approaches to the analysis of political ideas, the 'doctrinal' aspect that is explicated here refers exclusively to the former aspect: to 'the logical entities belonging to the abstract world of thought', as George H. Sabine described it many years ago.[95] He contrasts this specification with 'theories' (or, for present purposes, 'doctrines') which are 'also beliefs, events in people's minds and factors in their conduct'. In this 'latter role they are influential . . . because they are believed', and hence constitute 'events, or . . . actual factors in historical situations and as such

are part of the data which the historian of politics has to deal with'.[96]
Sabine's classic distinction should, indeed, always be kept before us
when we are conceiving of the role of ideas in politics. To define the
former (as both Sartori and Seliger do) in terms of their function in
the latter is to bar quite effectively any subsequent empirical determination of this complex but crucial relationship. This happens
whenever the notion of 'belief systems' is introduced as a definitional characteristic of 'doctrines'.

A similar charge can be levelled against Robert Heeger's
definition of ideology as highlighted – and much praised – by
Vedung is his exemplification of the 'explicative' method (which,
however, he interprets almost exclusively in terms of Sartori's rather
than Oppenheim's approach to conceptualization). In Vedung's
translation, Heeger proposes the following stipulative definition of
ideology: 'Ideology = Df (i) a set of convictions that is held by (ii) a
large social group and that (iii) contains values and factual
conceptions that covary and that (iv) fills political functions and that
(v) contains elements of action-oriented political thought.'[97] Here we
have a definition which not only happily mixes 'function-oriented'
and 'content-oriented' conceptual elements, but which also conjoins
these in such a manner that the meaning of 'ideology' is made
contingent upon the operation and verification of specific empirical
factors (or functions). One consequence of this procedure is that a
'set of convictions', which – in so far as it fulfils all conditions
posited above – constitutes an ideology at one point in time, is
subsequently in grave danger of losing this status simply by no
longer being held by a large group of people and/or because it has
lost its political function(s). It would thus imply, e.g., that Musso-
lini's fascism can today no longer be treated as an ideology, even
though its contents – as reposited in research libraries, home
bookcases and, it should not surprise us, fond memory – have
remained unchanged since the early decades of this century. (It
could, however, become one overnight – or tomorrow – again; but
we could only know this *ex post facto.*) This is certainly counter-
intuitive and contrary to ordinary usage, particularly since it seems
to imply that the meaning of ideology depends on whether it 'works'
or not. Such a view 'is ... dangerous on simple logical grounds',
W. G. Runciman has also written a propos of Weber's warning

against trying to define the 'state' by what it does. For if 'the state is defined by what it does . . . it must cease to be a state if it doesn't.'[98] It is also a typical example of how concepts are rendered otiose by being 'functionalized' in the operational sense exemplified here, or when their meaning is conflated with their reference.

Indeed, to make the meaning (and hence applicability) of a concept dependent in this way on empirical verification – e.g., the number of people sharing a given set of convictions – is patently a case of putting the empirical cart before the conceptual horse. Sartori himself has, in fact, most emphatically warned us against this type of semantic 'fuzziness'. He thus wrote some years ago:

> The definitional requirement for a concept is that its *meaning* is declared, while operational definitions are required to state the conditions, indeed the operations, by means of which a concept can be *verified* and, ultimately, measured . . . It should be understood, therefore, that operational definitions implement, but do not replace, definitions of meaning. Indeed there must be a conceptualization before we engage in operationalization.[99]

The problem with this defintion is thus not only that it, too, has a core element – 'a set of convictions' – which does not logically separate ideas from their effects in political life (or Sabine's 'logical entities' from 'events in people's minds'), but that it compounds this shortcoming by introducing operational elements into the proper definition itself.

Thirdly, the normative aspects attending the notion of 'doctrine' need to be considered briefly at this point. In his discussion of ideology, Sartori has defined 'ideology' not only in terms of its cognitive structure but also with respect to its emotional or emotive characteristics. He thus writes that '*Per se* the ideological mentality is not necessarily conducive to an active involvement and thereby to "ideological activism". Thus . . . reference should be made to the emotional component, and thereby to the notion of ideological affect, or passion.'[100] Willard A. Mullins, in his critique of Sartori's article, has suggested that although it is difficult to ascribe with any certainty an 'emotivist' label to the view expressed above, this positivist stance all the same seems to be the import of Sartori's brief remarks regarding the normative aspects of ideology. If this is indeed the case, I fully concur with Mullins's claim that the 'use of emotivist conceptions to explain the normative terms employed in ideology obscure the vital role these terms play in evaluating political purposes and the programs, strategies, and reasons related to them. This is because evaluation ... is not the equivalent of expressing or arousing emotions, even though both activities involve the use of normative terms.'[101] In any case, my position is that doctrines – be they political or theological, scientific or metaphysical – necessarily possess a normative dimension; and that it, too, is to be regarded *not* in terms of belief systems but as descriptions without any built-in functional or 'causal' characteristics. Mullins thus reflects a viewpoint that I fully share when he notes that 'Here we are not concerned with what "causes one to do", but with the factors that "give one cause for doing" ... The normative terms of ideology describe political purposes and provide warrants, grounds, or justifications for them.'[102] As we shall have reason to emphasize more fully in the concluding chapter, doctrines in this sense belong quintessentially to the intentional rather than to the dispositional dimension of explanation. As such they refer to ideational entities which logically are wholly disconnected from such Sartorian conceptions as 'triggering mechanisms', 'ideological heating', 'ideological passion' and similar causal–dispositional notions.

A final point about 'doctrines' will detain us only momentarily. Although it is implicit in what has been said above, it nevertheless deserves special emphasis inasmuch as it constitutes a central dividing line between two very different conceptions of ideology itself. Doctrines as here conceived are perforce *manifest* ideational constructions and should hence be distinguished from 'commitments that are not usually explicitly verbalized'.[103] Being 'forensic' rather than 'latent', they constitute 'elaborate, self-conscious word systems', as William Bluhm has written, and are as such diametrical in thrust to Shapiro's elaboration of the 'latent ideological level of political cultures'.[104] In short, we are not concerned here with 'constitutive discourses' of any kind but, rather, with a much less problematic (and hence more prosaic) phenomenon of political life: the explicit verbalization of the principles that are intended to motivate political action.

Although the meaning of 'political' has been touched upon more than once already, the nature of the present exercise requires a somewhat more explicit specification of this term. The question is whether as a qualifier of the concept of doctrine, the notion of 'political' needs to be clarified further, given the way that it has been used above to distinguish between the 'public' and 'private' realms of social life. In my view, the only addendum which is necessary at this juncture is the following. When Eckstein speaks about 'politicalization' as the increase – relative to the private sphere – of the public (or 'princely') domain, he has in mind a realm specified in concrete, institutional terms: as the penetration of society by an increasingly powerful and embracing *government*. However, in his discussion of the meaning of 'political' he also refers to those putatively *political relations* within a society which 'involve, say, legitimate power, or conflict management, or the regulation of social conduct, and the like', even though 'these may simply exist throughout society and not be located in any clearly defined social domain or institution.'[105] For our special purposes only the former specification and usage will be incorporated into the meaning of 'political', even though the latter – as a contingent factor – is closely intertwined with it. In other words, a doctrine will be regarded here as 'political' only if and when it refers to the functions and activities of the 'publicly' institutionalized domain of society.

The advantage of this delimitation is that it counteracts any temptation to politicize arbitrarily – i.e., by definition – all and sundry social or economic relations. In my view, this is precisely what Shapiro does when he speaks about the 'politics of constitutive rules', quoting Foucault's maxim that we need to 'conceive of sex without the law, the power without the king'.[106] It may very well be that the 'constitutive rules of phenomena, which are sequestered in language in general and speech practices in particular, contain a politics worth investigating': but *this* is certainly not the politics that I have in mind here.[107] Seliger, too, posits a notion of politics – as implying the pursuit of policy, i.e., 'a somehow interconnected sequence of projects of action' – which is so broad that it comes as no surprise that he is subsequently quite hard put to distinguish between it and almost everything else (including ideology).[108] The historical fact of the growth of the political domain at the expense of private interactions is itself too palpable, sweeping and important to be slighted – inadvertently or not – by such definitional sleights of hand.

(b)   *Motivational purport*

The range of 'political doctrines' as discussed above is still so broad that it easily covers not only the Monroe Doctrine's forceful and effective specification of territorial spheres of interest, but also, e.g., complicated and wholly abstruse lucubrations in the field of eighteenth-century constitutional theory. Indeed, it can be used to discuss not only political history and philosophy, but also contemporary domestic and international politics in its many guises. In other words, nothing which has hitherto been specified about 'political doctrines' has implied that they are ideological in any general or particular sense. (This fact has not, of course, prevented many scholars from treating them as coterminous with 'ideology' itself.) As a crucial step towards such a determination, we shall now distinguish between political doctrines which 'purport' – in some form or other – to 'motivate' political action, and those (a much larger class) which are not action-oriented in this sense. We shall discuss the latter concept first, before considering the implications of qualifying it in terms of the notion of 'purport'.

It is clear that in their very different ways both Destutt de Tracy's *idéologie* and Lenin's socialist ideology are predicated as action-oriented systems of thought, i.e., as ideational levers to be applied towards some desired political end. As we have previously noted, the French *philosophes* here had in mind the formation of republican citizenship, while Lenin's avant-garde ideologists were allotted the more resolute task of formulating and constantly instilling a revolutionary animus within the masses. In the case of the former, the motivational component is almost wholly intellectualized, since the premise is that once all the accretions on the individual mind of bias, prejudice and the so-called affections have been removed, the resulting ideas in their pristine form will create and sustain a new 'public' dispensation in France. That is to say, the apperception of these 'general ideas' – resulting from the salubrious programme of establishing the 'real' and fundamental nature of ideas by means of the more abstersive aim of eliminating all *préjugés* from the mind (both being part of *idéologie* as a *science des idées*) – will *as such* provide the requisite impetus for acting in accordance with the 'ideas' *and* the 'ideals' contained in the 'scientific' undertaking thus propounded. Lenin, on his part, spoke of a socialist ideology which will *use* ideas as an effective instrument for collective action in history – as a vehicle, in the hands of the dedicated ideologist, for arousing and channelling the potential revolutionary consciousness of the oppressed masses. In his view, this aim is best pursued in terms of a cognitively 'closed' – that is, dogmatic and authoritarian – system of ideas; and in so doing he reduces the role of ideas to a tool for mass politicization, since in the final analysis he justifies the conceptual nature and value of ideas in terms of the strategic considerations of affective mass mobilization.

This is obviously a very different kettle of fish from the 'idealistic' notions held by Destutt de Tracy and the group of *savants* and *philosophes* who had formed themselves around him in the Institut de France a century earlier. Nevertheless, as subsequent usage of the term during this century testifies, both of these types of ideo-motivational components have continued to remain a core element of the meaning of our concept. Herz thus writes that 'where efforts are made to instill overall ideas and attitudes ... into passive publics, or where both elites and masses are equally imbued with ideas leading to action, we may ... legitimately speak of ideology.'[109] Zbigniew Brzezinski defines ideology as 'an action program suitable for mass consumption, derived from certain doctrinal assumptions about the general nature of the dynamics of social reality', while H. M. Drucker's more succinct views that in so far as ideas about society 'can be marshalled into arguments and programmes, these ideas are ... ideological.'[110] Carl Friedrich's often quoted definition is equally germane in this connection, namely, that ideologies are 'reasonably coherent bodies of ideas concerning practical means of how to change, reform or maintain a political order.'[111] Charles E. Lindblom has latterly spoken of official ideologies that serve 'simultaneously both as a guide to "truth" and as a guide to practical political action to achieve the new society', which comes very close to specifying precisely those two dimensions which in their respective senses are shared by Destutt de Tracy and Lenin.[112] Seliger, as usual somewhat more prolix, writes that ideologies 'are "systems", in as much as certain values, factual assessments and commitments to ends and means are deliberately fused in order to ensure that through concerted action, certain forms of social organization will be defended, abolished, reconstructed or modified.'[113] Daniel Bell, another central contributor to our concept, conceives of ideology as *inter alia* an 'interpretative system of political ideas . . . which . . . demands . . . a commitment to action in the effort to realize . . . beliefs'.[114] However, it is perhaps Plamenatz who has made this point most effectively in his distinction between two fundamental functions of theories: that of describing and explaining, on the one hand, and of justifying and encouraging behaviour, on the other. He calls the first function descriptive and the second persuasive, and adds that ordinarily, 'when we speak of ideology, we have in mind persuasive theories.'[115] Since this general motivational aspect of ideology is clearly very common in the literature, I shall not justify it further here.

However, this aspect needs to be *explicated* somewhat more fully, if only to clarify what is meant specifically when one attributes motivational characteristics to doctrinal ideas. First of all, it is clear that such traits are not to be viewed in non-ideational terms – i.e., in terms of how ideas function and are responded to – since we are dealing exclusively here with the *content* of ideas. However, they can (in the sense adumbrated by Plamenatz above) be specified with reference to their substantive import, i.e., as being either descriptive or persuasive, or both. There is, in other words, a fundamental difference between ideas which have a persuasive content, and ideas which are predicated structurally in terms of 'how one believes' (as Sartori writes).[116] However, when he dismisses 'ideology in know-ledge' in favour of 'ideology in politics' because the former puta-tively does not 'explain . . . essential features of politics', he is surely throwing the baby out with the bathwater. To pit the sociology of knowledge against a psycho-functional (or behavioural) approach to the study of ideology as the only two available alternatives is certainly an odd way of structuring this issue. But this is precisely what he does when he writes that 'the relation between ideology and "idea" (i.e., conceptual thinking) bears on the genesis of ideological doctrines, on how they originate and are born, and is eventually conducive to an epistemological discussion', whereas 'ideologies [conceived in terms of "ideology in politics"] are no longer ideas, in the sense that ideological doctrines no longer fall under the jurisdiction of logic and verification.' Instead, when 'we pass on to consider ideologies we are confronted with "the conversion of ideas into social levers", i.e., with a *persuasive treatment* (not a logical treatment) of ideas leading to action-oriented ideals.'[117] Against this extreme function-oriented analysis – predicated on an exclusively genetic notion of the meaning of 'ideological doctrines' – I wish to posit the view that doctrines of a motivational (or persuasive) kind can very well be specified and analysed in a fully logical fashion; that this is possible without implicating any genetic factors or epistemological conclusions; and that it would be very strange indeed if this were not the case.

As previously suggested, Sartori here seems to base his distinction between an epistemological and a functional role of ideas – and thus his whole analysis as such – on a philosophical view that is no longer regarded as tenable by contemporary philosophers of social science. Clearly, the logical positivism which, once upon a time, was made popular by A. J. Ayer, and which in the field of ethics and normative analysis has perhaps found its most enduring formulation in Charles Stevenson's *Ethics and Language*, is no longer alive and well – especially not as a viable tool for analysing the role of ideas in political action.[118] The whole discussion of the philosophy of social action in chapter 2 is meant to be an explicit reflection of this state of affairs, as well as of the supposition that persuasive ideas are logically and otherwise fully explicable in both non-functional and non-genetic terms.

This leads us directly to my second point, namely, that it is imperative – precisely for the reasons suggested above – that it be stressed once more that the types of motivational doctrines with which we are concerned here are doctrines which *purport* to motivate action, and are hence not necessarily doctrines which *de facto* obtain an intended effect. This is as fundamental a point as it is – at least on closer reflection, given our premises – an almost self-evident consequence of our previous discussion. And yet it is often neglected entirely, probably because ideology is so often conceived behaviourally or functionally in terms of its actual or predicted effects on polities, groups or individuals. As I have argued above, this in turn is a consequence of the common practice of defining ideologies as belief systems rather than doctrines.

But there is also a further reason for stressing the motivational purport *per se* of ideological doctrines. For it is often maintained that the goals which ideologies are intended to accomplish are different from those which are ostensibly expressed in the doctrines themselves; and hence, that ideology *qua* ideational subterfuge is essentially geared towards manipulating people against their own wishes or without their being fully conscious of it. The whole tradition stretching from Marx's conception of ideology as 'false consciousness' to Habermas's approach in terms of distorted symbols of communication exemplifies this usage of the term. (It is also, for obvious reasons, a tradition fostering the *critique* of ideology as a major task of the social theorist.) By emphasizing the purport of doctrines rather than their assumed, implicit or imputed goals, my aim is – once again – to stress that our definition should pertain wholly to characteristics that are explicitly stated, thus removing any temptation to seek 'underlying' or 'real' as opposed to 'spurious' motives behind promulgated ideological doctrines. The requirement is, in other words, that the action-orientation that is ascribed to doctrines be that which is explicitly contained in the doctrines themselves. Julius Gould has expressed this point in his definition of ideologies as 'patterns of beliefs and concepts which purport to explain complex social phenomena with a view to directing and simplifying socio-political choices facing individuals or groups'.[119] This is also, in my interpretation, what Plamenatz means when he speaks about the persuasive character of ideologies: their purport, by means of whatever message they contain, is to function as a mobilizing factor in social action.

(c)   *Collective interest*

The final definitional characteristic of ideology that will be discussed here appears at first sight also to have the closest affinities to Marx's (and Engels's) way of using our concept. In *The German Ideology*, for example, Marx has written that the 'ideas of the ruling class are in every epoch the ruling ideas', and that 'each new class which puts itself in the place of the one ruling before it, is compelled, merely in order to carry through its aim, to represent its interest as the interest of all members of society.'[120] However, let me emphasize immediately that all apparent similarities between these two conceptions are wholly terminological, since I have in mind a definiens which resolutely tries to steer clear of all the methodological and philosophical problems associated with Marx's definition of ideology in terms of class interests and the substructure/superstructure metaphor. Thus, while his conception is almost entirely normative and metaphysical (as I have argued extensively elsewhere), the notion that is posited here simply claims not only that ideological doctrines contain a manifest motivational purport, but that these action-oriented ideas also refer to goals defined explicitly in terms of the putative interest of social groups or collectivities of one kind or another. This is a far cry from any Marxian (or Marxist) conceptions of ideology as both a function and an expression of class interests.[121]

However, the notion of a 'collective interest' has for a long time been impugned for another reason as well, namely, for being a subjective term meaning different things to different people, and hence really nothing at all. Many years ago Arnold Wolfers thus wrote of such 'political formulas' that 'while appearing to offer guidance and a basis for broad consensus, they may be permitting everyone to label whatever policy he favours with an attractive and possibly deceptive name.'[122] This is a view which still remains more or less accepted as a valid general criticism of all such notions.[123] However, I believe that this problem, while genuine, is easily resolved by making it plain that we are not speaking here of 'interest' in any normative sense whatsoever, but merely as that interest which a group or collectivity imputes to itself. Or as Gray has recently written (commenting on Barry's viewpoint, which I share, that preferences determine interests), 'the only relevant authority to which appeal may be made to settle questions about a man's interests is the judgment of the man himself.'[124] This is also what Herz must have had in mind when he wrote that 'a system of thought ... that becomes effective in movements ... implies a connection between ideologies and "masses" ', and hence that we can meaningfully speak of 'ideology where nationalism or socialist ideas embue entire populations.'[125] Obviously, as Plamenatz has noted, this type of mobilization entails 'making the members of the group more aware than they otherwise would be that they share certain aims and that certain conditions favour their achievement.'[126] Barry's definition of ideology – as 'a set of beliefs attributing to the movement some significance over and above the self-interest of the participants' – seems to be in line with this conception as well.[127] He also reminds us of Edmund Burke's definition 'of a party as a body of men united by a common view of the public good', which is clearly a notion that constitutes an embryonic conception of how contemporary 'denominational, Marxist, and nationalistic parties are able to maintain their appeal and to shape the society according to their ideological creeds', as Sartori has described present day parties in the first volume of his book on *Parties and Party Systems*.[128] For it is probably safe to claim that this 'ideological patterning of society' is a consequence of creeds which emphasize appeals to collective political interest – be they denominational, Marxist, nationalist or whatever.

The reason for including this factor as an essential characteristic of our definiendum lies in the historical transformation of politics which we have previously discussed, and within which, it has been asserted of the past two centuries, the role of ideology has been seminal.

Let us briefly recall Eckstein's claim that politics before the French Revolution consisted mainly of the interplay between the interests of small and privileged groups surrounding and headed by a sovereign in terms of whose paramount interest all other interests were defined. Hence, as E. H. Carr has put it, 'The essential characteristic of the period was the identification of the nation with the person of the sovereign', in consequence of which the 'national interest' *qua raison d'état* constituted a value which was not only simple to determine – inasmuch as it was the ruler's prerogative to define it – but it also had little relation to any ideology in the sense that the term has been understood during the past century. Herz thus notes that 'We hardly speak of ideology in reference to the motivations of a ruler in the age of monarchical absolutism, even where he is motivated by certain theories (such as that of *raison d'état*) in his foreign policy.'[129] However, as George and Keohane have written:

With the 'democratization' of nationalism . . . the relative simplicity of the concept of 'raison d'état' was eroded, and the state itself came to be seen as composed of different interests. In the era of liberal democracy, 'l'état, c'est moi' was no longer an acceptable answer to the question of sovereign legitimacy. The national interest came to reflect a weighing of various diverse interests . . . as different groups within the polity competed to claim it as a legitimizing symbol for their interests and aspirations, which might by no means be shared by many of their compatriots.[130]

In short, the transition from the politics of 'interests' to that of 'incorporation' and 'incumbency' was accompanied – and probably more often than not precipitated – by mobilizing doctrines appealing to various collective interests, be they nationalistic, as in the above case, or politically more exclusive in some sense or other. Indeed, this is a common characteristic of all the big 'isms' of the past two centuries: their claim to represent the interests of 'the people', 'the state', 'the nation', a given 'class' or 'race', and so forth.

Furthermore, this characteristic also explains the actual mobilizing power of ideologies in all their various configurations. Without forceful and explicit appeals to ostensibly common or collective interests, political doctrines would – and will – remain nothing but political doctrines, however forceful and intellectually persuasive their claims. It should perhaps also be added that the recognition of the importance of this factor in political change remains one of Marx's enduring observations: and one which, as we all know today, Lenin put into practice with both consummate skill and, sad to say, the most profound of effects. Thus, in this sense at least, its Marxian connotations are, after all, not entirely misplaced.

5

Conclusion

Ideology as conceptualized in the previous chapter pertains to political behaviour in general, and is hence intended to be equally applicable within all areas of political inquiry. In this concluding chapter I shall once again narrow the focus of discussion by returning briefly to the query which occasioned this analysis in the first place: the specific applicability of this concept to the comparative study of foreign policy. In the process I also intend to tie together the assorted contents of the previous chapters into a single conceptual package.

Since ideologies are doctrinal, they belong to the intentional dimension of our explanatory framework. As I have already suggested, the import of this specification is both far-reaching and contrary to much of the conventional literature; and its implications are at least as pertinent to the study of foreign policy as they are to the analysis of politics in general. Indeed, it has been one of my major purposes in this study as a whole to argue for the utter necessity, particularly in the study of foreign policy, of divorcing the concept of ideology from its conceptual beholdenness to the dispositional notion of belief systems, and especially the normative and cognitive–perceptual components defining the latter. Ideology is to political analysis what dogmatics is to theology: the explicit formalization of the doctrines, tenets or creeds which are posited as the objects *of* faith, *of* belief, *of* commitment, rather than being these properties *as such*. This conception constitutes the basic premise of the following extension of 'ideology' to the study of foreign policies.

Principally, this extension will involve leaving the definitional aspect and (1) turning instead to a discussion of the particular *functions* or *purposes* which ideologies can be considered to perform with respect to foreign policy actions; and (2) relating this empirical aspect to the *explanatory* framework presented in chapter 3. This will not, however, entail any changes in the conceptualization of our term; it means, rather, that the ensuing discussion will be about the role of ideologies *in* the actual conduct of foreign policy, and how this function should be conceived when *explaining* such conduct. This dual question at the same time leads us straight back to our starting-point: the problematic nature of conventional wisdom in regard to the role in general of ideational–normative factors in foreign policy analysis.

A THE FUNCTIONS OF IDEOLOGY

Rather than indulging in a litany on how something that for decades had been effectively shunned was suddenly – with little epistemic fuss or reflection – seen to function in all the nooks and crannies of foreign policy behaviour, I shall instead avail myself of a particular instance of this conventional wisdom as a foil for a more constructive discussion of the potential utility of ideology as conceptualized above. My aim in so doing is not, in other words, to single out this particular example for purposes of emphasizing any special short-comings that it may have. On the contrary, I have chosen it simply because it so well – in terms both of clarity and of insight into the literature – represents the mainstream use of our concept in the study of foreign policy. As such it also exemplifies the major problem with this conventional tradition: its failure, much of the time, to distinguish between two different but common functional notions in the study of political behaviour, namely, function in the sense of *purpose*, and function in the sense of *effect* or *consequence*. In the first sense we speak, e.g., of the function of a spade as that of digging furrows or holes; but we can impute to it functions of the other kind as well, such as constituting an object for pecuniary enrichment or horticultural enjoyment. To convenience the discussion somewhat, we can refer to this distinction in terms of *function*$_1$ and *function*$_2$.

In his book on *Soviet Bargaining Behaviour*, Christer Jönsson gives the concept of ideology a prominent place in the framework that he uses to analyse the nature of international negotiations. The meaning of the concept itself is specified by citing Zbigniew Brzezinski's definition of it as

> an action programme suitable for mass consuption, derived from certain doctrinal assumptions about the general nature of the dynamics of social reality, and combining some assertions about the inadequacies of the past and/or present with some explicit guides to action for improving the situation and some notions of the desired eventual state of affairs.[1]

This notion of the concept is then immediately used to make the following claims: 'As this definition suggests, ideology performs diverse functions. We may distinguish a cognitive function, serving as an "analytic prism", and a normative function, providing specific policy prescriptions, a "guide to action". In these respects, ideology coincides with images.' But ideology has further functions as well, 'one of which is to furnish a common political language. Still another related function is legitimation: to legitimize the regime and justify or rationalize changes in policy.'[2] On the face of it, these functional extrapolations from Brzezinski's definition seem quite unexceptionable, particularly since they represent the pertinent literature so well. (The diligent reader is referred back to the first chapter of this book.) Nevertheless, I shall argue below that we have here a typical instance of how the concept is 'functionalized' into a notion possessing little – if any– discriminating power.

First of all, the thrust of Brzezinski's definition is, clearly, to emphasize the explicit nature and function of ideologies as 'action programmes' designed for large-scale societal change; and as such it conforms unusually well with the doctrinal conception of ideology as discussed in the previous chapter. (Indeed, since Brzezinski exemplifies a typical 'Leninist' view of the role of ideology in political change, it should come as no surprise that his conception is so close to the one that has been advocated here.) In other words, we have here a clear-cut example of how ideology is seen to function$_1$ in political life. Secondly, however, it is equally obvious that although Jönsson purportedly bases his discussion of the various functions of ideology on Brzezinski's conception of the latter, it is couched almost wholly in terms of functions which belong to a fundamentally different category of phenomena, that is to say, that of observed consequences rather than of intended behaviour.

This conflation of functions$_1$ and functions$_2$ is most clearly in evidence when he discusses the relationship between 'ideology' and 'images'. Of it he writes, on the one hand, that we 'can think of ideology and images as [either] partly overlapping' or – in the case of the normative and cognitive functions of ideology – as 'coinciding' entities. On the other hand, 'images are not the same things as ideologies': for not only can 'ideological tenets ... represent ... images' – they can also both 'determine' *and* be 'caused' by them.[3] But clearly, inasmuch as the same relationship is predicated in logical, causal and semantic–iconic terms, Jönsson is speaking here in incompatible tongues. This situation is a common result of the type of thinking that occurs when, as Robert Merton has written in his classic confutation of the functionalist fallacy, 'concepts of subjective disposition [i.e., motives and purposes] are ... erroneously merged with the related, but different, concepts of objective consequences of attitude, belief and behaviour.'[4] He has also described this problem in terms of the 'tendency to confuse the subjective category of *motive* with the objective category of *function*'; and it was in order to inhibit this – often inadvertent – functionaliza-tion$_1$of functions$_2$ that he introduced his famous distinction between manifest and latent functions. Ideologies as conceived by Brzezinski are obviously motivational (and hence manifest) in the above sense, whereas Jönsson's on the whole do *not* pertain to 'those objective consequences for a specified unit ... which contribute to its adjust-ment or adaptation *and were so intended*', to cite Merton's description of manifest functions.[5]

With specific reference to my previous discussion, the problem with the conventional wisdom that Jönsson mediates is, first of all, that whereas the conception endorsed by him belongs squarely within our intentional dimension, the notion of images is a quint-essential dispositional conception. This pertains in particular to images as defined by him, namely, 'the organized representation of an object or a situation in an actor's cognitive system', in the sense that this 'system of images serves as a kind of mental and emotional filter, which mediates and orders incoming messages', and 'deter-mines the actor's focus of attention ... as well as his interpretation ...

and ... affects the actor's perception both of events and of alternatives open to him'.[6] Indeed, this description comes very close to the one contained in my own discussion of the dispositional dimension. Secondly, and in view of this distinction, it also follows from my previous discussion that whereas images *qua* perceptions can be related causally to ideologies with respect to the same action, the converse is logically not feasible. This also pertains to all notions of 'overlapping' and 'coincidence': belonging to logically different classes of phenomena, images and ideologies can as little 'overlap' or 'coincide' as can the many apples and pears of philosophic folklore. Thirdly, the reason why it is so difficult to avoid this type of fuzziness is that both the intentional and the dispositional dimensions of action are composed of ideational entities, while at the same time referring to fundamentally different methodological aspects of ideas. Here we should once more remind ourselves of George Sabine's distinction between 'logical entities' and 'events in people's minds', both of which are referred to as 'ideas'.[7] Whenever such entities are discussed without reference to this distinction, the result is an open invitation to commit the variant of the functional fallacy illustrated above.[8] Thus, while one can believe in a doctrine (i.e., a special configuration of ideas), and while this belief can be described in terms of specific doctrinal elements (i.e., ideas), beliefs can never become doctrines, or doctrines beliefs, even though both constitute ideational phenomena *par excellence*. In short, although in the beginning was the *logos*, it makes all the difference, in the world thus created, what subsequent roles it is allowed to play. It certainly cannot play them all at the same time.

The immediate consequences of all this for Jönsson's discussion of the functions of ideology are as follows. When he avers that ideology has the 'cognitive' function of serving as an 'analytic prism', he is speaking about a dispositional attribute, and hence about a possible psychological–cognitive *effect* of ideological doctrines on *belief systems*. This empirical consequence is, of course, something very different from the notion that the role of ideology consists of *being* such a prism. (The latter claim would be tantamount to saying that the function of a spade consists of its being 'a flattish rectangular iron blade socketed on a wooden handle', to quote the *Shorter Oxford English Dictionary*.) The same must be said about Jönsson's 'normative' function, except that here we have a notion that is so vague that both types of functions are in principle possible. Ideologies can thus have numerous normative consequences for the belief systems of people (not the least of which is to turn them *against* such doctrines); but it is only when their purpose is to constitute specific policy prescriptions *qua* motivating guides to political action that we can speak of their normative function in a manifest sense. The 'symbolic' function is clearly one of dispositional effect as well, except in those special instances then the political role of language itself is at issue as a doctrine.

Finally, Jönsson's 'legitimating' function is, once more, a mixed bag of function$_1$ and function$_2$, although – I surmise – with very little of the former in it. In any event, when he refers to William Zimmermann's observation that 'during the Krushchev era, Soviet specialists on international relations, rather than letting Lenin do their thinking for them, found they could utilize Lenin to legitimate their thinking no matter how un-Leninistic those thoughts may be', he is certainly *not* speaking in terms of function$_1$.[9] This example represents little more than a common instance of intellectual subterfuge and sophistry (although in the final analysis it remains somewhat unclear who – Lenin or his latter-day avatars – is being bamboozled by whom).

Since the role of ideology must necessarily be stated in terms of intended consequences, the question pertaining to the specific nature of these intentions must at least be raised before we can consider this discussion concluded. What is there specifically about the consequences of ideology which makes them so important and desirable in the eyes of modern politicians? Although this is one of the most intriguing questions that political inquiry can tackle, here I shall merely offer a few preliminary suggestions and reflections before ending this study by considering the explanatory issue raised above.

First of all, I believe that with the advent of modern politics we also entered into a basically non-Hobbesian era of political manipulation. This, in my reading, is one of the major implications of the introduction – less than two centuries ago – of what Harry Eckstein has called the politics of incorporation (as discussed in the previous chapter). Jon Elster has intimated the logic underlying this historical development in his suggestion that when 'acting with fervour rather than with calculation the ruling classes can succeed in reaching and shaping the minds of their subjects, with consequences beneficial for their rule.'[10] Insight on the part of political elites into the mechanics of this manipulatory tool – especially in the form of various kinds of nationalism – constitutes, in my view, one of the major watersheds of post-Renaissance political history. This is also, I surmise, one of the reasons for the success of the politics of incorporation as well as for its development into the politics of incumbency: demands from below for power (fed by ideas from Rousseau and Montesquieu rather than Hobbes and Machiavelli) could effectively be manipulated for their own purposes by incumbent and new holders of the reins of government.

Marx's insight, in his vehement attack on the so-called 'German ideologists' of the 1840s, was to recognize this role which ostensibly 'new' and 'revolutionary' ideas – usually of a Hegelian coinage – played in consolidating rather than eroding the power of the German *Bürgertum* of his time. To call these ideas 'ideological' was Marx's particular way of emphasizing their wishy-washy Enlightenment character: their function$_2$, in the name of the principles of rationalism and equality, of inhibiting any demands for a genuinely revolutionary upheaval. It is in this light – of recognizing the 'ideational fervour' of the ruling classes as merely a new type of manipulatory instrument against radical demands for change – that we have to understand his aim 'of uncloaking these sheep, who take themselves and are taken for wolves; of showing how their bleating merely imitates in a philosophic form the conceptions of the German middle class; how the boasting of these philosophic commentators only mirrors the wretchedness of the real conditions of Germany.'[11] This insight also underlies one of Marx's most famous remarks, namely, that the ideas of the ruling class are in every historical epoch also its ruling ideas.[12] Although problematic as an empirical proposition, this statement nevertheless catches the essence of the point that I am trying to make here: the role, in modern politics, of ideas as persuasive instruments not only for motiviating action towards change (the politics of incorporation), but also for retaining and consolidating the status quo (the politics of incumbency).

In other words, while ideological doctrines are most often thought of as revolutionary in thrust, they are in fact equally – and perhaps even better – suited for the purposes suggested by Elster above (and previously discussed by Eckstein). This is also, in my interpretation, a central notion underlying the claim that 'total' or 'extremist' ideologies have over the past three of four decades given way to more 'moderate' or 'pragmatic' party doctrines in Western societies. When Seymour Martin Lipset writes (in the new concluding chapter of his updated edition of *Political Man*) that 'because revolutionary mass politics in early industrial society was largely a phenomenon of the working-class struggle for citizenship, its ideological commitments were eroded when "the workers . . . achieved industrial and political citizenship, [and] the conservatives . . . accepted the welfare state" ', he is therefore suggesting an empirical hypothesis that does *not* deny the continued presence of ideologies in public life.[13] Rather, his claim is that the ideological commitments of the major Western political parties have tended to change their characteristics along a radical–moderate dimension. Implicit in the above statement, and explicitly discussed elsewhere in his extensive analysis of this topic, is also a distinction between the ideological commitments of intellectuals, on the one hand, and those characterizing the main political parties, on the other. Thus, while it would be fatuous to deny that the former have continued intermittently to achieve radical forms of expression (e.g., in the New Politics of the student movement of the 1960s and early 1970s), it is also undeniable that their effect on the major-party protagonists in Western democracies during the past decades have not – to say the least – been especially profound. By explaining this loss in the *mass* appeal of radical movements in terms of the moderating effects of post-war social and economic developments on class-related partisan conflict, Lipset et al. have, in other words, not denied the continued existence and force of such radical movements among intellectuals, students and other *minority* groups. On the contrary, the acknowledgement of this fact has been part of the end-of-ideology thesis itself. In so far as the critics of this claim have ignored the distinction between types of ideologies as well as between different belief publics, it is not surprising that so much of the subsequent criticism of this hypothesis has so often been beside the point.

Secondly, whatever the basic contents of ideological doctrines, the psycho-logic underlying them requires the conscious manipulation of the dispositional properties of individual actors. This is also the reason why it is so important, when conceptualizing the functions of ideology, to view 'ideology' and 'images' (or 'doctrines' and 'belief systems') in terms of mutually exclusive dimensions. In failing to do this, the tradition expounded by Jönsson also fails fundamentally in accounting for the *logic* of *ideological manipulation.* For as long as images and ideology in any sense whatsoever either 'overlap', 'coincide' or by definition 'determine' each other, we have no logical or empirical way of accounting for the dynamics of the phenomenon of ideological persuasion. Or as John Plamenatz has observed, 'to say that the thought that forms part of an action affects it is like saying that the shape of something affects it. The thought that affects human behaviour is external to the behaviour it affects.'[14] In the conceptualization posited here, no such circularities inhibit our understanding of the basic mechanics of action-oriented programmes of political suasion.

In my view, the skeletal outline of such a logic is as follows. One of the pre-eminent functions$_1$ of ideological doctrines is to affect the *belief systems* – i.e., the values and perceptions – of individuals, with the view of creating and/or sustaining certain types of *intentions* in the pursuit of political goals. Therefore, in so far as ideology has a politico-socializing function in political systems, it constitutes a dynamic factor in both changing and sustaining political goals within a polity. It is this persuasive effect of doctrines that is of interest when discussing the nature of 'open' and 'closed' minds, and how these relate to the query (raised by Giovanni Sartori) of '*how* one believes'. As an empirical problem it allows us to pose some very intriguing questions, for example, whether certain types of political doctrines have the effect of fostering certain types of belief systems; and hence, whether and how changes in the doctrinal commitments of political parties have led to the demise of dogmatic or extremist belief systems within a polity. However, since the relationship between *what* one believes and *how* one believes is both complex and dynamic, this is a query which – if it is to avoid some of the fundamental problems inhering in the conventional wisdom criticized above – must be couched in terms of a framework premised on a clear logical distinction between the intentional, dispositional and situational dimensions of explanation. This is one of the pre-eminent arguments of this study.

But how, given this view of the general function of ideology in politics, can we use this concept to *explain* foreign policy actions? First of all, it must immediately be noted that whereas the functions of ideological doctrines have been viewed in terms of an empirical process in which doctrines – as socializing ideas – are dynamically related both to dispositional behaviour and to the subsequent pursuit of political goals defined in terms of such doctrines, the explanatory framework that has been posited above is not intended to represent a *model* of this dynamic relationship, but – on the contrary – constitutes a logical framework restricted to the conceptualization of foreign policy actions (our explanandum) in terms of the methodological links between three basic explanatory dimensions (or types of explanans) in the social sciences. It, so to speak, 'freezes' reality into logical categories for purposes of scientific analysis.

Thus, while the functions of ideology are viewed empirically in the dynamic way described above, the role of the concept in explaining foreign policy actions must of necessity be made subservient to a logic of explanation which does not include the notion of function as an explanatory factor. Indeed, in so far as our framework does not admit of the notion of functional explanation in any sense whatsoever, it stands in marked contrast to some of the prevalent models for explaining foreign policy. This methodological restriction is a consequence of (1) viewing foreign policy in terms of actions pursued by specific actors for clearly specified purposes; and (2) disregarding the outcomes of such actions. However, since the logic of this framework has been discussed and justified in some detail above, there is no need to repeat that discussion here. Instead, I shall give a brief example from a recent Swedish foreign policy controversy to illustrate both its practical utility and its limitations. (Being a national of Sweden, I beg the foreign reader's indulgence for this temporary parochialism.) Thereafter I will indicate the role of the concept of ideology in this type of analysis.

Following a series of submarine encroachments of Swedish territorial waters in the early 1980s, an intensive public debate ensued between the incumbent Social Democratic government and the leadership of the Conservatives. The main issue concerned the manner in which the Swedish government should respond to the Soviet Union, on whom an official commission had put the blame for this illegal activity in the Baltic. The Conservative party argued for the strictest possible response, whereas the government – or more specifically, the late Swedish prime minister, Olof Palme – tended to favour a somewhat less unaccommodating stance. This resulted in a controversy about the nature of Swedish foreign policy as such, in which each side accused the other of compromising Sweden's long-standing doctrine of neutrality.

Two types of arguments have been used to explain this unusual political conflict regarding Swedish foreign policy (which had previously enjoyed a long history of political non-partisanship). The *first* argument maintains that whereas the Social Democrats have retained an essentially 'optimistic' view of Soviet intentions and policies, the Conservatives are inherently 'pessimistic' in this respect. Consequently, while both parties wish to pursue the traditional Swedish policy of armed neutrality in their dealings with the Soviet Union, their actual policies *vis-à-vis* her tend for this reason to diverge on some central issues. The *second* argument states that Swedish foreign policy is faced with a choice between two fundamental options in the pursuit of international affairs. The first option, represented by former foreign minister Östen Undén's post-war policies, is to make a clear distinction between questions pertaining to (1) Swedish national security, (2) international disarmament and (3) the pursuit of human rights and democratic principles on the international arena. According to this view, these three issue-areas should be pursued in their own right as separate but equally important policy domains. In other words, no one issue-area should be made to impinge on the others. The second option, most vigorously defended by Herbert Tingsten (formerly editor-in-chief of *Dagens Nyheter*, Sweden's main newspaper), is *not* to view these three issues as watertight policy areas; rather, in a thoroughly Wilsonian fashion he argued that the first two questions should always be made subservient to a fundamental Swedish commitment to human rights and democratic values in her international dealings. In the view of the advocates of this interpretation, the government's relations with the Soviets can be explained in terms of its commitment to Undén's principles, whereas the Conservative view can be shown to be a reflection of Tingsten's essentially moral point of view.[15]

How are we to choose between these two contending explanations of the same phenomenon? Or rather: how is one to argue for the superior validity of the one over the other? In my view, this is simply not possible, for the reason that, *qua* putative explanations, they are in principle incommensurable: they pertain to two fundamentally different dimensions of explanation. More specifically, the one does not exclude the other, since one's perceptions of Soviet intentions along an optimistic–pessimistic scale do not necessarily predetermine one's foreign policy stance in terms of the Undén–Tingsten options. Rather, since the latter type of explanation is an *intentional* one, expressed in terms of two different types of doctrinal policy commitments, while the former is a typical *dispositional* explanation in terms of cognitive–normative perceptions, the link between them is entirely empirical and hence an open question. Undén's doctrine may – or may not – be a consequence of an optimistic view of Soviet intentions; but we can only determine this by means of an empirical inquiry in which the intentional factor is clearly distinguished from cognitive–psychological aspects.

Although to my knowledge the following argument has not been made in the above controversy, it is in principle also possible to argue in terms of a *third* type of explanation for the conflict between these two Swedish political parties. This type of explanation would be couched in terms of what I have called the situational dimension, i.e., with reference to the objective and structural conditions which constrain the behaviour of actors, be they single or collective. It could thus, for example, be claimed that once a political party or leader attains the responsibilities of government, it (or he/she) will *ipso facto* act differently from a party or leader in opposition.

Once again, however, this putative explanation is not *per se* an alternative to either of the explanations posited above. Thus if this situational factor does indeed play a role in Swedish foreign policy, it does so in terms of its influence on the dispositional factors affecting

Swedish foreign policy actions, i.e., as a structural constraint on the belief systems of the relevant decision-makers. As such it, too, is an empirical variable which must be clearly distinguished from both dispositional and intentional factors. Hence, although it is possible that the doctrine underlying Sweden's present policies *vis-à-vis* the Soviet Union is indeed a consequence of, say, an optimistic view of Soviet intentions; and although it is arguable that this optimism is *inter alia* a function of the structural conditions of incumbency, both of these hypotheses are entirely empirical and can, furthermore, be validated only in the logical, step-by-step manner discussed in chapter 3. In short, being neither causal nor teleological, a situational explanation can by definition never rival either a dispositional or an intentional explanation. The three are interrelated, not mutually exclusive.

The methodological implications of this example are – at least – the following. First of all, it illustrates the confusion which arises when our three explanatory dimensions are not clearly distinguished from one another. Secondly, this example shows why intentional explanations logically precede dispositional ones, and that situational explanations are appropriate only when expressed in terms of their link to the dispositional dimension. We must first determine the stated rationale for a foreign policy choice before attempting to explain foreign policy actions in terms of such causal factors as perceptions and values; and we can only introduce constraining (i.e., situational) factors into the explanation once such causal factors have been identified. In other words, by themselves either dispositional or situational explanations of foreign policy actions will always tend to beg the question. This is essentially the case with the first type of explanation referred to above; as such it also represents a typical example of the fallacy of psychologism. Similarly, the third type of explanation would – were it to be adduced by itself – qualify as a case of the ecological fallacy. Finally, this example emphasizes, once again, the fundamental importance of intentional factors in the analysis of foreign policy actions. Given the logic of the analysis expounded here, an explanation of a foreign policy action must of necessity always contain an intentional dimension; it may also, but need not, be augmented by – in turn – dispositional and situational variables.

This final point also leads us back to the central query of this study as a whole, namely, the role of the concept of ideology in foreign policy analysis. For in addition to the more general methodological issues raised above, our example suggests the restricted but at the same time significant scope of this concept in the study of foreign policy behaviour. Both of these roles are illustrated by the doctrines associated with Undén and Tingsten: for theirs are obviously typical foreign policy ideologies in the sense defined in the previous chapter, i.e., doctrines intended to motivate an actor (or actors) to pursue certain actions for the sake of the collective interest of the nation.

The restrictive aspect is indicated by the fact that ideological foreign policy doctrines are as such nothing more than *descriptions of intentional behaviour.* Furthermore, once we have identified them as ideological, i.e., made a conceptual determination in terms of our formal definition, the content of such a description will depend entirely on the characteristics of the specific instance in each given case. This may lead the reader to conclude that the concept is, after all, little more than an empty conceptual container, lacking wholly in the systematic import – Carl Hempel's classic criterion – which all truly scientific concepts possess and which distinguishes them from mere notational devices in the language of social analysis.

However, such a faint-hearted response is most certainly misplaced in this context. Conceptualization is not the end station of scientific analysis; it is, rather, its proper point of departure. And the starting-point that has been suggested in this study is certainly intended – if anything – to be systematic in Hempel's sense. The reason for this bold claim is that, although as a concept 'ideology' constitutes only a specific type of descriptive category in the intentional dimension of social action, it at the same time implicates a host of additional explanatory factors, once we extend our analysis to include dispositional and situational variables. Indeed, herein lies not only the crucial importance of situating the concept within a larger explanatory framework, but also the reason why a purely semantic explication of ideology is bound to remain an exercise in mere linguistic usage. Hence, while ideologies are by definition not causal factors in the explanation of foreign policy actions (they are 'merely' logical entities of a specific kind), they are nevertheless always – given their dynamic, empirical function$_1$ in actual politics, as suggested above – directly linked to such dispositional variables in one way or another. In other words, while ideologies are not belief systems, the former can in practice never exist without being empirically rooted in the latter. It is this fact which underwrites the systematic import of our concept.

This brings us to my concluding remark. If our concept is eventually to attain the hallmark of all scientific concepts, namely, that of being not only clear and precise, but also able to function in hypotheses and theories with explanatory and predictive force, it must be further elaborated in terms of characteristics extending beyond those defining its meaning. In my view, such an elaboration must be based not only on a classification and analysis of types of ideological doctrines, but also – given the functional$_1$ role of ideologies in politics – on the kinds of causal linkages which can be shown to exist between dispositional and intentional factors, i.e., between belief systems and ideologies.

The prototypical questions in such an in-depth analysis will include the following: what kinds of belief systems – i.e., perceptions and values – tend to cause what types of ideological doctrines; what is the role of situational factors in these cognitive and normative processes; and hence, why – in the final analysis – do given actors pursue given foreign policy actions? Comparatively, such analyses can be couched in terms of the foreign policies of various states, or those pertaining to a single state over time. The same holds for case studies of the kind discussed above. To establish these kinds of linkages constitutes, in my view, the prime reason for retaining the concept of ideology as an *explanatory* tool of potentially the first rank in the comparative analysis of social action.

However, since the aim of this book has been limited to the most fundamental methodological problems relating to the *conceptualization* of ideology in the analysis of foreign policy, it has perforce left aside the further exploration of ideology in such systematic empirical terms. In other words, although I have attempted to go at least some of the way towards achieving this additional goal, the crucial task of propounding a *theory* of the role of ideology in the conduct of foreign policy still remains to be tackled.

Notes

CHAPTER 1   INTRODUCTION

1   An interesting comparison is to be found in Giovanni Sartori's important article entitled 'Politics, Ideology, and Belief Systems', *American Political Science Review*, vol. 63 (1969), p. 398, in which he notes that while the *International Encyclopedia of the Social Sciences*, published in 1968, contains no less than two articles under the heading 'Ideology', its forerunner, the *Encyclopedia of the Social Sciences*, dating from the 1930s, does not contain even a rubric bearing the name of the concept. It is perhaps also indicative that in a British series on 'Key Concepts in Political Science' the contribution on *Ideology* (London, 1970) by John Plamenatz is one of the first on a long list; indeed, it takes precedence over such traditionally important concepts as 'power', 'representation', 'legitimacy', 'liberty', 'tradition and authority', and other hallowed notions of the social science canon.

2   Zbigniew Brzezinski and Samuel P. Huntington, *Political Power: US/USSR* (New York, 1963), p. 67.

3   Michael Brecher, 'The Subordinate State System of Southern Asia', in James N. Rosenau, ed., *International Politics and Foreign Policy* (New York, 1969), p. 155. Brecher is here basically summarizing the viewpoint presented in John Herz's *International Politics in the Atomic Age* (New York, 1959). Political scientists are not, however, wholly of one mind in their historical interpretations of the genesis of ideology in international relations. K. J. Holsti, e.g., thus writes that the 'third development of the nineteenth century [sic] with major consequences on the structure and processes of the European state system was the use of ideological principles and political doctrines as a major motive or guide to foreign policy behaviour.' K. J. Holsti, *International Politics* (2nd edn: London, 1974), p. 69.

4   For a wide-ranging collection of essays on this theme, see Ali A. Mazrui, *Africa's International Relations: The Diplomacy of Dependency and Change* (London, 1977).

5   Arne Naess, Jens Christophersen and Kjell Kvalø, *Democracy, Ideology and*

Objectivity: Studies in the Semantics and Cognitive Analysis of Ideological Controversy (Oslo, 1956), p. 171.

6 Willard A. Mullins, 'On the Concept of Ideology in Political Science', *American Political Science Review*, vol. 64 (1970), p. 1043; and Sartori, 'Politics, Ideology', p. 398.

7 Quoted in Martin Seliger, *Ideology and Politics* (London, 1976), p. 87.

8 Stanislav Ossowski, as quoted by William E. Connolly, *Political Science and Ideology* (New York, 1967), p. 18.

9 Richard S. Rudner, *Philosophy of Social Science* (Englewood Cliffs, NJ, 1966), p. 8.

10 Kenneth W. Thompson and Roy Macridis, 'The Comparative Study of Foreign Policy' in Roy Macridis, ed., *Foreign Policy in World Politics* (4th edn: Englewood Cliffs, NJ, 1972), pp. 1ff. Gross's definition is to be found in *Foreign Policy Analysis* (New York, 1954), p. xv.

11 Ole R. Holsti, 'Foreign Policy Decision Makers Viewed Psychologically: "Cognitive Process" Approaches', in G. Matthew Bonham and Michael J. Shapiro, eds. *Thought and Action in Foreign Policy* (Basel, 1977), pp. 22f. See also Ole R. Holsti, 'The Study of International Politics Makes Strange Bedfellows: Theories of the Radical Right and the Radical Left', *American Political Science Review*, vol. 68 (1974), pp. 217ff.

12 Stephen D. Krasner, *Defending the National Interest: Raw Materials Investments and US Foreign Policy* (Princeton, NJ, 1978), p. 344. The reference to Hartz is on p. 335.

13 See Charles Reynolds, *Theory and Explanation in International Politics* (London, 1973), pp. 126ff., and especially pp. 140ff.

14 Krasner, *Defending the National Interest*, p. 15.

15 Franz Schurmann, *The Logic of World Power* (New York, 1974).

16 Ibid., p. 188.

17 Idem. For another discussion of the distinction between 'national interest' and 'ideology', see Stephen Kirby, 'National Interest *Versus* Ideology in American Diplomacy', in Robert Benewick, R. N. Berki and Bhikhu Parekh, eds, *Knowledge and Belief in Politics* (London, 1973), pp. 225ff.

18 Herbert C. Kelman, 'Patterns of Personal Involvement in the National System: A Social–Psychological Analysis of Political Legitimacy', in Rosenau, ed., *International Politics*, p. 276.

19 Evan Luard, *Types of International Society* (New York, 1976), p. 68.

20 For an analysis, somewhat dated, of the ambiguities involved in the 'nationalisms' of the African states, see my 'A Conceptual Analysis of African Nationalism', in C. A. Hessler, ed., *Idéer och ideologier* (Stockholm, 1969), pp. 249ff. A lucid historical and analytical discussion of the rise of nationalism in Europe is to be found in Otto Pflanze's 'Nationalism in Europe, 1848–1871', *The Review of Politics*, vol. 28 (1966), pp. 129ff. Also see Anthony D. Smith, *Theories of Nationalism* (London, 1971).

21 Macridis, ed., *Foreign Policy*, pp. 2, 1.

22 Bernard C. Cohen, 'Foreign Policy', in David L. Sills, ed. *International Encyclopedia of the Social Sciences*, vol. 5 (New York, 1968), p. 530.

23 Ian Clark, *Reform and Resistance in the International System* (Cambridge, 1980), p. 11.

24 Ibid., p. 31.

25 Ibid., pp. 31f.

26 K. J. Holsti, *International Politics*, p. 353.

27 Macridis, ed., *Foreign Policy*, p. 12.

28 Vernon V. Aspaturian, 'International Politics and Foreign Policy in the Soviet System', in R. Barry Farrell, ed., *Approaches to Comparative and International Politics* (Evanston, Ill., 1966), p. 222.

29 Stanley Hoffmann, *Gulliver's Troubles: Or the Setting of American Foreign Policy* (New York, 1968), pp. 115, 114.

30 Henry A. Kissinger, *Nuclear Weapons and Foreign Policy* (New York, 1957).

31 R. W. Cottam, *Foreign Policy Motivation* (Pittsburgh, Pa, 1977) pp. 39f.

32 Gabriel A. Almond, *The American People and Foreign Policy* (New York, 1960), pp. 158, 159.

33 Hans J. Morgenthau, *Politics Among Nations* (3rd edn: New York, 1961), pp. 87f. This viewpoint is in contrast to Nathan Leites's in *The Operational Code of the Politburo* (New York, 1951).

34 Cottam, *Foreign Policy Motivation*, p. 16.

35 Thomas W. Robinson, 'National Interest', in Rosenau, ed., *International Politics*, p. 188.

36 Werner Levi, 'Ideology, Interests, and Foreign Policy', *International Studies Quarterly*, vol. 14 (March 1970), p. 7.

37 Almond, *The American People*, p. 159.

38 Ibid., p. 29.

39 R. Barry Farrell, 'Foreign Policies of Open and Closed Political Societies', in Farrell, *Approaches*, ed., p. 556.

40 Johan Galtung, 'Foreign Policy Opinions as a Function of Social Position', in Rosenau, ed., *International Politics*, p. 556.

41 See ibid., pp. 557, 553ff. Cf. E. J. Meehan, *The British Left Wing and Foreign Policy: A Study of the Influence of Ideology* (New Brunswick, NJ, 1960).

42 John P. Raser, 'Learning and Affect in International Politics', in Rosenau, ed., *International Politics*, p. 437fn.

43 See Henry A. Kissinger, *American Foreign Policy: Three Essays by Henry A. Kissinger* (New York, 1969), pp. 17ff. The essay relevant here, on 'Domestic Structure and Foreign Policy', can also be found in Rosenau, ed., *International Politics*, pp. 261ff.; see especially pp. 267ff.

44 K. J. Holsti, *International Politics*, p. 389.

45 See Michael Brecher, B. Steinberg and J. Stein, 'A Framework for Research on Foreign Policy Behaviour', *Journal of Conflict Resolution*, vol. 13 (1969), pp. 75ff., especially pp. 88ff.; Michael Brecher, 'Image, Process and Feedback in Foreign Policy: Israel's Decision on German Reparations', *American*

Political Science Review, vol. 67 (1973), pp. 73ff.; and Michael Brecher, *Decisions in Israel's Foreign Policy* (London, 1974), pp. 3ff.

46 Quoted in Brecher et al., 'A Framework', p. 87.

47 Idem.

48 A term first introduced by Harold and Margaret Sprout; see ibid., p. 86fn.

49 Rudolph J. Rummel, 'Some Dimensions of the Foreign Policy Behaviour of Nations', in Rosenau, ed., *International Politics*, p. 607.

50 Hedley Bull, *The Anarchical Society: A Study of Order in World Politics* (London, 1977), pp. 247f.

51 Morton A. Kaplan, 'Variants on Six Models of the International System', in Rosenau, ed., *International Politics*, p. 296. It is probably this function of 'ideology' which Kirby has in mind when he writes:

> Thus an ideological foreign policy is one that seeks the transformation of international society, and is marked off from a more traditional diplomacy by the scope and the inclusiveness of its values and the goals that reflect them, and also by the zeal and enthusiasm with which they are pursued. But the disruptive force of an ideological foreign policy may be of two kinds. It may encourage a deliberate rejection of the circumspect, cautious and ultimately accommodatory style of balance-of-power diplomacy, as Kennan believed communist ideology did for Soviet foreign policy ... Or alternatively, an ideology, in the looser sense of a body of altruistic values, can disrupt international society unintentionally.
>
> (Kirby, 'National Interest *Versus* Ideology', pp. 230f.)

Also see Luard, *Types of International Society*, pp. 67ff.

52 K. J. Holsti, *International Politics*, pp. 366f.

53 Ibid., p. 367. See also ibid., pp. 356, 357.

54 Brzezinski and Huntington, *Political Power*, p. 56.

55 Idem. For a critique of this conception in the name of an even wider definition of ideology, see William Taubman, 'Political Power: USA/USSR – Ten Years Later', *Studies in Comparative Communism*, vol. 8, nos 1/2 (1975), pp. 192ff.

56 F. S. Northedge, ed., *The Foreign Policies of the Powers* (rev. edn: London, 1974), p. 13.

57 Charles Taylor, 'Neutrality in Political Science', in Peter Laslett and W. G. Runciman, eds, *Philosophy, Politics and Society*, 3rd series (Oxford, 1969), p. 30.

58 Kenneth N. Waltz, *Theory of International Politics* (Reading, Mass., 1979), p. 11.

59 Abraham Kaplan, *The Conduct of Inquiry* (San Francisco, 1964), p. 370.

60 A. James Gregor, *An Introduction to Metapolitics* (New York, 1971).

61 Anatol Rapoport, 'Some Systems Approaches to Political Science', in David Easton, ed., *Varieties of Political Theories* (Englewood Cliffs, NJ, 1966), p. 132.

62 Harry Eckstein, 'Case Study and Theory in Political Science', in Fred I. Greenstein and Nelson W. Polsby, eds, *Handbook of Political Science: Strategies of Inquiry* (vol. 7) (Reading, Mass., 1975), p. 86.

63 Idem.
64 Ibid., p. 87.
65 Idem.
66 For the details of his argumentation under each heading, see ibid., pp. 88ff.
67 Harry Eckstein, ed., *Internal War* (New York, 1964), pp. 7f.
68 Felix E. Oppenheim, 'The Language of Political Inquiry: Problems of Clarification', in Fred I. Greenstein and Nelson W. Polsby, eds, *Handbook of Political Science: Scope and Theory* (vol. 1) p. 283.
69 See ibid. for the latter, and for the former, J. Donald Moon, 'The Logic of Political Inquiry: A Synthesis of Opposed Perspectives', in Greenstein and Polsby, eds, *Handbook*, vol. 1, pp. 131ff.
70 On this distinction, see Oppenheim, 'The Language of Political Inquiry', pp. 309ff.
71 On this whole problem, see Giovanni Sartori, Fred W. Riggs and Henry Teune, *Tower of Babel: On the Definition and Analysis of Concepts in the Social Sciences* (Pittsburgh, Pa, 1975).
72 Oppenheim, 'The Language of Political Inquiry', p. 284.
73 Karl Popper, *Conjectures and Refutations* (London, 1973), p. 28.
74 Gregor, *An Introduction*, p. 54.
75 J. L. Austin, *Philosophical Papers* (2nd edn: London, 1970), p. 185.
76 Oppenheim, 'The Language of Political Inquiry', p. 309.
77 See Sartori et al., *Tower of Babel*, pp. 7ff.
78 Gregor, *An Introduction*, p. 134, and Oppenheim, 'The Language of Political Inquiry', p. 284.
79 Gregor, *An Introduction*, p. 134.
80 Kaplan, *The Conduct of Inquiry*, p. 309.
81 Oppenheim, 'The Language of Political Inquiry', p. 309.

CHAPTER 2   FOREIGN POLICY ACTIONS

1 Giovanni Sartori, 'Concept Misformation in Comparative Politics', *American Political Science Review*, vol. 64 (1970), p. 1043.
2 See ibid., passim, and Harry Eckstein, ed., *Internal War* (New York, 1964), pp. 8ff.
3 Arthur L. Kalleberg, 'The Logic of Comparison', *World Politics*, vol. 19 (July 1966), pp. 72f.
4 John G. Gunnell, 'Social Science and Political Reality: The Problem of Explanation', *Social Research*, vol. 35 (1968), p. 165.
5 Arthur L. Kalleberg, 'Concept Formation in Normative and Empirical Studies: Toward Reconciliation in Political Theory', *American Political Science Review*, vol. 63, no. 1 (1969), p. 26.
6 Murray Edelman, *Political Language: Words That Succeed and Policies that Fail* (New York, 1977), p. 23. Theodore J. Lowi has written the following on this matter: 'There is more to the urge for classification than the desire for

complexity. Finding different manifestations or types of a given phenomenon is the beginning of orderly control and prediction. Moreover, to find the *basis* for classification reveals the hidden meanings and significance of the phenomenon, suggesting what the important hypotheses ought to be concerned with.' Lowi, 'Four Systems of Policy, Politics, and Choice', *Public Administration Review*, vol. 32, no. 4 (July/August 1972), p. 299.

7   For a succinct and clarifying discussion of the distinction between delimitation and classification, see Eckstein, ed., *Internal War*, pp. 7ff. In it you will also find that rarest of things: an acknowledgement by an editor of having failed.

8   John Galtung, *Theory and Methods of Social Research* (New York, 1967), p. 37.

9   For two unpublished but excellent contributions to this discussion, see Edward L. Morse, 'Defining Foreign Policy for Comparative Analysis: A Research Note', mimeo, Princeton, NJ, June 1971; and Patrick J. McGowan, 'The Unit-of-Analysis Problem in the Comparative Study of Foreign Policy', paper presented at the Events Data Measurement Conference, Michigan State University, East Lansing, Mich., 15–16 April 1970.

10   See Sartori, 'Concept Misformation', pp. 1040ff.

11   See ibid., pp. 1041ff.

12   May Brodbeck, 'General Introduction', in May Brodbeck, ed., *Readings in the Philosophy of the Social Sciences* (New York, 1968), p. 5.

13   Carl G. Hempel, 'Fundamentals of Concept Formation in Empirical Science', in *International Encyclopedia of Unified Science*, vol. 11, no. 7 (Chicago, 1952), pp. 2, 6. Also see Karl R. Popper, *The Poverty of Historicism* (New York, 1957), pp. 26ff.

14   See McGowan, 'The Unit-of-Analysis Problem', pp. 1ff., and especially pp. 7ff., 10ff.

15   See Sartori, 'Concept Misformation', p. 1045.

16   Carl G. Hempel, 'A Logical Appraisal of Operationalism', in Philipp G. Frank, ed., *The Validation of Scientific Theories* (New York, 1961), p. 56.

17   See Hempel, *Fundamentals*, p. 60.

18   Sartori, 'Concept Misformation', p. 1045.

19   John D. Steinbruner, *The Cybernetic Theory of Decision* (Princeton, NJ, 1974), p. 9.

20   For a discussion of the conceptual difference between international *politics* and international *relations*, see, e.g. K. J. Holsti, *International Politics* (London, 1974), pp. 20ff., and F. A. Sondermann, 'The Linkage between Foreign Policy and International Politics', in James N. Rosenau, ed., *International Politics and Foreign Policy* (New York, 1969), pp. 8ff. Also note the distinction between foreign policy analysis and capabilities analysis as presented in Harold and Margaret Sprout, *The Ecological Perspective in Human Affairs* (Princeton, NJ, 1965), pp. 222f., and in their 'Environmental Factors in the Study of International Politics', in Rosenau, ed., *International Politics*, pp. 41ff. See also Charles Hermann, 'Policy Classification: A Key to the

Comparative Study of Foreign Policy', in James N. Rosenau, Vincent Davis and Maurice A. East, eds, *The Analysis of International Politics* (New York, 1972), pp. 58ff.

21 For examples of such usages, see, e.g., Talcott Parsons and Edward Shils, *Toward a General Theory of Action* (New York, 1962), p. 53; Sprout, *The Ecological Perspective*, p. 23; and Richard C. Snyder, H. W. Bruch and Burton Sapin, eds, *Foreign Policy Decision-Making* (New York, 1962), p. 64.

22 Abraham Kaplan, *The Conduct of Inquiry* (San Francisco, 1964), p. 57.

23 Carl G. Hempel, 'The Theoretician's Dilemma', in H. Feigl, M. Scriven and G. Maxwell, eds, *Minnesota Studies in the Philosophy of Science*, vol. 11 (Minneapolis, 1958) p. 42.

24 See Sartori, 'Concept Misformation', p. 1040.

25 George C. Homans, 'Bringing Men Back In', in Alan Ryan, ed., *The Philosophy of Social Explanation* (London, 1973), p. 63.

26 See, e.g., the essays contained in ibid., and Alan R. White, ed., *The Philosophy of Action* (London, 1968); G. H. von Wright's *Explanation and Understanding* (London, 1971), as well as the contributions to May Brodbeck, ed., *Readings in the Philosophy of the Social Sciences* (London, 1968), pp. 738ff.

27 For a discussion of this controversy, see *inter alia* von Wright, *Explanation and Understanding*, which also contains a useful bibliography. Today the lines are generally drawn between the partisans of 'deductive–nomological' explanation, on the one hand, and 'rational' explanation, on the other.

28 See Alisdair MacIntyre, 'Antecedents of Action', in B. Williams and A. Montefiori, eds, *British Analytic Philosophy* (London, 1966), pp. 215f.; and T. F. Daveny, 'Intentions and Causes', *Analysis*, vol. 27 (1966), p. 23ff., who strongly advocate this position. In one form or another, this argument has been given by Stuart Hampshire, *Thought and Action* (London, 1959), Anthony Kenny, *Action, Emotion and Will* (London, 1963), and A. I. Melden, *Free Action* (London, 1961). It is also to be found in Peter Winch's famous *The Idea of Social Science and Its Relation to Philosophy* (London, 1958), and in R. S. Peters, *The Concept of Motivation* (London, 1958).

29 See MacIntyre, 'Antecedents', p. 215.

30 See Daveny, 'Intentions and Causes', pp. 23ff.

31 See Jens Henrik Olsen, 'Causation and the Explanatory Patterns of Human Action' (Copenhagen, mimeo, 1975), pp. 64ff. Like the first version, this one has been deeply influenced by Gilbert Ryle's classic *The Concept of Mind* (London, 1949); and it is also to be found in, and is defended by, Charles Taylor, 'The Explanation of Purposive Behaviour', in Robert Borger and Frank Cioffi, eds, *Explanation in the Behavioural Sciences* (London, 1970), pp. 49ff., and von Wright, *Explanation and Understanding*, passim.

32 A. J. Ayer, 'Man as a Subject for Science', in P. Laslett and W. G. Runciman, eds, *Philosophy, Politics and Society*, 3rd series (Oxford, 1969), p. 13. Also see Charles Taylor, *The Explanation of Behaviour* (London, 1964), and Taylor, 'The Explanation of Purposive Behaviour'.

33 See Peters, *The Concept of Motivation*.
34 See, e.g., A. R. Louch, *Explanation and Human Action* (Oxford, 1966), pp. 50ff.
35 This argument is taken from Olsen, *Causation*, pp. 162f. The argument itself is a variant of the logical connection argument, but should be distinguished from it in so far as it has peculiar methodological consequences of its own.
36 Martin Hollis, *Models of Man* (Cambridge, 1977), p. 114.
37 Quoted in Jon Elster, *Ulysses and the Sirens: Studies in Rationality and Irrationality* (Cambridge, 1979), p. 33.
38 See Donald Davidson, 'Actions, Reasons, and Causes', *The Journal of Philosophy*, vol. 60, no. 23 (1963), pp. 693ff.; and Olsen, *Causation*, pp. 64ff.
39 'Items which have such a partial noncontingent connection,' Oppenheim adds, 'may also be related causally ... Once the view that reasons cannot logically be causes of actions has been undermined, a strong presumption can be provided in favour of the ordinary view that such a causal connection actually exists.' Felix E. Oppenheim, 'The Language of Political Inquiry: Problems of Clarification', in Fred I. Greenstein and Nelson W. Polsby, eds, *Handbook of Political Science: Scope and Theory* (vol. 1) (Reading, Mass., 1975), p. 296. He also quotes here from an article by Keith S. Donnellan in the *Encyclopedia of Philospohy*, in which the latter makes the point that 'It is not enough merely to point out *some* logical connection between the concept of desire, belief, and feeling and that of action; the connection must be one which is clearly absent in undisputed cases of causal connections.'
40 See, e.g., G. E. M. Anscombe, *Intention* (Oxford, 1957), pp. 23f., and C. H. Whiteley, *Mind in Action* (London, 1973), p. 66.
41 D. Locke, 'Reasons, Wants, and Causes', *American Philosophical Quarterly*, vol. 10 (1974), p. 177.
42 Brian Fay and J. Donald Moon, 'What Would an Adequate Philosophy of Social Science Look Like?', *Philosophy of the Social Sciences*, vol. 7, no. 3 (1977) p. 215.
43 See Olsen, *Causation*, pp. 12ff., and the short discussion in Oppenheim, 'The Language of Political Inquiry', pp. 294ff., in which, *inter alia*, he notes the following: 'My reasons for acting in a certain way cannot, it seems, be *my reasons* unless *they* lead me also to act that way, that is, unless I act *because* of those reasons. The difference between a reason and a rationalization is precisely that the former is causally related to action but the latter is not.' Ibid., pp. 296f. Also note the discussion in Russell Keat and John Urry, *Social Theory as Science* (London, 1975), p. 154ff. Von Wright has argued against his previous view in this respect; or at least he has admitted that 'it is difficult to argue for it correctly.' See Von Wright, 'Determinism and the Study of Man', in Juha Manninen and Raimo Tuomela, eds, *Essays on Explanation and Understanding* (Dordrecht, 1976), pp. 421ff.
44 Ayer, 'Man as a Subject', p. 14.
45 Ayer, idem.
46 See Taylor, 'The Explanation of Purposive Behaviour', pp. 49ff. Cf. Borger's

arguments against Taylor's exclusivist teleological position in ibid., pp. 80ff.; also consult Olsen, *Causation*, pp. 107ff.

47 See Richard J. Bernstein, *The Restructuring of Social and Political Theory* (Oxford, 1976), pp. 65ff.

48 See Louch, *Explanation.*

49 See Olsen, *Causation*, pp. 37ff.

50 Paul A. Samuelson, 'Some Notions on Causality and Teleology in Economics', in D. Lerner, ed., *Cause and Effect* (New York, 1965), p. 99.

51 R. F. Atkinson, *Knowledge and Explanation in History* (London, 1978), p. 145.

52 MacIntyre, 'Antecedents', pp. 209ff. The third kind is thoroughly discussed in H. L. A. Hart and A. M. Honoré, *Causation and the Law* (London, 1959).

53 Quoted in Oppenheim, *Political Concepts: A Reconstruction* (Oxford, 1981), p. 192.

54 Ibid., pp. 192f.

55 Very pertinent here is the discussion on 'quasi-causality' and 'practical inferences' to be found in von Wright, *Explanation and Understanding*, pp. 34ff., and J. Donald Moon, 'The Logic of Political Inquiry: Synthesis of Opposing Perspectives', in Greenstein and Polsby, eds, *Handbook*, vol. 1, pp. 161ff. See also John Gunnell, 'Interpretation and the History of Political Theory: Apology and Epistemology', *American Political Science Review*, vol. 76 (June 1982), pp. 317ff., and Quentin Skinner's contribution to this topic, discussed in Gunnell's article.

56 Quentin Skinner, in ' "Social Meaning" and the Explanation of Social Action', in P. Gardiner, ed., *The Philosophy of History* (London, 1974), pp. 106ff., distinguishes between 'intentions', on the one hand, which are explained in terms of the illocutionary redescription of actions (a non-naturalist assignation of meaning), and motives, reasons, etc., on the other, leading him to a position between the 'naturalists' (like the more recent MacIntyre and Ayer) and the 'anti-naturalists' (Melden and Winch in particular). Runciman makes a similar distinction when he writes that 'I am constantly puzzled by questions of meaning as opposed to cause and of appositeness as opposed to validity, and my persistent awareness of descriptive discretion in the practice of sociological research is not to be appeased by mere dismissal out of hand.' W. G. Runciman, *A Critique of Max Weber's Philosophy of Social Science* (Cambridge, 1972), p. 98; and see pp. 79ff. Also see Bernstein, *The Restructuring*, pp. 69ff.

57 Alisdaire MacIntyre, 'The Idea of a Social Science', in Alan Ryan, ed., *The Philosophy of Social Explanation* (London, 1973), p. 26.

58 Fay and Moon, 'What Would an Adequate Philosophy?', p. 221.

59 Peter Winch, *The Idea of a Social Science and Its Relation to Philosophy* (London, 1958).

60 Kaplan, *The Conduct of Inquiry*, p. 358. Also consult pp. 323ff., 358ff. for further elaborations on these distinctions.

61 Kalleberg, 'Concept Formation', p. 32.

62 Kaplan, *The Conduct of Inquiry*, p. 35. Charles Taylor has written:

> It is not just that people in our society all or mostly have a given set of ideas in their heads and subscribe to a given set of goals. The meanings and norms implicit in these practices are not just in the minds of the actors but are out there in the practices themselves, practices which cannot be conceived as a set of individual actions, but essentially modes of social relation, of mutual action.
>
> (Taylor, 'Interpretation and the Sciences of Man',
> *Review of Metaphysics*, vol. 25 [1971], p. 27)

63 For a discussion of the philosophical implications of 'description', see W. G. Runciman, 'Describing', *Mind*, vol. 81 (1975), pp. 372ff.

64 Ernest Nagel, *The Structure of Science* (New York, 1961), pp. 475, 484f. Also see Richard S. Rudner, *Philosophy of Social Science* (Englewood Cliffs, NJ, 1966), p. 72.

65 Ibid., p. 83. For an incisive discussion of the non-psychological nature of *Verstehen* (and for arguments against Rudner's standpoint), see Moon, 'The Logic of Political Inquiry', pp. 177ff. For a short introduction to the early facets of the 'hermeneutical' method in German sociology, see my *The Concept of Ideology and Political Analysis* (Westport, Conn., 1981), pp. 170ff.

66 Gunnell, 'Social Science and Political Reality', p. 177. On this matter Moon says:

> Is interpretation a necessary condition of social inquiry, or is it just one *possible* form such inquiry can take? There is no obvious reply to this question. But we can note that what most political scientists are interested in explaining is what people *do* in *political* contexts. And both their 'doings' and the concept of 'political' are part of the field of meanings which it is the task of a hermeneutical science to explicate. The natural scientist may be free to shape his concepts in any way he sees fit, but the social scientist's subject matter is the social relations and the ideas constituting those relations, which are part of our experience as social actors. If he ignores those ideas, he is, so to speak, no longer studying the same object. If we are interested in legislative behaviour, for example, we must take the criteria of what is to count as legislative behaviour from the self-understandings of the actors involved. It is the conventions of the political system that determine what a 'legislature' is, who is a member of it, and which of a member's actions are done in his 'official' capacity and which are not.
>
> (Moon, 'The Logic of Political Inquiry', p. 181)

Also see W. G. Runciman, 'Ideology and Social Science', in Robert Benewick, R. N. Berki and Bhikhu Parekh, eds, *Knowledge and Beliefs in Politics* (London, 1973), pp. 13ff.

67 As quoted in Gunnell, 'Interpretation', p. 177. A more elaborate definition is provided by Weber as follows:

> Sociology is a science which attempts the interpretative understanding of social action in order thereby to arrive at a causal explanation of its course and effects. In 'action' is included all human behaviour when and in so far as the acting individual attaches a subjective meaning to it ... Action is social in so far as, by virtue of the subjective meaning attached to it by the acting individual (or individuals), it takes account of the behaviour of others and is thereby oriented in its course.
>
> (Max Weber, *The Theory of Social and Economic Organization* [New York, 1964], p. 88)

For a deeper penetration into the debate regarding *Verstehen*, see, *inter alia*: ibid., pp. 175ff.; Kalleberg, 'Concept Formation', pp. 28ff.; T. Abel, 'The Operation Called *Verstehen*', *American Journal of Sociology*, vol. 54 (1948), pp. 211ff.; Murray L. Wax, 'On Misunderstanding *Verstehen*: A Reply to Abel', *Sociology and Social Research*, vol. 51 (1966–7), pp. 323ff.; Lee Braude, '*Die Verstehende Soziologie*: A New Look at an Old Problem', *Sociology and Social Research*, vol. 50 (1965–66); and Peter A. Munch, 'Empirical Science and Max Weber's *Verstehende Soziologie*', *American Sociological Review*, vol. 22 (1957), pp. 26ff.

68 James N. Rosenau, *The Adaptation of National Societies: A Theory of Political Systems Behaviour and Transformation* (New York, 1970), pp. 4f. For other articles in which he has explained his conceptualization of 'adaptation', see especially his 'Compatibility, Consensus, and the Emerging Political Science of Adaptation', *American Political Science Review*, vol. 61 (1967), pp. 983ff., and 'Foreign Policy as Adaptive Behaviour', *Comparative Politics*, vol. 2 (1970), pp. 365ff. See also his 'Comparing Foreign Policies: Why, What, How', in James N. Rosenau, ed., *Comparing Foreign Policies* (New York, 1974), pp. 3ff. His most recent views on the notion of adaptation are to be found in 'A Pretheory Revisited: World Politics in an Era of Cascading Interdependence', *International Studies Quarterly*, vol. 28, no. 3 (September 1984), pp. 245ff.

69 See my criticisms of Mannheim on this score in Carlsnaes, *The Concept of Ideology*, pp. 200ff.

70 Charles Reynolds, *Theory and Explanation in International Politics* (London, 1973), p. 56.

71 It is of this fallacy that Marion Levy has written: 'In science this leads to errors; in morality it leads to self-pity; in governance it leads to irresponsibility.' Marion J. Levy, ' "Does It Matter If He's Naked?" Bawled the Child', in Klaus Knorr and James N. Rosenau, eds, *Contending Approaches to International Relations* (Princeton, NJ, 1969), p. 99.

72 For an excellent if old – though not dated – discussion of the problems involved in the method of imputation, see Arthur Child, 'The Problem of

Imputation in the Sociology of Knowledge', *Ethics*, vol. 51 (1940–1), pp. 202ff.

73 Michael K. O'Leary, 'Foreign Policy and Bureaucratic Adaptation', in Rosenau, ed., *Comparing Foreign Policies*, p. 56. But I think that he is quite right when he adds:

> There is, of course, an obvious alternative perspective. It is that foreign policy is most profitably viewed as being productive of private benefits for various parts of the national society. What varies most significantly as a consequence of foreign policy is not adaptation as a society-wide phenomenon, but rather the extent to which individual groups and institutions within a society are able to persist, thrive, or otherwise adapt.
>
> (Ibid., p. 57)

For a discussion and critique of Rosenau's 'adaptive' model from a somewhat different point of view, see Steve Smith, *Foreign Policy Adaptation* (Farnborough, 1981), as well as his summary of this discussion in Steve Smith, 'Rosenau's Adaptive Behaviour Approach – A Critique', *Review of International Studies*, vol. 7 (1981), pp. 107–26. Also see the same author's 'Rosenau's Contribution', *Review of International Studies*, vol. 9 (1983), pp. 137–46, and 'Theories of Foreign Policy: An Historical Overview', *Review of International Studies*, vol. 12 (1986), pp. 13–29.

74 Quoted in Jon Elster, *Sour Grapes: Subversion of Rationality* (Cambridge, 1983), p. 142.

75 Émile Durkheim, 'Social Facts', in Brodbeck, ed., *Readings*, pp. 254, 248, respectively. For an exhaustive and chronological bibliography of this great debate, see Steven Lukes, 'Methodological Individualism Reconsidered', in Ryan, ed., *The Philosophy of a Social Science*, pp. 120f., fn. 12. For some illuminating flashbacks – again in chronological order – see the series of quotations in I. C. Jarvie, *Concepts and Society* (London, 1972), pp. 173ff.

76 For an explication of the differences between, respectively, ontological holism and individualism, and methodological holism and individualism, see Jarvie, *Concepts*, pp. 155ff.; the quote is from Runciman, *A Critique*, p. 30.

77 See Joachim Israel's article, 'The Principle of Methodological Individualism and Marxian Epistemology', *Acta Sociologica*, vol. 14 (1971), pp. 149f.; Runciman, *A Critique*, p. 11; Karl R. Popper, *The Poverty of Historicism* (New York, 1961), pp. 152ff. and *The Open Society and Its Enemies*, vol. 2 (London, 1962), pp. 90ff. Also see May Brodbeck's discussion in Brodbeck, ed., *Readings*, pp. 286ff.

78 See Israel, 'The Principle'.

79 Runciman, *A Critique*, pp. 25f. Also see Weber's definition in note 67 above.

80 Ernest Gellner, *Cause and Meaning in the Social Sciences* (London, 1973), p. 14.

81 Idem.

82 Oppenheim, 'The Language of Political Inquiry', p. 299.

83 Jarvie, *Concepts*, p. 156.

84 J. O. Wisdom, 'Situational Individualism and the Emergent Group Properties', in Borger and Cioffi, eds, *Explanation*, pp. 271ff. It is because of the irreducible situational factor that Wisdom speaks of 'situational individualism', a viewpoint which he finds compatible with Popper's.

85 This is in fact Jarvie's definition of methodological individualism; see Jarvie, *Concepts*, p. 32.

86 Joseph Agassi's views on this issue are to be found in his 'Methodological Individualism', *British Journal of Sociology*, vol. 11 (1960), pp. 24ff., and are referred to in Jarvie, *Concepts*, pp. 155ff. Lukes's unfortunate definition is to be found in Lukes, 'Methodological Individualism' p. 122, where he writes: 'Methodological individualism, therefore, is a prescription for explanation, asserting that no purported explanations of social (or individual) phenomena are to count as explanations, or (in Watkins's version) as rock-bottom explanations, unless they are couched *wholly* in terms of facts about individuals.' My emphasis.

87 Runciman, *A Critique*, p. 30.

88 See, e.g., Christopher Peacocke, *Holistic Explanation: Action, Space, Interpretation* (London, 1979), and 'Holistic Explanation: An Outline of a Theory', in Ross Harrison, ed., *Rational Action: Studies in Philosophy and Social Science* (London, 1979), pp. 61ff.

89 I should add, however, that the former dangers of ontological individualism – so prevalent in older history books – seem to be almost completely absent. However, some perhaps still tend to take de Gaulle too literally at his word on those occasions when he sought to give the impression that for all ontologically essential purposes he and France could be conflated.

90 See, e.g., Rosenau, *The Adaptation*, pp. 4f.

91 In this connection see Steinbruner, *The Cybernetic Theory*, pp. 36ff.

92 Rosenau, *The Adaptation*, p. 2.

93 Rosenau, 'Compatibility', p. 986.

94 Kaplan, *The Conduct of Inquiry*, p. 81. McGowan writes in an essay:

> Rosenau never defines national societies, and since this concept is time and place specific, we can substitute the more general term, actor, in its place. For Rosenau, the actors that produce the attitudes and activities of interest can be identified because they are characterized by having four 'essential structures'. These actor structures are 'essential' to the actor because they are 'preconditions for their survival'. The essential structures are defined behaviourally as 'interaction patterns' of individuals and groups within the actor.
>
> (Patrick J. McGowan, 'Problems in the Construction of Positive Foreign Policy Theory', in Rosenau, ed., *Comparing Foreign Policies*, pp. 27f)

In this redescription we have, once again, the pathetic fallacy: an 'actor', which is an analytical construct, is defined as 'producing' 'attitudes' and 'activities'; and furthermore, *within* this 'actor' we have 'individuals' and 'groups' as well, which leads us to wonder if these too are 'produced' by the 'actor'. In this connection, a further criticism, made by Stuart J. Thorson, is relevant. Discussing the Rosenau/McGowan conceptualization of 'adaptation', he writes:

> In the preceding discussion 'adaptive' has been used in two ways. First, mention was made of an adaptive political system. Second, certain foreign policy behaviours were said to be adaptive or maladaptive. Although at first glance these uses may appear the same, they are not. An adaptive system may at times behave maladaptively ... For to require that the foreign policies of a nation always be adaptive if the nation is to continue to exist (as McGowan seems to require), is very different than the simple assertion that foreign policy behaviours result from adaptive systems.
>
> (Stuart J. Thorson, 'National Politic Adaptation', in ibid., pp. 74f.)

My point of view is, of course, that only individual actions are adaptive or maladaptive, and that the determination of these consequences in each case rests on the particular goals towards which purposive behaviour is directed.

95 Herbert C. Kelman, 'The Role of the Individual in International Relations: Some Conceptual and Methodological Considerations', *Journal of International Affairs*, vol. 24 (1970), pp. 3f.

96 See Reinhard Bendix, *Max Weber: An Intellectual Portrait* (Garden City, NJ, 1962), p. 476. Thus, e.g., Weber, in adopting Tönnies's famous distinction between *Gesellschaft* and *Gemeinschaft*, preferred to use, respectively, the terms *Vergesellschaftung* and *Vergemeinschaftung*. These are active nouns and are unfortunately not translatable into English.

97 Sprout, *The Ecological Perspective*, p. 11. Also see Kelman, 'The Role of the Individual', pp. 1ff. For a handy collection of essays on this topic, see John O'Neill, ed., *Modes of Individualism and Collectivism* (London, 1973).

98 See Dina A. Zinnes, 'Some Evidence Relevant to the Man–Milieu Hypothesis', in Rosenau, Davis and East, eds, *The Analysis*, pp. 209ff.

99 See F. A. von Hayek, *Studies in Philosophy, Politics and Economics* (London, 1967), p. 100 (especially fn. 12); Popper, *The Poverty*, p. 65, *The Open Society*, especially pp. 93ff. and fn. 11 on pp. 323f., and *Objective Knowledge* (London, 1972), pp. 106ff., 160, fn. 9. In his *Conjectures and Refutations: The Growth of Scientific Knowledge* (London, 1972), p. 124, Popper notes:

> In all social situations we have individuals who do things; who want things; who have certain aims. In so far as they act in the way in which they want to act, and realize the aims which they intend to realize, no problem arises for the social sciences (except the problem whether their wants and aims can perhaps be socially explained, for example by

certain traditions). The characteristic problems of the social sciences arise only out of our wish to know the *unintended consequences*, and more especially the *unwanted consequences* which may arise if we do certain things. We wish to foresee not only the direct consequences but also these unwanted or indirect consequences.

Also see Wisdom's discussion in Wisdom, 'Situational Individualism', pp. 275ff.

100 Anthony Giddens, *Central Problems in Social Theory* (London, 1979), p. 7.
101 Popper, *Conjectures and Refutations*, pp. 124f.
102 Fay and Moon, 'What Would an Adequate Philosophy?', p. 223.
103 For a discussion of Alfred Schutz's 'typifications', and of phenomenology in general, see Bernstein, *The Restructuring*, pp. 115f.
104 Fay and Moon, 'What Would an Adequate Philosophy?' p. 223.
105 Ibid., pp. 223f.
106 John Elster, 'Anomalies of Rationality: Some Unresolved Problems in the Theory of Rational Behaviour', in Louis Levy-Garboua, *Sociological Economics* (London, 1979), p. 81.
107 Fay and Moon, 'What Would an Adequate Philosophy?', pp. 220f.
108 Ibid., p. 220.
109 For a discussion of the distinction between 'notational' and 'substantive' uses of a term, see Kaplan, *The Conduct of Inquiry*, pp. 49f.
110 Stanley Hoffmann, *Gulliver's Troubles: Or the Setting of American Foreign Policy* (New York, 1968), p. 208.
111 K. J. Holsti, *International Politics*, p. 20.
112 Hermann, 'Policy Classification', p. 70.
113 James N. Rosenau, 'Moral Fervor, Systemic Analysis, and Scientific Consciousness', in Austin Ranney, ed., *Political Science and Public Policy* (Chicago, 1968), p. 215.
114 Richard Rose, 'Comparing Public Policy – An Overview', *European Journal of Political Research*, vol. 1 (April 1973), p. 73.
115 George D. Greenburg, Jeffrey A. Miller, Lawrence B. Mohr, and Bruce C. Vladeck, 'Developing Public Policy Theory: Perspectives from Empirical Research', *American Political Science Review*, vol. 71 (December 1977), p. 1533.
116 Morse, 'Defining Foreign Policy', pp. 13ff. Within the first class Morse has placed the following definitions: those defined in terms of, respectively, (1) political goals, especially the 'national interest', (2) principles of action, (3) a set of orientations, (4) ideology, and (5) foreign policy acts. Under the second rubric he places those definitions defined in terms of, respectively, (1) institutional machinery, (2) outputs or decisions, and (3) motives of men. Finally, policy effects are defined in terms of (1) role or (2) process of adjustment.
117 Ibid., p. 16. See also Donna H. Kerr, 'The Logic of "Policy" and Successful Policies', *Policy Sciences*, vol. 7 (September 1976), pp. 351ff.
118 Hermann, 'Policy Classification', p. 59.
119 Morse, 'Defining Foreign Policy', p. 40.

120   Michael Brecher, *Decisions in Israel's Foreign Policy* (London, 1974), pp. 1ff.
121   McGowan, 'The Unit-of-Analysis Problem', pp. 10ff.
122   Brecher, *Decisions*, pp. 1f. Brecher rejects the classification of decisions under actions for the following reason, which he gives as a quotation from Joseph Frankel:

> an important distinction between decisions and actions lies in their spheres of operation: decisions take place in the decision-maker's mind whereas actions take place in his environment. By decision-making here is understood an act of determining in one's mind a course of action, following a more or less deliberate consideration of alternatives, and by decision is understood that which is thus determined. By action is understood a thing done, a deed, or the process of acting or doing.

It is also for this reason that he rejects the explication contained in Parsons and Shils, *Toward a General Theory*, pp. 4ff. The Frankel quote is to be found in Michael Brecher, *The Foreign Policy System of Israel* (New Haven, Conn., 1972), pp. 617f.
123   Brecher, *Decisions*, pp. 1f.
124   Herman M. Weil writes:

> The few analyses of foreign governments suggests that one of the greatest difficulties in studying foreign policy decision-making is acquiring some information about the behaviour of key actors. Unless the decision maker is willing to make recollections about sensitive national security decisions public, these efforts are stymied. The problem [he adds, perhaps a bit naïvely] has not stifled analyses of U.S. decisions in part because American ideology is consistent with public disclosure of the perceptions, motivations, and decisions of key actors.
> (Herman M. Weil, 'Can Bureaucracies Be Rational Actors? Foreign Policy Decision-Making in North Vietnam', *International Studies Quarterly*, vol. 19 [1975], pp. 433ff.)

125   Ole R. Holsti, 'Foreign Policy Formation Viewed Cognitively', in Robert Axelrod, ed., *Structure of Decision* (Princeton, NJ, 1976), p. 35.
126   McGowan, 'The Unit-of-Analysis Problem', p. 11. Another aspect of this problem of reliability is of relevance here. Weil thus writes:

> After a decision has been made and implemented, the decision maker usually has much more information about his options than he did when the decision was required. It is at least possible, then, that recollection of the decision process is coloured by the additional information so that its use as a source data for analysis will result in an unrealistic portrayal of the problems confronted when the decision was required.
> (Weil, 'Can Bureaucracies?', p. 435)

127 Quoted in William Wallace, *The Foreign Policy Process in Britain* (London, 1975), p. viii.
128 Morse, 'Defining Foreign Policy', pp. 53ff.
129 Idem.
130 See Robert K. Merton, *On Theoretical Sociology* (New York, 1967), pp. 115ff.
131 See Marion J. Levy, Jr, *The Structure of Society* (Princeton, NJ, 1952), p. 87.
132 Steinbruner, *The Cybernetic Theory*, p. 16.
133 Morse, 'Defining Foreign Policy', p. 57.
134 A related argument has been made with reference to the meaning of 'power', defined in terms of one actor's dependence on another actor. David Baldwin thus writes that the 'dependence of B on A may or may not be the result of A's preferences. Indeed, A may be rather unhappy with the situation. If some states find themselves dependent in some respects on other states, it does not follow that this situation is attributable to the preferences of the dominant states.' David A. Baldwin, 'Interdependence and Power: A Conceptual Analysis', *International Organization*, vol. 34 (Autumn 1980), p. 499.
135 Jack A. Nagel, *The Descriptive Analysis of Power* (New Haven, Conn. 1975), p. 16.
136 Baldwin, 'Interdependence and Power', p. 499.
137 See Arthur Child, 'The Problem of Imputation in the Sociology of Knowledge', *Ethics*, vol. 51 (1940–1), and 'The Problem of Imputation Resolved', *Ethics*, vol. 54 (1943–4), passim. See also my own discussion in Carlsnaes, *The Concept of Ideology*, pp. 197ff.
138 Charles W. Kegley, 'Introduction: The Generation and Use of Events Data', in Charles W. Kegley, Gregory A. Raymond, Robert M. Good and Richard A. Skinner, eds, *International Events and the Comparative Analysis of Foreign Policy* (Columbia, SC, 1975), pp. 92f.
139 Ibid., p. 97.
140 Following immediately upon the above quotation, Kegley writes: 'events are empirical referents for foreign policy actions that are *official* and *governmental*, that is, external behaviour which is a direct result of governmental action.' Idem. I of course agree with the statement as it stands, although I would distinguish between 'events' and 'governmental action' as an operational unit of observation, as distinguished from a theoretical (or formal) definition of our unit of analysis. Edward E. Azar, writing in the same collection of essays, appears to have recognized this distinction. 'Foreign policy,' he thus notes, 'is a sequential, constantly unfolding set of actions. Its purposes relate to its sources (the process by which it is determined), which in turn relate to the forms through which it manifests itself. Operationally, we assume that the foreign policy of a nation manifests itself as that nation's overt external actions, reactions, and interactions (events).' Azar, 'Behavioural Forecasts and Policy-Making: An Events Data Approach', in Kegley et al., p. 222.

141 See Samuel Beer and Adam Ulam, eds, *Patterns of Government: The Major Political Systems of Europe* (2nd edn: New York, 1967), pp. 60f.

142 See James N. Rosenau, 'Pre-Theories and Theories of Foreign Policy', in James N. Rosenau, ed., *The Scientific Study of Foreign Policy* (London, 1980), pp. 115ff.; William Zimmermann, 'Issue Area and Foreign Policy Process: A Research Note in Search of a General Theory', *American Political Science Review*, vol. 67 (December 1973), pp. 120ff.; and William C. Potter, 'Issue Area and Foreign Policy Analysis', *International Organization*, vol. 34 (Summer 1980), pp. 405ff.

143 Sartori, 'Concept Misformation', pp. 1034ff.

144 See Rupert Emerson, *From Empire to Nation* (Cambridge, Mass., 1960), passim, for a discussion of the concept of nationalism, as well as my essay 'A Conceptual Analysis of African Nationalism', in C. A. Hessler, ed., *Idéer och ideologier* (Stockholm, 1969), pp. 294ff., and the references contained in it. Also consult Oran Young, 'The Actors in World Politics', in Rosenau et al., eds, *The Analysis* pp. 125ff.; and, for a discussion of the differences between a 'state' and a 'nation', J. P. Nettl, 'The State as a Conceptual Variable', *World Politics*, vol. 10 (July 1968), pp. 559ff.

145 Sartori, 'Concept Misformation', p. 1034.

146 Ibid., p. 1053. Arend Lijphart, in his article on 'Comparative Politics and Comparative Method', *American Political Science Review*, vol. 65 (September 1971), pp. 682ff., argues for the importance of 'controlled variables' in the comparative study of politics, i.e., variables that can be held constant. As I understand him (and I think that he is correct in this), comparability increases in direct proportion (loosely speaking) to the number of variables which can be held constant. Conceptual stretching, while aiming at such control of variables, in fact involves a process of decreasing the number of *empirically viable* constants and substituting for them constants of such generality that they have little empirical relevance. This, I believe, is the point that Sartori is making.

147 See Sartori, 'Concept Misformation', p. 1050. To this list can be added such typically stretched terms as 'nationalism' and 'ideology'.

148 Young, 'The Actors', p. 126. For a discussion of the principle of sovereignty, see F. H. Hinsley, *Sovereignty* (New York, 1966), and of territoriality, John Herz, *International Politics in the Atomic Age* (New York, 1959), and his 'Rise and Demise of the Territorial States', *World Politics*, vol. 9 (1957), pp. 437ff. For the latter's revised views, see his 'The Territorial State Revisted: Reflections on the Future of the Nation–State', in Rosenau, ed., *International Politics*, pp. 76ff. In the same reader, also note Fred W. Riggs, 'The Nation–State and Other Actors', pp. 90ff.

149 This dichotomy occurs in an article by Richard N. Rosecrance and Arthur Stein, entitled 'Interdependence: Myth or Reality?', *World Politics*, vol. 26 (October 1973), pp. 1ff.

150 See, e.g., ibid., p. 12.

151 See my paper, 'Interdependence and Foreign Policy Actions', delivered at the European Consortium for Political Research workshops in Grenoble, April 1978.

152 Edward Morse, 'The Politics of Interdependence', *International Organization*, vol. 23, no. 2 (Spring 1969), pp. 320f.; also see his 'Crisis Diplomacy, Interdependence, and the Politics of International Economic Relations', *World Politics*, vol. 24 (supplement) (Spring 1972), pp. 123ff. and 'Interdependence in World Affairs', N. Rosenau, Kenneth W. Thompson and Gavin Boyd, eds, *World Politics: An Introduction* (New York, 1976), pp. 660ff., as well as the references in this last book.

153 See Robert O. Keohane and Joseph S. Nye, Jr, *Power and Interdependence: World Politics in Transition* (Boston, Mass., 1977).

154 In addition to the above, see Richard N. Cooper's *The Economics of Interdependence* (New York, 1968), pp. 3ff. and 'Economic Interdependence and Foreign Policy in the Seventies', *World Politics*, vol. 24, no. 2 (January 1972), pp. 159ff. For arguments against the notion of increased interdependence, see in particular Kenneth N. Waltz, 'The Myth of National Interdependence', in Charles P. Kindleberger, ed., *The International Corporation* (Cambridge, Mass., 1970), pp. 205ff.

155 Wolfram F. Hanrieder, 'Compatibility and Consensus: A Proposal for the Conceptual Linkage of External and Internal Dimensions of Foreign Policy', *American Political Science Review*, vol. 61 (1967), p. 974.

156 See Edward L. Morse, *Modernization and the Transformation of International Relations* (New York, 1976), and the references contained in it.

157 Andrew M. Scott, 'The Logic of International Interaction', *International Studies Quarterly*, vol. 21 (September 1977), pp. 443f.; and Morse, *Modernization*, pp. 87, 81.

CHAPTER 3   COMPARATIVE ANALYSIS AND FOREIGN POLICY EXPLANATIONS

1 J. Donald Moon, 'The Logic of Political Inquiry: A Synthesis of Opposed Perspectives', in Fred I. Greenstein and Nelson W. Polsby, eds, *Handbook of Political Science: Scope and Theory* (vol. 1) (Reading, Mass., 1975), p. 182.

2 Robert Boardman, 'Comparative Method and Foreign Policy', in *The Year Book of World Affairs*, vol. 27 (1973), p. 382.

3 David E. Apter, 'Comparative Studies: A Review with Some Projections', in Ivan Vallier, ed., *Comparative Methods in Sociology* (Berkeley, Calif., 1971), p. 3.

4 Harry Eckstein, 'A Perspective on Comparative Politics, Past and Present', in Harry Eckstein and David E. Apter, eds, *Comparative Politics: A Reader* (New York, 1963), p. 29.

5 Guy E. Swanson, 'Frameworks for Comparative Research: Structural Anthropology and the Theory of Action', in Vallier, ed., *Comparative Methods*, p. 141.

6 Ibid., p. 145.

7 Oscar Lewis, 'Comparisons in Cultural Anthropology', in F. W. Moore, ed., *Readings in Cross-Cultural Methodology* (New Haven, Conn., 1961), p. 55; W. J. M. Mackenzie, *Politics and Social Science* (Harmondsworth, 1967), pp. 310f.

8 See R. M. Marsh, *Comparative Sociology* (New York, 1967), especially chapter 1.

9 D. P. Warwick and S. Osherson, 'Comparative Analysis in the Social Sciences', in D. P. Warwick and S. Osherson, eds, *Comparative Research Notes* (Englewood Cliffs, NJ, 1973), pp. 6f.

10 Quoted in Boardman, 'Comparative Method', p. 373.

11 Patrick McGowan, 'Meaningful Comparisons in the Study of Foreign Policy: A Methodological Discussion of Objectives, Techniques and Research Designs', in Charles W. Kegley, Gregory A. Raymond, Robert M. Good and Richard A. Skinner, eds, *International Events and the Comparative Analysis of Foreign Policy* (Columbia, SC, 1975), p. 53.

12 Morris Zelditch, 'Intelligible Comparisons', in Vallier, ed., *Comparative Methods*, p. 270.

13 Evert Vedung, 'The Comparative Method and Its Neighbours', in Brian Barry, ed., *Power and Political Theory: Some European Perspectives* (London, 1976), p. 199.

14 Zuleika Dobson is, of course, the Oxonian heroine of Max Beerbohm's preposterous love story bearing her name, published in 1911. Reputedly, she was so enravishingly beautiful that even the statues of Broad Street perspired when she happened to pass them. The undergraduates went one step further: their infatuation with her was so utter that they drowned themselves *en masse* in the Thames at the conclusion of the crew races.

15 Zelditch, 'Intelligible Comparisons', pp. 269f.

16 Ibid., pp. 270f., 273.

17 Warwick and Osherson, 'Comparative Analysis', p. 8.

18 Zelditch, 'Intelligible Comparisons', pp 270f. My emphasis.

19 Harry Eckstein, 'Case Study and Theory in Political Science', in Fred I. Greenstein and Nelson W. Polsby, *Handbook of Political Science: Strategies of Inquiry* (vol. 7) (Reading, Mass., 1975), p. 85.

20 Arthur L. Kalleberg, 'The Logic of Comparison', *World Politics*, vol. 19 (July 1966), p. 81. My emphasis.

21 See, e.g., Vedung, 'The Comparative Method', pp. 210ff., whose misinterpretation of Kalleberg's logic in the above respect leads him to posit a definition which, precisely because it ignores the requirement of a common dimension in terms of which comparisons can be made, is fundamentally flawed.

22 Charles W. Kegley, *The Comparative Study of Foreign Policy: Paradigm Lost?* (Columbia, SC, 1980), p. 17.

23 Ibid., p. 20.

24 Eckstein, 'Case Study', p. 80.

25   Idem.
26   Arend Lijphart, 'Comparative Politics and the Comparative Method', *American Political Science Review*, vol. 65 (September 1971), p. 691.
27   Neil J. Smelser, 'The Methodology of Comparative Analysis', in Warwick and Osherson, *Comparative Resarch Notes*, p. 57.
28   Lijphart, 'Comparative Politics', pp. 691ff.
29   Ibid., p. 693.
30   Eckstein, 'Case Study', pp. 92f.
31   Ibid., p. 84.
32   Giovanni Sartori, 'Concept Misformation in Comparative Politics', *American Political Science Review*, vol. 64 (1970), p. 1042.
33   J. David Singer, 'The Level-of-Analysis Problem in International Relations', *World Politics*, vol. 14 (1961), p. 77.
34   Oran Young, *A Systemic Approach to International Politics* (Princeton, NJ, 1968), p. 11.
35   Ibid., p. 18.
36   Moon, 'The Logic of Political Inquiry', p. 183.
37   Martin Hollis, *Models of Man* (Cambridge, 1977), p. 140.
38   See, e.g., Amartya Sen, *Choice, Welfare and Measurement* (Oxford, 1982), passim.
39   Martin Seliger, *Ideology and Politics* (London, 1976), pp. 171ff.
40   G. H. von Wright, *Explanation and Understanding* (London, 1971), p. 99.
41   Alexander L. George, *Presidential Decisionmaking in Foreign Policy: The Effective Use of Information and Advice* (Boulder, Colo., 1980), p. 221.
42   Donald Davidson, *Essays on Actions and Events* (Oxford, 1980), pp. 3f.
43   Quoted by Jon Elster in his essay 'Anomalies of Rationality: Some Unresolved Problems in the Theory of Rational Behaviour', in Louis Lévy-Garboua, ed., *Sociological Economics* (London, 1979), p. 81.
44   See von Wright, *Explanation and Understanding*, passim, and the essays in Juha Manninen and Raimo Tuomela, eds, *Essays on Explanation and Understanding* (Dordrecht, 1976).
45   John D. Steinbruner, *The Cybernetic Theory of Decision* (Princeton, NJ, 1974), p. 45.
46   Ibid., p. 108.
47   George, *Presidential Decisionmaking*, p. 28.
48   Ibid., p. 29.
49   I. M. Destler, *Presidents, Bureaucrats, and Foreign Policy: The Politics of Organizational Reform* (Princeton, NJ, 1972), p. 56.
50   See ibid., pp. 70f.
51   Alexander L. George and Robert O. Keohane, 'The Concept of National Interests: Uses and Limitations', in George, *Presidential Decisionmaking*, p. 221. My emphasis.
52   Idem.
53   Charles E. Lindblom, *Politics and Markets: The World's Political—Economic Systems* (New York, 1977), p. 52.

54 Robert K. Merton, *Social Theory and Social Structure* (New York, 1957), pp. 421f.

55 Anatol Rapoport, 'Various Meanings of "Rational Political Decisions" ', in Leif Lewin and Evert Vedung, eds, *Politics as Rational Action: Essays in Public Choice and Policy Analysis* (Dordrecht, 1980), p. 59.

56 Donald R. Kinder and Janet A. Weiss, 'In Lieu of Rationality: Psychological Perspectives on Foreign Policy Decision-Making', *Journal of Conflict Resolution*, vol. 22 (December 1978), p. 708.

57 See, *inter alia*, H. A. Simon, *Administrative Behaviour* (New York, 1946), and his 'Theories of Decision Making in Economics and Behavioural Science', *American Economic Review*, vol. 49 (1959), pp. 253–83; David Braybrooke and Charles E. Lindblom, *A Strategy of Decision* (New York, 1963); R. Cyert and J. March, *A Behavioural Theory of the Firm* (Englewood Cliffs, NJ, 1963); George T. Allison, *Essence of Decision* (Boston, Mass., 1971); Kinder and Weiss, 'In Lieu of Rationality', pp. 707–34; and Elster, 'Anomalies of Rationality', pp. 65–94.

58 Steinbruner, *The Cybernetic Theory*, p. 45.

59 Kinder and Weiss, 'In Lieu of Rationality', p. 708.

60 Ibid., p. 720.

61 See, e.g., G. Matthew Bonham and Michael Shapiro, eds, *Thought and Action in Foreign Policy* (Basel, 1977).

62 Kinder and Weiss, 'In Lieu of Rationality', p. 320.

63 George, *Presidential Decisionmaking*, pp. 71f.

64 Robert Jervis, *Perception and Misperception in International Politics* (Princeton, NJ, 1976).

65 Kinder and Weiss, 'In Lieu of Rationality', pp. 718f.

66 Ibid., p. 723.

67 Quoted in ibid., p. 711.

68 Arthur A. Stein, 'When Misperception Matters', *World Politics*, vol. 34, no. 4 (July 1982), pp. 505–26.

69 George, *Presidential Decisionmaking*, p. 62.

70 Ibid., p. 65.

71 See, e.g., Ole R. Holsti, 'The "Operational Code" Approach to the Study of Political Leaders: John Foster Dulles's Philosophical and Instrumental Beliefs', *Canadian Journal of Political Science*, vol. 3 (1970), pp. 123–57.

72 George, *Presidential Decisionmaking*, p. 56.

73 Ibid., pp. 58ff.

74 J. Wilkenfeld, Gerald W. Hopple, Paul J. Rossa and Stephen J. Andrioli, *Foreign Policy Behaviour: The Inter-State Behaviour Analysis Model* (Beverly Hills, Calif., 1980), p. 205.

75 George, *Presidential Decisionmaking*, p. 45.

76 For an example of the 'motivational approach' to foreign policy analysis, see Stephen G. Walker and Lawrence S. Falkowski, 'The Operational Codes of US Presidents and Secretaries of State: Motivational Foundations and

Behavioral Consequences', paper presented to the 1982 annual meeting of the International Society for Political Psychology, Washington, DC, June 1982.

77 Kinder and Weiss, 'In Lieu of Rationality', pp. 732, 733.
78 Ibid., p. 728.
79 Harold and Margaret Sprout, *The Ecological Perspective in Human Affairs* (Princeton, NJ, 1965), p. 11.
80 Elster, 'Anomalies of Rationality', p. 65.
81 Ibid., p. 66.
82 In this connection, see Hyam Gold, 'Foreign Policy Decision-Making and the Environment: The Claims of Snyder, Brecher, and the Sprouts', *International Studies Quarterly*, vol. 22, no. 4 (December 1978), pp. 569–86.
83 On the structural characteristics of the market concept in the study of domestic and international politics, see Kenneth N. Waltz, *Theory of International Politics* (Reading, Mass., 1979).
84 Quoted in ibid., p. 80.
85 Ibid., p. 8. My emphasis.
86 See Anthony Giddens's discussion of praxis *qua* social practices in his *Central Problems in Social Theory* (London, 1979), pp. 1ff.
87 William I. Bacchus, *Foreign Policy and the Bureaucratic Process: The State Department's Country Director System* (Princeton, NJ, 1974), p. 15.
88 Steinbruner, *The Cybernetic Theory*, p. 140.
89 Bacchus, *Foreign Policy*, p. 38.
90 George, *Presidential Decisionmaking*, p. 109.
91 Destler, *Presidents*, p. 64.
92 Allison, *Essence*, pp. 162f.
93 Quoted in Destler, *Presidents*, p. 64.
94 Ibid., p. 65.
95 Allison, *Essence*, pp. 67f.
96 See references in note 57 above, but also, e.g., J. P. Olsen and J. G. March, *Ambiguity and Choice in Organizations* (Bergen, 1979).
97 Allison, *Essence*, pp. 78ff.
98 See whole of chapter 3 in ibid., pp. 67ff.
99 Destler, *Presidents*, pp. 56f.
100 See Anthony Downs, *Inside Bureaucracy* (Boston, Mass., 1967), pp. 211ff.
101 Waltz, *Theory*, p. 111.
102 See Destler, *Presidents*, p. 78.
103 Quoted in ibid., p. 75.
104 Allison, *Essence*, p. 81.
105 Steinbruner, *The Cybernetic Theory*, p. 124.
106 Giddens, *Central Problems*, p. 52.
107 Ibid., p. 54.
108 Steinbruner, *The Cybernetic Theory*, p. 125.

CHAPTER 4   THE CONCEPT OF IDEOLOGY

1   Giovanni Sartori, 'Guidelines for Concept Analysis', in Sartori, ed., *Social Science Concepts: A Systematic Analysis* (Beverly Hills, Calif., 1984), pp. 57f.

2   Felix Oppenheim, *Political Concepts: A Reconstruction* (Oxford, 1981), p. 177.

3   Michael J. Shapiro, *Language and Political Understanding: The Politics of Discursive Practices* (New Haven, Conn., 1981), p. 20.

4   Karl Popper, 'Normal Science and Its Dangers', in I. Lakatos and A. Musgrave, eds, *Criticism and the Growth of Knowledge* (Cambridge, 1970), p. 56.

5   Carl G. Hempel, *Fundamentals of Concept Formation in Empirical Science* (Chicago, 1952), p. 12.

6   See Carl G. Hempel, *Aspects of Scientific Explanation* (New York, 1965), pp. 46ff.

7   Sartori thus quotes George Thompson in Sartori, 'Guidelines', p. 9.

8   See Abraham Kaplan, *The Conduct of Inquiry* (San Francisco, 1964), pp. 48ff.

9   Evert Vedung, *Political Reasoning* (Beverley Hills, Calif., 1982), p. 68.

10 Brian Barry, 'Power: An Economic Analysis', in Brian Barry, ed., *Power and Political Theory* (London, 1976), p. 94. My emphasis.

11 Vedung, *Political Reasoning*, p. 68; and Sartori, 'Guidelines', pp. 57f.

12 Oppenheim, *Political Concepts*, p. 3, and Oppenheim, 'The Language of Political Inquiry: Problems of Clarification', in Fred I. Greenstein and Nelson W. Polsby, eds, *Handbook of Political Science: Scope and Theory* (vol. 1) (Reading, Mass., 1975), p. 283.

13 Oppenheim, *Political Concepts*, pp. 3f.

14 John Lyons, *Semantics*, vol. 1 (Cambridge, 1977), p. 23.

15 Oppenheim quoting Arthur Pap and Abraham Kaplan in *Political Concepts*, p. 4.

16 Sartori, 'Guidelines', p. 58.

17 W. G. Gallie, *Philosophy and Historical Understanding* (London, 1964), p. 158.

18 John Gray, 'On the Contestability of Social and Political Concepts', *Political Theory*, vol. 5 (August 1977), p. 338.

19 Idem.

20 Barry Clarke, 'Eccentrically Contested Concepts', *British Journal of Political Science*, vol. 9 (January 1979), p. 123.

21 As reported in Gray, 'On the Contestability', p. 337.

22 Quoted in ibid., p. 333.

23 Martin Landau, 'Comment: On Objectivity', *American Political Science Review*, vol. 46 (September 1972), p., 847.

24 See Clarke, 'Eccentrically Contested Concepts', p. 122.

25 Roger Trigg, *Reason and Commitment* (London, 1973), p. 25.

26 Clarke, 'Eccentrically Contested Concepts', p. 125.

27 Quoted in Gray, 'On the Contestability', p. 335.

28 See my *The Concept of Ideology and Political Analysis: A Critical Examination of Its Usage By Marx, Lenin and Mannheim* (Westport, Conn. 1981), pp. 210ff.

29 Thomas Kuhn, *The Structure of Scientific Revolutions* (2nd edn: Chicago, 1970), p. 199.
30 Ibid., p. 200.
31 Carl R. Kordig, *The Justification of Scientific Change* (Dordrecht, 1971), p. vii.
32 See my *The Concept of Ideology*, pp. 206ff.
33 See Kordig, *The Justification*, pp. 85ff.
34 William E. Connolly, *The Terms of Political Discourse* (Lexington, Mass., 1974), p. 6. Also see Oppenheim, *Political Concepts*, pp. 150ff., whose disagreement with Connolly is substantial on this score.
35 See, e.g., some of the essays – and especially titles – in C. I. Waxman, ed., *The End of Ideology Debate* (New York, 1968).
36 Ibid., respectively, pp. 276, 318.
37 Ernest Nagel, *The Structure of Science* (New York, 1961), pp. 492ff. For references to Kalleberg and Kaplan, see above, pp. 39f.
38 Oppenheim, *Political Concepts*, p. 196.
39 See ibid., pp. 198ff.
40 Connolly, *The Terms*, p. 128.
41 See Karl Popper, *The Open Society and Its Enemies*, vol. 2 (London, 1962), pp. 216ff.
42 Sartori, 'Guidelines', p. 16. See pp. 15–85 for a step-by-step description of the method for conceptualization advocated by Sartori.
43 Ibid., pp. 18, 17.
44 Oppenheim, *Political Concepts*, p. 181.
45 Oppenheim, 'The Language of Political Inquiry', p. 284.
46 See note 5 above. He quotes it in 'The Language of Political Inquiry', p. 291.
47 Oppenheim, *Political Concepts*, p. 187.
48 See Carl G. Hempel, *Philosophy of Natural Science* (Englewood Cliffs, NJ, 1966), pp. 94ff.
49 Kaplan, *The Conduct of Inquiry*, p. 50. Hempel notes of such concepts that 'those characteristics of the elements which serve as criteria of membership in a given class are associated, universally or with a high probability, with more or less extensive clusters of other characteristics.' Hempel, *Aspects*, pp. 146f.
50 Hempel writes, however, that a scientific discipline often proceeds from an 'intitial "natural history" stage, which primarily seeks to describe the phenomena under study and to establish simple empirical generalizations concerning them', only to arrive at a more scientific level at a later stage in its development. See ibid., pp. 139f.
51 Fred M. Frohock, 'The Structure of "Politics" ', *American Political Science Review*, vol. 72 (September 1978), p. 860.
52 Ibid., p. 861.
53 Ibid., p. 860. Also see my paper on 'Foreign Policy and the Democratic Process', *Scandinavian Political Studies*, vol. 4 (new series), no. 2 (1981), pp. 81ff., where various conceptions of the democratic process are discussed.
54 Sartori, 'Guidelines', pp. 42, 30. See pp. 22ff. for his discussion of the relationship between, and characteristics of, 'intension' and 'extension'.

55 Ibid., p. 54.
56 Ibid., p. 55.
57 Ibid., p. 56.
58 Lyons, *Semantics*, p. 207.
59 Sartori, 'Guidelines', p. 25.
60 Frohock, 'The Structure', p. 865.
61 Ibid., p. 867.
62 See Vedung, *Political Reasoning*, pp. 68ff. The fundamental problem with Vedung's discussion of the intension/extension dichotomy is that he posits it in terms of a triangle – consisting of 'word', 'intension' and 'extension' – which, although it is presented as a 'somewhat revised version' of the famous Ogden/Richards semantic triangle (and is referred to as such), in fact constitutes a wholly different *conceptual* configuration (and should hence – if anything – be called the Vedung triangle). While Sartori, too, has emended this triangle, he has done so only in the form of slight *linguistic* modifications. Thus, instead of the traditional triangular relationships between 'word', 'meaning' and 'object', he speaks of 'term', 'meaning' and 'referent'. One result of Vedung's transubstantiation of the traditional triangle is that whereas the meanings of 'intension' and 'extension' are usually defined or understood *in terms of the relationship between* a word, its meaning and its reference, they acquire wholly different characteristics when made to constitute two of the three *component elements of the triangle itself*. As a consequence, Vedung's subsequent discussion of 'intensional' and 'extensional definitions' becomes extremely puzzling when – as is quite explicitly the case – it continues to be couched in terms of the Ogden/Richards framework and Sartori's elaboration of it. See Sartori, 'Guidelines', pp. 22ff.
63 Giovanni Sartori, Fred W. Riggs and Henry Teune, *Tower of Babel: On the Definition and Analysis of Concepts in the Social Sciences* (Pittsburgh, Pa., 1975), p. 8.
64 Quentin Skinner, 'Meaning and Understanding in the History of Ideas', *History and Theory*, vol. 8, no. 1 (1969), p. 38.
65 H. L. A. Hart, *The Concept of Law* (Oxford, 1961), p. 5.
66 See Kaplan, *The Concept of Inquiry*, pp. 49ff.
67 Quoted in Harry Eckstein, 'The Idea of Political Development: From Dignity to Efficiency', *World Politics*, vol. 34 (July 1982), p. 468.
68 Ibid., pp. 461ff.
69 Ibid., pp. 469f.
70 See W. G. Runciman, *Social Science and Political Theory* (Cambridge, 1965), pp. 22ff., and especially p. 37. Also see Jürgen Habermas, *Strukturwandel der Öffentlichkeit* (Neuwied, 1962).
71 Eckstein, 'The Idea', p. 482.
72 Idem.
73 John Herz, 'International Relations: Ideological Aspects', in David L. Sills, ed., *International Encyclopedia of the Social Sciences*, vol. 8 (New York, 1968), p. 70.

74   Anthony Giddens, *Central Problems in Social Theory* (London, 1979), p. 175.
75   V. I. Lenin, *Selected Works*, vol. 1 (Moscow, 1967), p. 644.
76   George Lichtheim, *The Concept of Ideology and Other Essays* (New York, 1967), p. 8.
77   See my *The Concept of Ideology*, pp. 50ff.
78   See ibid., pp. 170ff.
79   Oppenheim, *Political Concepts*, p. 4.
80   Ibid., p. 5.
81   See Robert Dahl, 'The Concept of Power', in R. Bell, D. Edwards and R. H. Wagner, eds, *Political Power: A Reader in Theory and Research* (New York, 1969), p. 80; and P. Bachrach and M. S. Baratz, *Power and Poverty: Theory and Practice* (London, 1970), p. 21.
82   Quoted by Oppenheim, *Political Concepts*, p. 16.
83   Ibid., p. 7.
84   Giovanni Sartori, 'Politics, Ideology, and Belief Systems', *American Political Science Review*, vol. 63 (June 1969), pp. 398ff. For a similar critique, see Willard A. Mullins, 'Sartori's Concept of Ideology: A Dissent and an Alternative', in Allen R. Cox, ed., *Public Opinion and Political Attitudes* (New York, 1974), pp. 223ff.
85   Carlsnaes, *The Concept of Ideology*, p. 246.
86   As quoted in Giddens, *Central Problems*, p. 187.
87   N. Berdyaev, *The Origin of Russian Communism* (London, 1937), pp. 139f.
88   Lichtheim, *The Concept*, p. 8.
89   Aside from Webster's, these quotations come, respectively, from the following sources: E. A. Shils, 'The Concept and Function of Ideology', in David L. Sills, ed., *International Encyclopedia of the Social Sciences*, vol. 7 (New York, 1968), p. 66; J. Gould as quoted in Harry M. Johnson, 'Ideology and the Social System', in Sills, ed., *International Encyclopedia*, vol. 7, p. 76; N. Birnbaum, 'The Sociological Study of Ideology (1940–1960): A Trend Report and Bibliography', *Current Sociology*, vol. 9, no. 2 (1960), pp. 91f.; C. J. Friedrich, *Man and His Government* (New York, 1963), p. 90; Talcott Parsons, *The Social System* (Glencoe, Ill., 1951), p. 349; and Herz, 'International Relations', p. 69.
90   John Plamenatz, *Ideology* (London, 1970), p. 123.
91   See Sartori, 'Politics, Ideology', pp. 398ff.
92   Ibid., p. 399.
93   With regard to this aspect I cannot but agree with Seliger's criticism of Sartori when he writes that the latter

>   associates 'openness' and 'closedness' with different categories of doctrines and in the process subsumes alike under 'ideological mentality' what pertains to personal belief systems and to doctrines. Thus not only are the structural elements which he relates in an undifferentiated manner to general doctrines and personal attitudes as much philosophical (or epistemological) as they are psychological, but his use of 'ideological mentality' for both personality and cultural traits,

and the explicit assumption of their confluence lead Sartori eventually to attribute, at least by implication, a specific mentality to 'isms'.

(Martin Seliger, *Ideology and Politics* [London, 1976], pp.100f.)

Clearly, when Milton Rokeach – to whose work Sartori refers – speaks about 'open' and 'closed' minds he is speaking in terms of the minds of *persons*, or, more specifically, about the *belief systems* of such persons. See in particular chapter 3 of his *The Open and Closed Mind* (New York, 1960), pp. 54ff.

94 See, in particular, Sartori's article, 'Politics Ideology', and the references contained in it. The two main sources of this tradition are, surmisably, Rokeach's book above and P. E. Converse, 'The Nature of Belief Systems in Mass Publics', in David Apter, ed., *Ideology and Discontent* (New York, 1964), pp. 206–61.

95 Vedung, *Political Reasoning*, pp. 19ff. Sabine is quoted on p. 19.

96 Ibid., p. 19.

97 Ibid., p. 84. In its original version, this definition is to be found in Robert Heeger, *Ideologie und Macht* (Stockholm, 1976), p. 40.

98 W. G. Runciman, *Social Science*, p. 39.

99 Giovanni Sartori, 'Concept Misformation in Comparative Politics', *American Political Science Review*, vol. 64, no. 4 (December 1970), p. 1045.

100 Sartori, 'Politics, Ideology', p. 403.

101 Mullins, 'Sartori's Concept', p. 234.

102 Ibid., pp. 234f.

103 Shapiro, *Language*, p. 219.

104 The 'forensic/latent' distinction is discussed in Robert E. Lane, *Political Ideology* (New York, 1962), p. 16 and passim; Bluhm quoted by Shapiro, *Language*, p. 215; while Shapiro's own words are on p. 218.

105 Eckstein, 'The Idea', p. 470.

106 Quoted by Shapiro, *Language*, p. 218.

107 Idem.

108 Seliger, *Ideology and Politics*, p. 99.

109 Herz, 'International Relations', p. 70.

110 Zbigniew Brzezinski, *Ideology and Power in Soviet Politics* (New York, 1967), p. 5; H. M. Drucker, *The Political Uses of Ideology* (London, 1974), p. 107.

111 Friedrich, *Man*, p. 90.

112 Charles E. Lindblom, *Politics and Markets: The World's Political—Economic Systems* (New York, 1977), p. 239.

113 Seliger, *Ideology and Politics*, p. 99.

114 Daniel Bell, quoted in ibid., pp. 65f.

115 Plamenatz, *Ideology*, pp. 70f.

116 Sartori, 'Politics, Ideology', p. 399.

117 Idem.

118 See especially A. J. Ayer's *Language, Truth and Logic* (2nd edn: New York, 1950); C. L. Stevenson, *Ethics and Language* (New Haven, Conn., 1944).

119 Gould as quoted in Johnson, 'Ideology and the Social System', p. 315.

120 Karl Marx and Friedrich Engels, *The German Ideology* (Moscow, 1968), pp. 61f.

121 For a recent critical discussion of these Marxian conceptions of ideology with which I can only sympathize whole-heartedly, see Jon Elster, *Sour Grapes: Subversion of Rationality* (Cambridge, 1983), pp. 143ff. Sad to say, this sympathy does not extend to Elster's definition of ideology itself.

122 Quoted in Fred A. Sondermann, 'The Concept of the National Interest', *Orbis*, vol. 21, no. 1 (Spring 1977), p. 127.

123 See, e.g., James N. Rosenau, 'National Interest', in David L. Sills, ed., *International Encyclopedia of the Social Sciences*, vol. 11 (New York, 1968), pp. 34–9.

124 John Gray, 'Political Power, Social Theory, and Essential Contestability', in David Miller and Larry Siedentop, eds, *The Nature of Political Theory* (Oxford, 1983), p. 85.

125 Herz, 'International Relations', pp. 69f.

126 Plamenatz, *Ideology*, p. 98.

127 Brian Barry, *Sociologists, Economists and Democracy* (2nd edn: Chicago, 1978), p. 39.

128 Ibid., pp. 155f.; and Giovanni Sartori, *Parties and Party Systems* (Cambridge, 1976), pp. 137f.

129 E. H. Carr, *Nationalism and After* (London, 1945), p. 2; 'International Relations', p. 70.

130 Alexander L. George, *Presidential Decisionmaking in Foreign Policy: The Effective Use of Information and Advice* (Boulder, Colo, 1980), pp. 219f.

CHAPTER 5   CONCLUSION

1 Christer Jönsson, *Soviet Bargaining Behaviour: The Nuclear Test Ban Case* (New York, 1979), p. 13.

2 Idem.

3 Ibid., pp. 13ff.

4 Robert K. Merton, *Social Theory and Social Structure* (expanded edn: New York, 1968), p. 104.

5 Ibid., p. 117. My emphasis. In this connection also see W. G. Runciman's discussion in his *Social Science and Political Theory* (Cambridge, 1965), pp. 39ff., 110ff.

6 Jönsson, *Soviet Bargaining Behaviour*, pp. 11f.

7 George H. Sabine, 'What Is a Political Theory?', *Journal of Politics*, vol. 1 (1939), pp. 10f.

8 An even more illustrative example is the following passage in Jönsson's book:

> We have suggested that ideology and images may be thought of as partly overlapping entities and noted that the frequent charges of 'dogmatism' and 'revisionism' respectively indicate a difference in the *role* of *ideology* in Soviet and Chinese *images*. Although it would of course be a gross exaggeration to describe Chinese images as exclusively *flowing from*

ideology and Soviet images as *devoid* of ideological roots, it has generally been assumed that Chinese images are *ideologically determined* to a greater degree than Soviet images. However, as Clemens has pointed out, a more adequate description may be that different segments of Communist ideology are *operational* in Soviet and Chinese images.

(Jönsson, *Soviet Bargaining Behaviour*, p. 123. My emphasis.)

These claims make no sense at all to me.

9 Ibid., p. 14.
10 Jon Elster, *Sour Grapes: Subversion of Rationality* (Cambridge, 1983), p. 116.
11 Karl Marx and Friedrich Engels, *The German Ideology* (Moscow, 1968), p. 11.
12 Ibid., p. 61.
13 Seymour Martin Lipset, *Political Man: The Social Bases of Politics* (expanded and updated edn: London, 1983), p. 549.
14 John Plamenatz, *Ideology* (London, 1970), p. 66.
15 See, e.g., the pertinent editorial in *Dagens Nyheter* (Stockholm), 27 May 1984, and the ensuing discussion in the June 1st issue, p. 2, as well as in *Tiden* (Stockholm), nos 1, 2, and 3, 1985. It should be noted that I do not take a stand as to the validity of these respective claims. Quite conceivably both arguments are wrong; this, however, is immaterial with respect to the point I am trying to make.

Bibliography

Abel, T. 'The Operation Called *Verstehen*', *American Journal of Sociology* 54 (1948)

Agassi, Joseph. 'Methodological Individualism', *British Journal of Sociology* 11 (1960)

Allison, Graham T. *Essence of Decision*. Boston, Mass., 1971

Almond, Gabriel A. *The American People and Foreign Policy*. New York, 1960

Anscombe, G. E. M. *Intention*. Oxford, 1957

Apter, David E. 'Comparative Studies: A Review with Some Projections', in *Comparative Methods in Sociology*, ed. Ivan Vallier. Berkeley, Calif., 1971

Aspaturian, Vernon V. 'International Politics and Foreign Policy in the Soviet System', in *Approaches to Comparative and International Politics*, ed. R. Barry Farrell. Evanston, Ill. 1966

Atkinson, R. F. *Knowledge and Explanation in History*. London, 1978

Austin, J. L. *Philosophical Papers*. 2nd edn. London, 1970

Ayer, A. J. *Language, Truth and Logic*. 2nd edn. New York, 1950

—— 'Man as a Subject for Science', in *Philosophy, Politics and Society*, 3rd series, ed. P. Laslett and W. G. Runciman. Oxford, 1969

Azar, Edward E. 'Behavioural Forecasts and Policy-Making: An Events Data Approach', in *International Events and the Comparative Analysis of Foreign Policy*, ed. Charles W. Kegley, Gregory A. Raymond, Robert M. Good and Richard A. Skinner. Columbia, SC, 1975

Bacchus, William I. *Foreign Policy and the Bureaucratic Process: The State Department's Country Director System*. Princeton, NJ, 1974

Bachrach, P. and Baratz, M. S. *Power and Poverty: Theory and Practice*. London, 1970

Baldwin, David A. 'Interdependence and Power: A Conceptual Analysis', *International Organization* 34, (Autumn 1980)

Barry, Brian. 'Power: An Economic Analysis', in *Power and Political Analysis*, ed. Brian Barry. London, 1976

—— *Sociologists, Economists and Democracy*. 2nd edn., Chicago, 1978

Beer, Samuel and Ulam, Adam, eds. *Patterns of Government: The Major Political Systems of Europe*. 2nd edn. New York, 1967

Bell, R., Edwards, D. and Wagner, R. H., eds. *Political Power: Reader in Theory and Research*. New York, 1969

Bendix, Reinhard. *Max Weber: An Intellectual Portrait*. Garden City, NJ, 1962

Berdyaev, N. *The Origin of Russian Communism.* London, 1937

Bernstein, Richard J. *The Restructuring of Social and Political Theory.* Oxford 1976

Birnbaum, N. 'The Sociological Study of Ideology (1940–1960): A Trend Report and Bibliography', *Current Sociology* 9: 2 (1960)

Boardman, Robert. 'Comparative Method and Foreign Policy', in *The Year Book of World Affairs* 27 (1973)

Braude, Lee. '*Die Verstehende Soziologie*: A New Look at an Old Problem', *Sociology and Social Research* 50 (1965–6)

Braybrooke, David and Lindblom, Charles E. *A Strategy of Decision.* New York, 1963

Brecher, Michael. 'The Subordinate State System of Southern Asia', in *International Politics and Foreign Policy*, ed. James N. Rosenau. New York, 1969

—— *The Foreign Policy System of Israel.* New Haven, Conn., 1972

—— 'Image, Process and Feedback in Foreign Policy: Israel's Decision on German Reparations', *America Political Science Review* 67 (1973)

—— *Decisions in Israel's Foreign Policy.* London, 1974

——, Steinberg, B., and Stein, J. 'A Framework for Research on Foreign Policy Behaviour', *Journal of Conflict Resolution* 13 (1969)

Brodbeck, May. 'General Introduction', in *Readings in the Philosophy of the Social Sciences*, ed. May Brodbeck. New York, 1968

Brzezinski, Zbigniew. *Ideology and Power in Soviet Politics.* New York, 1967

—— and Huntington, Samuel P. *Political Power: US/USSR.* New York, 1963

Bull, Hedley. *The Anarchical Society.* London, 1977

Carlsnaes, Walter. 'A Conceptual Analysis of African Nationalism', in *Idéer och ideologier*, ed. C. A. Hessler. Stockholm, 1969

—— 'Interdependence and Foreign Policy Actions', paper presented at the European Consortium for Political Research workshops in Grenoble, April 1978

—— *The Concept of Ideology and Political Analysis: A Critical Examination of Its Usage by Marx, Lenin and Mannheim.* Westport, Conn., 1981

—— Foreign Policy and the Democratic Process', *Scandinavian Political Studies* 4: 2 (new series: 1981)

Carr, E. H. *Nationalism and After.* London, 1945.

Child, Arthur. 'The Problem of Imputation in the Sociology of Knowledge', *Ethics* 51 (1940–1)

—— 'The Problem of Imputation Resolved', *Ethics* 54 (1943–4)

Clark, Ian. *Reform and Resistance in the International System.* Cambridge, 1980

Clarke, Barry. 'Eccentrically Contested Concepts', *British Journal of Political Science* 9 (January 1979)

Cohen, Bernard C. 'Foreign Policy', in *International Encyclopedia of the Social Sciences* (vol. 5), ed. David L. Sills. New York, 1968

Connolly, William E. *Political Science and Ideology.* New York, 1967

—— *The Terms of Political Discourse.* Lexington, Mass., 1974

Converse, P. E. 'The Nature of Belief Systems in Mass Publics', in *Ideology and Discontent*, ed. David Apter. New York, 1964

Cooper, Richard N. *The Economics of Interdependence.* New York, 1968

—— 'Economic Interdependence and Foreign Policy in the Seventies', *World Politics* 24: 2 (January 1972)

Cottam, R. W. *Foreign Policy Motivation.* Pittsburgh, Pa, 1977

Cyert, R. and March, J. *A Behavioural Theory of the Firm.* Englewood Cliffs, NJ, 1963

Dagens Nyheter, Stockholm. 27 May and 1 June 1984

Daveny, T. F. 'Intentions and Causes', *Analysis* 27 (1966)

Davidson, Donald. 'Actions, Reasons, and Causes', *The Journal of Philosophy* 60: 23 (1963)

—— *Essays on Actions and Events.* Oxford, 1980

Destler, I. M. *Presidents, Bureaucrats, and Foreign Policy: The Politics of Organizational Reform.* Princeton, NJ, 1972

Downs, Anthony. *Inside Bureaucracy.* Boston, Mass., 1967

Drucker, H. M. *The Political Uses of Ideology.* London, 1974

Durkheim, Émile. 'Social Facts', in *Readings in the Philosophy of the Social Sciences*, ed. May Brodbeck. New York, 1968

Eckstein, Harry. 'A Perspective on Comparative Politics, Past and Present', in *Comparative Politics: A Reader*, ed. Harry Eckstein and David E. Apter. New York, 1963

—— 'Introduction', in *Internal War*, ed. Harry Eckstein. New York, 1964

—— 'Case Study and Theory in Political Science', in *Handbook of Political Science: Strategies of Inquiry* (vol. 7), ed. Fred I. Greenstein and Nelson W. Polsby. Reading, Mass., 1975

—— 'The Idea of Political Development: From Dignity to Efficiency', *World Politics* 34 (July 1982)

Edelman, Murray. *Political Language: Words That Succeed and Policies That Fail.* New York, 1977

Elster, Jon. *Ulysses and the Sirens: Studies in Rationality and Irrationality.* Cambridge, 1979

—— 'Anomalies of Rationality: Some Unresolved Problems in the Theory of Rational Behaviour', in *Sociological Economics*, ed. Louis Lévy-Garboua. London, 1979

—— *Sour Grapes: Subversion of Rationality.* Cambridge, 1983

Emerson, Rupert. *From Empire to Nation.* Cambridge, Mass., 1960

Farrell, R. Barry. 'Foreign Policies of Open and Closed Political Societies', in *Approaches to Comparative and International Politics*, ed. R. Barry Farrell. Evanston, Ill., 1966

Fay, Brian and Moon, J. Donald. 'What Would an Adequate Philosophy of Social Science Look Like?', *Philosophy of the Social Sciences* 7: 3 (1977)

Friedrich, C. J. *Man and His Government.* New York, 1963

Frohock, Fred M. 'The Structure of "Politics" ', *American Political Science Review* 72 (September 1978)

Gallie, W. G. *Philosophy and Historical Understanding.* London, 1964

Galtung, Johan. *Theory and Methods of Social Research.* New York, 1967

—— 'Foreign Policy Opinion as a Function of Social Position', in *International Politics and Foreign Policy*, ed. James N. Rosenau. New York, 1969

Gellner, Ernest. *Cause and Meaning in the Social Sciences*. London, 1973

George, Alexander L. *Presidential Decisionmaking in Foreign Policy: The Effective Use of Information and Advice*. Boulder, Colo, 1980

— and Keohane, Robert O. 'The Concept of National Interests: Uses and Limitations', in *Presidential Decisionmaking in Foreign Policy: The Effective Use of Information and Advice*, by Alexander L. George. Boulder, Colo, 1980

Giddens, Anthony. *Central Problems in Social Theory*. London, 1979

Gold, Hyam. 'Foreign Policy Decision-Making and the Environment: The Claims of Snyder, Brecher, and the Sprouts', *International Studies Quarterly* 22: 4 (December 1978)

Gould, J. and Kolb, W. L., eds. *A Dictionary of the Social Sciences*. New York, 1964

Gray, John. 'On the Contestability of Social and Political Concepts', *Political Theory* 5 (August 1977)

— 'Political Power, Social Theory, and Essential Contestability', in *The Nature of Political Theory*, ed. David Miller and Larry Siedentop. Oxford, 1983

Greenberg, George D., Miller, Jeffrey A., Mohr, Lawrence B. and Vladeck, Bruce C. 'Developing Public Policy Theory: Perspectives From Empirical Research', *American Political Science Review* 71 (December 1977)

Gregor, A. James. *An Introduction to Metapolitics*. New York, 1971

Gross, Felix. *Foreign Policy Analysis*. New York, 1954

Gunnell, John. 'Social Science and Political Reality: The Problem of Explanation', *Social Research* 35 (Spring 1968)

— 'Interpretation and the History of Political Theory: Apology and Epistemology', *American Political Science Review* 76 (1982)

Habermas, Jürgen. *Strukturwandel und Öffentlichkeit*. Neuwied, 1962

Hampshire, Stuart. *Thought and Action*. London, 1959

Hanrieder, Wolfram F. 'Compatibility and Consensus: A Proposal for the Conceptual Linkage of External and Internal Dimensions of Foreign Policy', *American Political Science Review* 61 (1967)

Hart, H. L. A. *The Concept of Law*. Oxford, 1961

— and Honoré, A. M. *Causation and the Law*. London, 1959

Hayek, F. A. von. *Studies in Philosophy, Politics and Economics*. London, 1967

Heeger, Robert. *Ideologie und Macht*. Stockholm, 1976

Hempel, Carl G. 'Fundamentals of Concept Formation in Empirical Science', in *International Encyclopedia of Unified Science* 11: 7 (Chicago, 1952)

— 'The Theoretician's Dilemma', in *Minnesota Studies in the Philosophy of Science*, vol. 11, ed. H. Feigh, M. Scriven and G. Maxwell. Minneapolis, 1958

— 'A Logical Appraisal of Operationalism', in *The Validation of Scientific Theories*, ed. Philipp G. Frank. New York, 1961

— *Aspects of Scientific Explanation*. New York, 1965

— *Philosophy of Natural Science*. Englewood Cliffs, NJ, 1966

Hermann, Charles. 'Policy Classification: A Key to the Comparative Study of Foreign Policy', in *The Analysis of International Politics*, ed. James N. Rosenau, Vincent Davis and Maurice A. East. New York, 1972

Herz, John. 'Rise and Demise of the Territorial States', *World Politics* 9 (1957)

—— *International Politics in the Atomic Age.* New York, 1959

—— 'International Relations: Ideological Aspects', in *International Encyclopedia of the Social Sciences*, vol. 8, ed. David L. Sills. New York, 1968

—— 'The Territorial State Revisited: Reflections on the Future of the Nation-State', in *International Politics and Foreign Policy*, ed. James N. Rosenau. New York, 1969

Hinsley, F. H. *Sovereignty.* New York, 1966

Hoffmann, Stanley. *Gulliver's Troubles: Or the Setting of American Foreign Policy.* New York, 1968

Hollis, Martin. *Models of Man.* Cambridge, 1977

Holsti, K. J. *International Politics.* 2nd edn. London, 1974

Holsti, Ole R. 'The "Operational Code" Approach to the Study of Political Leaders: John Foster Dulles's Philosophical and Instrumental Beliefs', *Canadian Journal of Political Science* 3 (1970)

—— 'The Study of International Politics Makes Strange Bedfellows: Theories of the Radical Right and the Radical Left', *American Political Science Review* 68 (1974)

—— 'Foreign Policy Formation Viewed Cognitively', in *Structure of Decision*, ed. Robert Axelrod. Princeton, NJ, 1976

—— 'Foreign Policy Decision-Makers Viewed Psychologically: "Cognitive Process" Approaches', in *Thought and Action in Foreign Policy*, ed. G. Matthew Bonham and Michael J. Shapiro. Basel, 1977

Homans, George C. 'Bringing Man Back In', in *Philosophy of Social Explanation*, ed. Alan Ryan. London, 1973

Israel, Joachim. 'The Principle of Methodological Individualism and Marxian Epistemology', *Acta Sociologica* 14 (1971)

Jarvie, I. C. *Concepts and Society.* London, 1972

Jervis, Robert. *Perception and Misperception in International Politics.* Princeton, NJ, 1976

Johnson, Harry M. 'Ideology and the Social System' in *International Encyclopedia of the Social Sciences*, ed. David L. Sills. New York, 1968

Jönsson, Christer. *Soviet Bargaining Behaviour: The Nuclear Test Ban Case.* New York, 1979

Kalleberg, Arthur L. 'Concept Formation in Normative and Empirical Studies: Toward Reconciliation in Political Theory', *American Political Science Quarterly* 60: 1 (1960)

—— 'The Logic of Comparison', *World Politics* 19 (July 1966)

Kaplan, Abraham. *The Conduct of Inquiry.* San Francisco, 1964

Kaplan, Morton A. 'Variants on Six Models of the International System', in *International Politics and Foreign Policy*, ed. James N. Rosenau. New York, 1964

Keat, Russell and Urry, John. *Social Theory as Science.* London, 1975

Kegley, Charles W. 'Introduction: The Generation and Use of Events Data', in *International Events and the Comparative Analysis of Foreign Policy*, ed. Charles W. Kegley, Gregory A. Raymond, Robert M. Good and Richard A. Skinner. Columbia, SC, 1975

—— *The Comparative Study of Foreign Policy: Paradigm Lost?* Columbia, SC, 1980

Kelman, Herbert C. 'Patterns of Personal Involvement in the National System: A

Social–Psychological Analysis of Political Legitimacy', in *International Politics and Foreign Policy*, ed. James N. Rosenau. New York, 1969
—— 'The Role of the Individual in International Relations: Some Conceptual and Methodological Considerations', *Journal of International Affairs* 24 (1970)
Kenny, Anthony. *Action, Emotion and Will*. London, 1963
Keohane, Robert O. and Nye, Joseph S. Jr. *Power and Interdependence: World Politics in Transition*. Boston, Mass., 1977
Kerr, Donna H. 'The Logic of "Policy" and Successful Policies', *Policy Sciences* 7 (1976)
Kinder, Donald R. and Weiss, Janet A. 'In Lieu of Rationality: Psychological Perspectives on Foreign Policy Decision-Making', *Journal of Conflict Resolution* 22 (December 1978)
Kirby, Stephen. 'National Interest *Versus* Ideology in American Diplomacy', in *Knowledge and Belief in Politics*, ed. Robert Benewick, R. N. Berki and Bhikhu Parekh. London, 1973
Kissinger, Henry A. *Nuclear Weapons and Foreign Policy*. New York, 1957.
—— *American Foreign Policy: Three Essays by Henry A. Kissinger*. New York, 1969
Kordig, Carl R. *The Justification of Scientific Change*. Dordrecht, 1971
Krasner, Stephen D. *Defending the National Interest: Raw Materials Investments and US Foreign Policy*. Princeton, NJ, 1978
Kuhn, Thomas. *The Structure of Scientific Revolutions*. 2nd edn. Chicago, 1970
Landau, Martin. 'Comment: On Objectivity', *American Political Science Review* 46 (September 1972)
Lane, Robert E. *Political Ideology*. New York, 1962
Leites, Nathan. *The Operational Code of the Politburo*. New York, 1951
Lenin, V. I. *Selected Works*, vol. 1. Moscow, 1967
Levi, Werner. 'Ideology, Interests, and Foreign Policy', *International Studies Quarterly* 14 (March 1970)
Levy, Marion J. Jr. *The Structure of Society*. Princeton, NJ, 1952
—— ' "Does It Matter If He's Naked?" Bawled the Child', in *Contending Approaches to International Relations*, ed. Klaus Knorr and James N. Rosenau. Princeton, NJ, 1969
Lewis, Oscar. 'Comparisons in Cultural Anthropology', in *Readings in Cross-Cultural Methodology*, ed. F. W. Moore. New Haven, Conn., 1961
Lichtheim, George. *The Concept of Ideology and Other Essays*. New York, 1967
Lijphart, Arend. 'Comparative Politics and the Comparative Method', *American Political Science Review* 65 (September 1971)
Lindblom, Charles E. *Politics and Markets: The World's Political–Economic Systems*. New York, 1977
Lipset, Seymour Martin. *Political Man: The Social Bases of Politics*. Expanded and updated edn. London, 1983
Locke, D. 'Reasons, Wants, and Causes', *American Philosophical Quarterly* 10 (1974)
Louch, A. R. *Explanation and Human Action*. Oxford, 1966
Lowi, Theodore J. 'Four Systems of Policy, Politics, and Choice', *Public Administration Review* 32: 4 (July/August 1972)

Luard, Evan. *Types of International Society*. New York, 1976

Lukes, Steven. 'Methodological Individualism Reconsidered', in *The Philosophy of Social Explanation*, ed. Alan Ryan. London, 1973

Lyons, John. *Semantics*, vol. 1. Cambridge, 1977

MacIntyre, Alisdaire. 'Antecedents of Action', in *British Analytic Philosophy*, ed. B. Williams and A. Montefiori. London, 1966

—— 'The idea of a Social Science', in *The Philosophy of Social Explanation*, ed. Alan Ryan. London, 1973

Mackenzie, W. J. M. *Politics and Social Science*. Harmondsworth, 1967

Marsh, R. M. *Comparative Sociology*. New York, 1967

Marx, Karl and Engels, Friedrich. *The German Ideology*. Moscow, 1968

Mazrui, Ali A. *Africa's International Relations: The Diplomacy of Dependency and Change*. London, 1977

McGowan, Patrick J. 'The Unit-of-Analysis Problem in the Comparative Study of Foreign Policy', paper presented at the Events Data Measurement Conference, Michigan State University, East Lansing, Mich., 15–16 April 1970

—— 'Problems in the Construction of Positive Foreign Policy Theory', in *Comparing Foreign Policies: Theories, Findings, and Methods*, ed. James N. Rosenau. New York, 1974

—— 'Meaningful Comparisons in the Study of Foreign Policy: A Methodological Discussion of Objectives, Techniques and Research Designs', in *International Events and the Comparative Analysis of Foreign Policy*, ed. Charles W. Kegley, Gregory A. Raymond, Robert M. Good and Richard A. Skinner. Columbia, SC, 1975

Meehan, E. J. *The British Left Wing and Foreign Policy: A Study of the Influence of Ideology*. New Brunswick, NJ, 1960

Melden, A. I. *Free Action*. London, 1961

Merton, Robert K. *Social Theory and Social Structure*. New York, 1957

—— *On Theoretical Sociology*. New York, 1967

—— *Social Theory and Social Structure*. Expanded edn. New York, 1968

Moon, J. Donald. 'The Logic of Political Inquiry: A Synthesis of Opposing Perspectives', in *Handbook of Political Science: Scope and Theory* (vol. 1), ed. Fred I. Greenstein and Nelson W. Polsby. Englewood Cliffs, NJ, 1975

Morgenthau, Hans J. *Politics Among Nations*. 3rd edn. New York, 1961

Morse, Edward L. 'The Politics of Interdependence', *International Organization* 23: 2 (Spring 1969)

—— 'Defining Foreign Policy For Comparative Analysis: A Research Note', mimeo. Princeton, NJ, June 1971

—— 'Crisis Diplomacy, Interdependence, and the Politics of International Economic Relations', *World Politics* 24 (supplement: Spring 1972)

—— *Modernization and the Transformation of International Relations*. New York, 1976

—— 'Interdependence in World Affairs', in *World Politics: An Introduction*, ed. James N. Rosenau, Kenneth W. Thompson and Gavin Boyd. New York, 1976

Mullins, Willard A. 'On the Concept of Ideology in Political Science', *American Political Science Review* 64 (1970)

—— 'Sartori's Concept of Ideology: A Dissent and an Alternative', in *Public Opinion and Political Attitudes*, ed. Allen R. Cox. New York, 1974

Munch, Peter A. 'Empirical Science and Max Weber's *Verstehende Soziologie*', *American Sociological Review* 22 (1957)

Naess, Arne, Christophersen, Jens and Kvalø, Kjell. *Democracy, Ideology and Objectivity: Studies in the Semantics and Cognitive Analysis of Ideological Controversy.* Oslo, 1956

Nagel, Ernest. *The Structure of Science.* New York, 1961

Nagel, Jack A. *The Descriptive Analysis of Power.* New Haven, Conn., 1975

Nettl, J. P. 'The State as a Conceptual Variable', *World Politics* 10 (July 1968)

Northedge, F. S. 'Introduction', in *The Foreign Policies of the Powers*, rev. edn., ed. F. S. Northedge. London, 1974

O'Neill, John. *Modes of Individualism and Collectivism*, London, 1973

O'Leary, Michael K. 'Foreign Policy and Bureaucratic Adaptation', in *Comparing Foreign Policies*, ed. James N. Rosenau. New York, 1974

Olsen, Jens Henrik. 'Causation and the Explanatory Patterns of Human Conduct', Copenhagen, mimeo.1975

—— and March, J. G. *Ambiguity and Choice in Organizations.* Bergen, 1979

Oppenheim, Felix E. 'The Language of Political Inquiry: Problems of Clarification', in *Handbook of Political Science: Scope and Theory*, (vol. 1) ed. Fred I. Greenstein and Nelson W. Polsby. Reading, Mass., 1975

—— *Political Concepts: A Reconstruction.* Oxford, 1981

Parsons, Talcott. *The Social System*. Glencoe, Ill., 1951

—— and Shils, Edward. *Toward a General Theory of Action.* New York, 1962

Peacocke, Christopher. *Holistic Explanation: Action, Space, Interpretation.* London, 1979

—— 'Holistic Explanation: An Outline of a Theory', in *Rational Explanation*, ed. Ross Harrison. London, 1979

Peters, R. S. *The Concept of Motivation*. London, 1958

Pflanze, Otto. 'Nationalism in Europe, 1848–1871', *The Review of Politics* 28 (1966)

Plamenatz, John. *Ideology*. London, 1970

Popper, Karl R. *The Poverty of Historicism*. New York, 1957

—— *The Open Society and Its Enemies*, vol. 2. London, 1962

—— 'Normal Science and Its Dangers', in *Criticism and the Growth of Knowledge*, ed. I. Lakatos and A. Musgrave. Cambridge 1970

—— *Conjectures and Refutations: The Growth of Scientific Knowledge*. Rev. edn. London, 1972

—— *Objective Knowledge*. London, 1972

Potter, William C. 'Issue Area and Foreign Policy Analysis', *International Organization* 34 (Summer 1980)

Rapoport, Anatol. 'Some Systems Approaches to Political Science', in *Varieties of Political Theories*, ed. David Easton. Englewood Cliffs, NJ, 1966

—— 'Various Meanings of "Rational Political Decisions" ' in *Politics as Rational Action: Essays in Public Choice and Policy Analysis*, ed. Leif Lewin and Evert Vedung. Dordrecht, 1980

Raser, John P. 'Learning and Affect in International Politics', in *International Politics and Foreign Policy*, ed. James N. Rosenau. New York, 1969

Reynolds, Charles. *Theory and Explanation in International Politics.* London 1973

Riggs, Fred W. 'The Nation–State and Other Actors', in *International Politics and Foreign Policy*, ed. James N. Rosenau. New York, 1969

Robinson, Thomas W. 'National Interest', in *International Politics and Foreign Policy*, ed. James N. Rosenau. New York, 1969

Rokeach, Milton. *The Open and Closed Mind.* New York, 1960

Rose, Richard. 'Comparing Public Policy – An Overview', *European Journal of Political Research* 1 (April 1973)

Rosecrance, Richard N. and Stein, Arthur. 'Interdependence: Myth or Reality?' *World Politics* 26 (October 1973)

Rosenau, James N. 'Compatibility, Consensus, and the Emerging Political Science of Adaptation', *American Political Science Review* 61 (1967)

—— 'Moral Fervor, Systemic Analysis, and Scientific Consciousness', in *Political Science and Public Policy*, ed. Austin Ranney. Chicago, 1968

—— 'National Interest', in *International Encyclopedia of the Social Sciences*, vol. 11, ed. David L. Sills. New York, 1968

—— *The Adaptation of National Societies: A Theory of Political Systems Behaviour and Transformation.* New York, 1970

—— 'Foreign Policy as Adaptive Behaviour', *Comparative Politics* 2 (1970)

—— 'Comparing Foreign Policies: Why, What, How', in *Comparing Foreign Policies*, ed. James N. Rosenau. New York, 1974

—— 'Pre-Theories and Theories of Foreign Policy', in *The Scientific Study of Foreign Policy*, ed. James N. Rosenau, London, 1980

—— 'A Pre-Theory Revisited: World Politics in an Era of Cascading Interdependence', *International Studies Quarterly* 28: 3 (September 1984)

Rudner, Richard S. *Philosophy of Social Science.* Englewood Cliffs, NJ, 1966

Rummel, Rudolph J. 'Some Dimensions of the Foreign Policy Behaviour of Nations', in *International Politics and Foreign Policy*, ed. James N. Rosenau. New York, 1969

Runciman, W. G. *Social Science and Political Theory.* Cambridge, 1965

—— *A Critique of Max Weber's Philosophy of Social Science.* Cambridge, 1972

—— 'Ideology and Social Science', in *Knowledge and Beliefs in Politics*, ed. Robert Benewick, R. N. Berki and Bhikhu Parekh. London, 1973

—— 'Describing', *Mind* 81 (1975)

Ryle, Gilbert. *The Concept of Mind.* London, 1949

Sabine, George H. 'What is a Political Theory?', *Journal of Politics* 1 (1939)

Samuelson, Paul A. 'Some Notions on Causality and Teleology in Economics', in *Cause and Effect*, ed. D. Lerner. New York, 1965

Sartori, Giovanni. 'Politics, Ideology, and Belief Systems', *American Political Science Review* 63 (June 1969)

—— 'Concept Misformation in Comparative Politics', *American Political Science Review* 64: 4 (December 1970)

—— *Parties and Party Systems.* Cambridge, 1976

— 'Guidelines for Concept Analysis', in *Social Science Concepts: A Systematic Analysis*, ed. Giovanni Sartori. Beverly Hills, Calif., 1984

——, Riggs, Fred W. and Teune, Henry. *Tower of Babel: On the Definition and Analysis of Concepts in the Social Sciences*. Pittsburgh, Pa, 1975

Schurmann, Franz. *The Logic of World Power*. New York, 1974

Scott, Andrew M. 'The Logic of International Interaction', *International Studies Quarterly* 21 (September 1977)

Seliger, Martin. *Ideology and Politics*. London, 1976

Sen, Amartya. *Choice, Welfare and Measurement*. Oxford, 1982

Shapiro, Michael J. *Language and Political Understanding: The Politics of Discursive Practices*. New Haven, Conn., 1981

Shils, E. A. 'The Concept and Function of Ideology', in *International Encyclopedia of the Social Sciences*, vol. 7, ed. David L. Sills. New York, 1968

Simon, H. A. *Administrative Behaviour*. New York, 1946

— 'Theories of Decision Making in Economics and Behavioural Science', *American Economic Review* 49 (1959)

Singer, J. David. 'The Level-of-Analysis Problem in International Relations', *World Politics* 14 (1961)

Skinner, Quentin. 'Meaning and Understanding in the History of Ideas', *History and Theory* 8: 1 (1969)

— ' "Social Meaning" and the Explanation of Social Action', in *The Philosophy of History*, ed. P. Gardiner. London, 1974

Smelser, Neil J. 'The Methodology of Comparative Analysis', in *Comparative Research Notes*, ed. D. P. Warwick and S. Osherson. Englewood Cliffs, NJ, 1973

Smith, Anthony D. *Theories of Nationalism*. London, 1971

Smith, Steve. *Foreign Policy Adaptation*. Farnborough, 1981

— 'Rosenau's Adaptive Behaviour Approach – A Critique', *Review of International Studies* 7 (1981)

— 'Rosenau's Contribution', *Review of International Studies* 9 (1983)

— 'Theories of Foreign Policy: An Historical Overview', *Review of International Studies* 12 (1986)

Snyder, Richard C., Bruch, H. W., and Sapin, Burton. 'Decision-Making as an Approach to the Study of Foreign Policy', in *Foreign Policy Decision-Making*, ed. Richard C. Snyder, H. W. Bruch and Burton Sapin. New York, 1962

Sondermann, F. A. 'The Linkage between Foreign Policy and International Politics', in *International Politics and Foreign Policy*, ed. James N. Rosenau. New York, 1969

— 'The Concept of the National Interest', *Orbis* 21: 1 (Spring 1977)

Sprout, Harold and Margaret. *The Ecological Perspective in Human Affairs*. Princeton, NJ, 1965

— 'Environmental Factors in the Study of International Politics', in *International Politics and Foreign Policy*, ed. James N. Rosenau. New York, 1969

Stein, Arthur A. 'When Misperception Matters', *World Politics* 34: 4 (July 1982)

Steinbruner, John D. *The Cybernetic Theory of Decision*. Princeton, NJ, 1974

Stevenson, C. J. *Ethics and Language*. New Haven, Conn., 1944

Swanson, Guy E. 'Frameworks for Comparative Research: Structural Anthropology and the Theory of Action', in *Comparative Methods in Sociology*, ed. Ivan Vallier. Berkeley, Calif., 1971

Taubman, William. 'Political Power: USA/USSR – Ten Years Later', *Studies in Comparative Communism* 8: 1/2 (1975)

Taylor, Charles. *The Explanation of Behaviour*. London, 1964

—— 'Neutrality in Political Science', in *Philosophy, Politics and Society*, 3rd series, ed. Peter Laslett and W. G. Runciman. Oxford 1969

—— 'The Explanation of Purposive Behaviour', in *Explanation in the Behavioural Sciences*, ed. Robert Borger and Frank Cioffi. London, 1970

—— 'Interpretation and the Sciences of Man', *Review of Metaphysics* 25 (1971)

Thompson, Kenneth W. and Macridis, Roy C. 'The Comparative Study of Foreign Policy', in *Foreign Policy in World Politics*, 4th edn, ed. Roy C. Macridis. Englewood Cliffs, NJ, 1972

Thorson, Stuart J. 'National Political Adaptation', in *Comparing Foreign Policies*, ed. James N. Rosenau. New York, 1974

Tiden, Stockholm. 1–3, 1985

Trigg, Roger. *Reason and Commitment*. London, 1973

Vedung, Evert. 'The Comparative Method and Its Neighbours', in *Power and Political Theory: Some European Perspectives*, ed. Brian Barry. London, 1976

—— *Political Reasoning*. Beverly Hills, Calif., 1982

Walker, Stephen G. and Falkowski, Lawrence S. 'The Operational Codes of US Presidents and Secretaries of State: Motivational Foundations and Behavioral Consequences', paper presented to the 1982 annual meeting of the International Society for Political Psychology, June 1982, Washington, DC

Wallace, William. *The Foreign Policy Process in Britain*. London, 1975

Waltz, Kenneth N. 'The Myth of National Interdependence', in *The International Corporation*, ed. Charles P. Kindleberger. Cambridge, Mass., 1970

—— *Theory of International Politics*. Reading, Mass., 1979

Warwick, D. P. and Osherson, S. 'Comparative Analysis in the Social Sciences', in *Comparative Research Notes*, ed. D. P. Warwick and S. Osherson. Englewood Cliffs, NJ, 1973

Wax, Murray L. 'On Misunderstanding *Verstehen*: A Reply to Abel', *Sociology and Social Research* 51 (1966–7)

Waxman, C. I., ed. *The End of Ideology Debate*. New York, 1968

Weber, Max. *The Theory of Social and Economic Organization*. New York, 1964

Weil, Herman M. 'Can Bureaucracies Be Rational Actors? Foreign Policy Decision-Making in North Vietnam', *International Studies Quarterly* 19 (1975)

White, Alan R. ed. *The Philosophy of Action*. London, 1968

Whiteley, C. H. *Mind in Action*. London, 1973

Wilkenfeld, J., Hopple, Gerald W., Rossa, Paula J. and Andrioli, Stephen J. *Foreign Policy Behaviour: The Inter-State Behaviour Analysis Model*. Beverly Hills, Calif., 1980

Winch, Peter. *The Idea of a Social Science and Its Relation to Philosophy*. London, 1958

Wisdom, J. O. 'Situational Individualism and the Emergent Group Properties', in

Explanation in the Behavioural Sciences, ed. Robert Borger and Frank Cioffi. London, 1970

Wright, G. H. von. *Explanation and Understanding*. London, 1971

—— 'Determinism and the Study of Man', in *Essays on Explanation and Understanding*, ed. Juha Manninen and Raimo Tuomela. Dordrecht, 1976

Young, Oran. *A Systemic Approach to International Politics*. Princeton, NJ, 1968

—— 'The Actors in World Politics', in *The Analysis of International Politics*, ed. James N. Rosenau, Vincent Davis and Maurice A. East. New York, 1972

Zelditch, Morris. 'Intelligible Comparisons', in *Comparative Methods in Sociology*, ed. Ivan Vallier. Berkeley, Calif., 1971

Zimmerman, William. 'Issue Area and Foreign Policy Process: A Research Note in Search of a General Theory', *American Political Science Review* 67 (December 1973)

Zinnes, Dina A. 'Some Evidence Relevant to the Man–Milieu Hypothesis', in *The Analysis of International Politics*, ed. James N. Rosenau, Vincent Davis and Maurice A. East. New York, 1972

Index